LANCASHIRE LEGENDS

Yours very truly,
J. Harland

ENGRAVED BY BANKS & CO., EDINBURGH, FROM A PHOTO. BY C. A. DUVAL & CO., MANCHESTER.

LANCASHIRE LEGENDS,

Traditions, Pageants, Sports, &c.

WITH AN APPENDIX

CONTAINING

A RARE TRACT ON THE LANCASHIRE WITCHES,

&c. &c.

BY

JOHN HARLAND, F.S.A.

AND

T. T. WILKINSON, F.R.A.S. &c.

LONDON:
GEORGE ROUTLEDGE AND SONS.
MANCHESTER: L. C. GENT.
1873.

FACSIMILE REPRINT 1993
BY LLANERCH PUBLISHERS,
FELINFACH. ISBN 1 897853 06 8

REPRINTED IN 1999

To

THE PRESIDENT AND COUNCIL OF THE
CHETHAM SOCIETY;

of which body

The Late JOHN HARLAND, F.S.A.

was so useful and worthy

a Member,

𝔗his 𝔙olume is 𝔇edicated

by

the Surviving Editor

T. T. WILKINSON.

PREFACE.

POPULAR legends and traditions are rapidly disappearing from the fireside literature of our county. Some of them pass away with the ancient mansions to which they were attached; others die out with the individuals who were wont to repeat them orally to their descendants; and not a few have become modified by the changes which have taken place in our social relationships to each other. Elementary education, also, is doing its work slowly, but surely, and with the spread of correct information amongst the masses, much of our popular superstition will cease to exist. That which remains will become modified according to prevalent ideas, just as Pagan rites, ceremonies, and beliefs, were Christianised by our forefathers and accepted under their modified forms.

How, or when, many of these popular legends took their rise cannot now be determined. Their origin is lost in the far distant past, and forms matter for mere conjecture. Some have probably been invented in order to account for certain unusual appearances, and a resort to the supernatural has been too frequently indulged in when natural phenomena have not admitted of an easy explanation to those who lacked the requisite information. The ringing of the curfew bell at Burnley, and other places, is plainly a relic of early Norman times, and the origin of the custom is well understood; but when the mysterious writing was found on the walls of the cellar at Barcroft Hall, the confinement of the heir to the estates until he became an idiot, by a younger brother, was needed to connect the writing with an item in the family pedigree. Many generations, no doubt looked with wonder upon the sculptured Paschal Lamb on the south front of the steeple at Burnley before it was connected with the demon pigs and the goblin builders, whose origin has never yet been satisfactorily explained. The same may be said of the rude figure of the pig and bell at Winwick church, and its curious legend, which Mr Worsley has proved to belong to St Anthony and his well-known badge.*

When readers were few it was necessary to give as much publicity as possible to important local transactions. Hence we can explain the custom of holding a ruler or wand when taking the oath in presence of a jury on being enrolled as a holder of property in a Manor; and the same necessity suggested the practice of paying money on the font of the parish church in the presence of the congregation. Paying pepper-corns, presenting gloves, spurs, &c., instead of rent for land, are obviously relics of military service handed down to us from feudal times; and when white gloves are presented to judges in courts of law, they intimate that the sheriff vacates his office with clean hands, which had a real significance when disembowelling formed one of the accessories to capital punishments.

The agency of the Devil is a frequent ingredient in the composition of our local legends. His bonds are always signed with the blood of his victims, and not a few of our localities can produce traditional instances of his crafty doings. He is also credited with the production

* Proceedings of the Liverpool Architectural and Archæological Society, 1871.

of certain natural appearances which seem to lie beyond the powers of human labour. The Roman roads which intersect our wild and still almost impassable moors, are said to have been formed by diabolical agency. Huge boulders which lie scattered on the crests of our hills, marking the outcrop of the millstone grit, are popularly said to have been hurled by him from their parent rocks when exhibiting his feats of strength, forcibly reminding us of the labours of Thor, one of the principal deities of our Scandinavian ancestors.

When we examine our minor superstitions we find many that will admit of no rational explanation. They have descended to us from remote antiquity and different races of people. Very many are relics of ancient faiths and ceremonial rites ; and not a few have served as explanations of natural phenomena, and were accepted as satisfactory by those to whom they were addressed. In certain cases their origin is tolerably clear. The custom of turning to the east is undoubtedly a relic of sun worship, to which our early ancestors are known to have been addicted. Looking backwards when leaving home is considered unlucky; and this has grown into a superstition from the fact of its having been disastrous to Lot's wife. Many religiously disposed persons object to a national census on the ground that it is sinful, and they adduce in proof the punishment which overtook David when he numbered the people. Hook-nosed persons are considered to be avaricious, because this characteristic attaches to the Jews, who have lain under this imputation for more than a thousand years. A superstitious regard for certain numbers has caused thirteen at dinner to be looked upon as ominous, since Judas was a traitor when he sat at meat with the twelve. In Courts Leet *once* calling suffices for ordinary cases, but *three* times are considered necessary when the authority of the sovereign is concerned. The origin of many of our pageants and pastimes is not difficult to trace. Most of them have degenerated from religious or civic festivals, some of which date from the very earliest colonisation of the county. Several might be noted that still retain marked characteristics of Pagan, early Christian, and mediæval times. With slight modifications, the same may be said of our punishments, whether legal or popular, and even of the games which are practised in nurseries and playgrounds by our children. The derivation of the great bulk, however, of all these, whether legend, pageant, or game, must for ever remain in a state of much uncertainty; and hence we have rarely ventured to enter upon a branch of the subject which is scarcely adapted for the general reader.

The following pages are intended to preserve a few of the more important legends, traditions, pageants, &c., as well as a portion of the more miscellaneous folk-lore of the county. In the first part of the work we have given a series of legends and traditions mostly attaching to our ancient mansions, and these are usually introduced by short genealogical notices of the principal persons named, together with the present state of the houses they either erected or improved. In the case of the Old Hall at Samlesbury it may be considered that more detail ought to have been given of the recent extensive renovations, but this has been so ably done by Mr James Croston in his exhaustive account of "Samlesbury Hall and its owners," that nothing more than a reference to that sumptuous work is required. It may be hoped, however, that this praiseworthy example will be followed by other owners of our historic mansions.

The second portion contains several curious accounts

of our local pageants, &c., including that of the still noted Preston Guild. Further information respecting this ancient pageant may be found in the very full and intering "History" of this guild by Mr William Dobson and my late colleague, who, amongst other matter, contributed a new translation of the "Custumal," which preserves some singular items from the ancient Breton laws. The wakes and rushbearings have engaged the attention of the historian as well as the novelist; and the description given by the latter enables us to live over again many episodes of youthful days.

The third portion relates to Lancashire sports and games. The division might have been much enlarged, but it was deemed unnecessary to include such as leapfrog, weights, ring by ring, sally water, &c., &c., since they are still well known and practised daily. The introductory article may be instanced as explaining many of our ancient games of which the names only now remain.

The fourth part contains an account of our old punishments, together with several still in use. Whipping has been revived as one of our legal punishments, and it is not improbable but that the occasional use of the stocks will shortly follow.

The fifth division contains a collection of popular rhymes, proverbs, similes, &c., in common use amongst our peasantry. Many of these are to be found in Collier's "Tummus and Meary" and other similar works; but more especially in the writings of Waugh and Brierley, respectively two of our most talented and popular Lancashire authors.

The sixth portion of the work is devoted to miscellaneous superstitions and observances, all of which have been collected within the past four or five years, and are still believed in, and practised at the present time. They

Preface.

have been classified under different heads as far as possible; but there are many curious items which do not readily admit of any special arrangement.

In the appendix will be found a reprint of a rare old chap-book on the Lancashire Witches, an account of the Lady in White of Samlesbury Hall, &c., all of which will probably be acceptable both to the general and the antiquarian reader.

We have now the pleasing duty of tendering our acknowledgments to R. W. Procter, Edwin Waugh, Benjamin Brierley, and William Beamont, Esqrs., and other authors whose writings are occasionally quoted. Our thanks are also due to W. C. Boulter, Esq., of Hull, and Joseph Chatwood, Esq., President of the Manchester Literary Club, for the poems and extracts contained in the memoir. We are also much indebted to W. A. Waddington, Esq., of Burnley, for his spirited and accurate sketch of the Foldys Cross, which forms so appropriate a vignette to the present volume. The inscription round the octagonal base runs thus :—"Orate pro anima Johannis Foldys cappellani qui istam crucem fieri fecit anno domini MCCCCCXX." This stately memorial was erected in the churchyard at Burnley by a Foldys of Danes House, who was then incumbent, and, after being thrown down many years ago in a drunken frolic, it was removed to Towneley, where it has been re-erected on the lawn behind the Hall. It is to be hoped that in a short time it will be restored to its original site, from which it ought never to have been removed.

T. T. W.

BURNLEY,
November 1872.

CONTENTS.

	PAGE
MEMOIR OF JOHN HARLAND, F.S.A.,	XV

PART I.
LEGENDS AND TRADITIONS.

Introduction,	1
Ashton Church and Ace of Spades,	3
Barcroft Hall and the Idiot's Curse,	4
Bernshaw Tower and Lady Sybil,	5
Burnley Cross and the Demon Pigs,	7
Clayton Hall and Kersal Cell,	8
Clegg Hall Tragedy,	10
Dildrum, King of Cats,	12
Dilworth Written Stone	13
Dule upo' Dun	15
Dun Cow and the Old Rib.	16
Eagle and Child.	19
Egerton Hall and "Old Madam,"	22
Entwisel, Sir Bertine,	23
Fairfax in Ashton Church,	26
Gorton, Reddish, and Nicker Ditch,	26
Habergham Hall and the Lady's Lament,	29
Hale, Chylde of,	31
Hanging Ditch, Manchester,	34
Hornby Chapel and Sir Edward Stanley,	34
Hulme Hall Treasure,	37
Ince Hall and the Dead Hand,	38
Kersal Hall Traditions,	41
Lostock Tower—"too late,"	43
Mab's Cross at Wigan,	45
Ormskirk Church,	47
Rhodes and Pilkington Traditions,	49
Rochdale Church, St Chad's,	52
Stretford Road, Great Stone,	53
Sykes's Wife at Lumb Farm.	55

xii *Contents.*

	PAGE
Towneley Hall Tradition,	57
Turton Tower,	59
Tyrone's Bed, near Rochdale,	60
Unsworth and its Dragons,	63
Wardley Hall Skull,	65
Wardley Hall Tradition,	70
Whalley Crosses,	73
Winwick Church and the Demon,	76
Worsley Giant, Tradition of the,	78
Wyecoller Hall and the Spectre Horseman,	79

PART II.
PAGEANTS, MASKINGS, AND MUMMINGS.

Introduction,	83
Aca's Fair, Manchester,	84
Ashton Gyst-Ale,	85
Burnley Waits,	87
Downham King and Queen,	88
Eccles Guising,	89
Hoghton Pageant in 1617,	93
Liverpool Fair, Custom at,	95
Liverpool May-Day Celebrations,	96
Preston Guild Merchant,	97
Pace Egg Mummers,	101
Robin Hood and Maid Marion,	108
Rushbearings,	109
Rushbearings on the Lancashire Border,	110
Rushbearing in East Lancashire,	111
Hambleton Fair, or Hapton Rushbearing,	112
Rochdale Rushbearings,	112
Warton Rushbearing,	121
Whalley Rushbearing,	121
Wakes in Lancashire,	123
Wakes at Didsbury,	125
Eccles Wakes and Eccles Cakes,	126

PART III.
SPORTS AND GAMES.

Introduction,	131
Ancient Customs in Games,	132
Barley Brake and Blindman's Buff,	141

Contents.   xiii

	PAGE
Clitheroe Sports and Pastimes,	142
Cockfighting at Manchester and Liverpool,	143
Cockfighting for Eccles Tithes,	145
Fighting "Up and Down,"	145
Hunting at Extwistle Hall,	147
Miscellaneous Games—Archery Butts, &c.,	148
Bullbaiting,	149
Hand Ball, Bandy Ball,	149
Spell and Nur,	149
Tip, Blackthorn, Fives,	150
Prison Bars, Quoits, Skates,	151
Slinging, Trippet,	152
Ignagning and Ignagnus,	153
Otter Hunting in the Fylde,	154
Kersal Moor Races,	154
Kersal Moor Races, eighteenth century,	155
Manchester Races; Castle Irwell,	157
Races by Nude Men,	159
School Holidays in 1790,	159
Treacle Dipping,	161

PART IV.
PUNISHMENTS—LEGAL AND POPULAR.

Introduction,	165
Stocks, Whipping Post, &c.,	166
Stocks at Burnley,	166
Scold's Brank or Bridle,	166
Cuck Stool or Ducking Stool,	167
Ducking Pits at Burnley,	167
Ducking Stool at Liverpool,	168
Ducking Stool in the Fylde,	169
Penance Stool at Bispham,	170
Kirkham Ducking Stool,	170
Manchester Gallows and Tumbrel,	171
Beheading a Thief,	172
The Old Appeal of Murder,	173
Penance in the Fylde,	174
Stang Riding, &c., in Lancashire,	174
Ringing the Pan,	176
Notchel Crying in East Lancashire,	176
Wife Selling,	177

Contents.

PART V.
POPULAR RHYMES, PROVERBS, SIMILES, &c.

	PAGE
Introduction,	181
Wigan Nursery Song,	182
Popular Rhymes,	183
Proud Preston—Christ's Croft,	184
Three Rivers at Mytton,	185
Lancashire Riddles,	186
Proverbs,	189-201
Similes,	190
Lancashire Sayings,	193
Farmer's Rhymes and Proverbs,	202
Sayings, &c.,	212
Wilson's Proverbs in Rhyme,	213

PART VI.
MISCELLANEOUS SUPERSTITIONS & OBSERVANCES.

Introduction,	217
Folklore of Birds,	218
Folklore of Cats,	219
Folklore of Children,	220
Superstitions respecting Courtship,	222
Superstitions respecting Fish and Bacon,	224
Superstitions respecting Hair,	224
Precepts in Medicine,	225
Observances as to Money,	227
Omens respecting events,	228
Weather Wisdom,	231
Witchcraft Superstitions,	234
Miscellaneous Observances, &c.,	235
The Devil at Cockerham,	241

APPENDIX.

Introduction,	247
Lancashire Witches Tract,	248
Eagle and Child,	259
Samlesbury Hall and the Lady in White,	261
The Dragon of Wantley,	264
Osbaldeston Hall,	270
Mellor Hall, or Abbot House,	272

MEMOIR

OF

JOHN HARLAND, F.S.A.

THE daily life of an antiquary is usually quiet and unobtrusive. His thoughts and actions relate more to the past than to the present; the common occurrences of the day are deemed of minor importance; he is most interested in things that were; and his special function is to rescue from oblivion that which the busy men of the world have had little inclination, or leisure, to preserve. He makes no conquests which absorb the attention, or elicit the applause of the public, for he is seldom either a general or a statesman; and yet his victories are frequently of greater importance than those which occur on the battle-field or in the senate. The actions of the former may affect the destinies of a nation— the measures of the latter may change the course of his country's policy; but the researches of the man of letters not unfrequently reverse the whole current of public opinion, and thus produce more permanent, and more widely extended effects than the arms of the one or the legislation of the other. Events occur at distant intervals which it would perhaps be impolitic, at the time, to illustrate in all their bearings. The secret causes which produced these events are therefore studiously concealed by the personages concerned; but after ages have passed away, some zealous antiquary carefully examines all the documents relating to such transactions; and then proceeds to assign to each his due meed of praise or blame, as in his opinion they deserve.

It is by such examinations into the public archives, or into the collections of private individuals, that modern generations have been led to reject many of the stereotyped assertions of our popular histories. Not a few of our kings, queens, and great personages, have suffered materially by the process; whilst others have regained their proper positions and legitimate characters, of which they ought never to have been deprived. National changes, both in religion and politics, have thus been assigned to their true causes; and even now we are beginning to learn that the political liberties which we are so rapidly acquiring involve nothing more than a return to those privileges which our ancestors enjoyed nine centuries ago under ancient Saxon rule.

When such results have followed from an examination of our national records; it is not too much to expect that similar modifications of opinion, in a less degree, must have been produced by an inspection of our local collections. Such is manifestly the case; and the many excellent local histories issued during the present century bear ample testimony to the fact. Local antiquaries have been silently, but effectually, at work, and the result is a mass of evidence with regard to local events and social polity which cannot be overlooked by any future historian. In the County of Lancaster the *Chetham* and *Historic* societies have issued numerous volumes, which lay open to our gaze both the public and the private lives of the principal personages who figure in our county history; and not a few of these volumes contain a fund of information relating to the domestic habits and family connections of our mediæval, and more recent ancestors. It is here that the labours of the plodding, careful antiquary make themselves felt; and it is thus that the value of his collections becomes known. He may have to wait long before his objects are accomplished; he may even be removed from earth before his works are duly appreciated; but sooner or later he will obtain his reward. This thought was ever present to the mind of the subject of this brief memoir; he knew the value of the volumes which he so liberally contributed to the *Chetham Society*, and although he has so recently "gone to his rest," it is already acknowledged that no one can hereafter write the history of this great county without being deeply indebted to the "*Mamecestre*," "*The Shuttleworth Accounts*," and his other works, for most valuable materials respecting families, places, men, manners, occupations, and prices; which are so plentifully scattered throughout those valuable volumes.

JOHN HARLAND, says the Rev. Brooke Herford, " whose great-grandfather was an enterprising farmer and grazier, living near Dunkeld in the middle of the last century, was born at Hull, May 27, 1806." He was the eldest child of John Harland and his wife Mary, daughter of John Breasley of Selby. His father followed the combined businesses of clock and watchmaker, and jeweller, in Scale Lane, Hull; and issued a medal in commemoration of the peace and end of the war in December 1813. "It was mainly to his mother" that their son "owed the elementary instruction which was the only foundation on which he built up his various and extensive knowledge. At the age of fourteen he went, on trial, into the office of Messrs Allanson and Sydney, the proprietors of the *Hull Packet* newspaper, and was apprenticed to them for seven years from January 1, 1821, to learn letterpress printing." The celebrated painter Etty was Mr Harland's predecessor as an apprentice; and when he removed from Hull to London he left a scrap-book, containing a series of early sketches, as a memento, in the hands of Mr George Walker, a journeyman printer in the same office. "From the beginning of his apprenticeship he gave all his energies to self-improvement; soon rose from compositor to reader; then was put into the office; and, teaching himself short-hand, was advanced to reporting. With indomitable industry, he made for himself during 1825-6, a system of short-hand in which he embodied all the best points of several stenographic systems, and soon became the most expert short-hand writer in the kingdom." During his residence at Hull he was first the playmate and then the companion of Benjamin Boulter, Esq., surgeon; to whom he wrote a series of characteristic letters during his five years' stay at Glasgow as a medical student. Only two of these letters are now in existence; but the following extracts from them will show that he was making rapid progress in self-instruction.

HULL, *March 9th*, 1827.

MY DEAR FRIEND—I received and read your letter with pleasure. . . You mistook my meaning respecting *Hogmanay* night. I did not mean to censure the jovialities of a single night, but to express a wish that these festivities should not be too often indulged in, as they are peculiarly unfitting for study. I am happy to find that I have no need to give you any such hints, since I hear you apply with a zeal which is worthy of its reward. I need not here say that it will afford me the most sincere gratification to hear of your complete success, and well merited diploma. Our theatrical campaign is drawing near to a close; but I am ill qualified to give you any particulars, as I have been but seldom this season. . . I have broken my flute and have not yet replaced it with a new one, so that I am out of practice. There is nothing new in the musical world at present. You have seen by the newspapers the steps our aristocracy are taking in the Fine Arts and Architecture. . . I have not *ten* months longer to stay in "servile chains"—and then—huzza for liberty—I shall be free! I hear that your studies will soon be varied by the comparatively delightful one of Botany; and this exercise in the morning will better enable you to support the tedium of confinement during the long summer days. Should Fate have willed us to meet again, either here or elsewhere, I shall rejoice in the happy hours we shall again enjoy; and should it be otherwise, I can only say, that I sincerely wish Fame, Fortune, and Beauty, may crown the efforts of the truly Brave, the arduous aspirant for Honours. Meanwhile, I hope, when opportunity permits, he will not forget in his correspondence, his sincere friend,

J. HARLAND.

MR B. BOULTER, *Glasgow.*

In the latter portion of the same year, Mr Boulter, who was still at Glasgow, is anxious to ascertain how he is progressing in his studies, and also what are his future prospects in life, now that his apprenticeship is drawing to a close. Mr Harland's reply fully proves that he was hard at work mentally and bodily, although suffering at times from an ailment which ultimately deprived him of the free use of his legs:—

HULL, *Oct.* 15, 1827.

MY DEAR FRIEND—You desire me to mention what books I have read, or am reading; with my critical judgment on the same. As, with some exceptions, they are principally light works which I now read, as novels, poetry, romances, &c., I am afraid they would afford you little gratification, either in the perusal of my critique, or of the works themselves. However, I will mention a few, requesting you to put your *veto* upon my not writing any more on this subject, if you find it at all tedious. I have lately waded through *four* out of *six* thick 8vo volumes of Dr. Franklin's "Life and Works." I would say of them that they are a bed of oysters from which the diligent searcher might collect many pearls; but a great portion of the work is interesting only to the statesman and the philosopher. "Babylon the Great" is a very fine picturesque portrait of London and its inhabitants in the present day. If you have commenced, or rather resumed, romance reading, I would recommend to your notice "Tales of the O'Hara Family," as possessing great interest. Lady Morgan's "Florence M'Carthy" I like very well. Miss Porter's "Village and Mariendorpt" is also a very amusing work. But if you want something in the grotesque style, read Hogg's "Winter Evening Tales," and, above all, *Blackwood's Magazine*. It is without exception the most delightful *emollient* I know for the gloom and dulness too often concomitants of severe study. I never miss reading it shortly after it makes its appearance, and there is inevitably some article, long or short, that proves a sure provocative of laughter and delight.

Your remarks on my progress in knowledge are, I think, more the effect of your good wishes than of your firm belief in my acquirements. However, I am obliged to you for the kindness and good wishes displayed by you in this respect, and will merely observe that I am nearer the summit of *stenographical* excellence than when I last wrote. I find you blame me for not giving you any idea what my proceedings will be after my apprenticeship expires. Though the time now draws so near, I must confess that I am more undetermined than when I parted from you. . . . I spent most of my last Hull fair at your father's. I need not say that at times I felt the want of your presence as the enlivener of the social board, and the mainspring of joy and cheerfulness. My bodily health is in general better than I could have supposed it would have been at this season of the year. I may speak in the same terms of my leg. . . . Hoping we may meet again soon, or if not, that we may congratulate each

other on having reached wealth, honour, and fame; endeared by the recollection that it will be by our own industry, which alone will pave the way to these blessings. That such may be our future lot ; that we and our children may be ever united in the bonds of friendship and companionship ; and that you and I may enjoy many hours of delightful intercourse and retrospection is the sincere wish of
Yours sincerely,
JOHN HARLAND.
Mr B. BOULTER,
Student of Medicine, College, Glasgow.

The wish expressed by Mr Harland in the last clause of the preceding letter, was ultimately realised. His early friend died very suddenly in November 1867; but in January of the same year, his son, the present W. Consitt Boulter, Esq., F.S.A., was in correspondence with him on antiquarian subjects. In addition to the two letters already given, Mr Boulter has kindly communicated the following extracts from the letters which passed between them :—

"I am very glad to find that a son of one of my oldest friends is so early [age 19] applying himself to the study of antiquities and archæology. I began about the same age ; but it is very rare to find *young* men caring about the history of the past" (30*th January* 1867).

"I annex a list of my volumes; besides which, I have printed many articles in *The Manchester Literary and Philosophical Society's Memoirs ;* in *The Journal of the British Archæological Association ; The Lancashire and Cheshire Historic Society's Transactions; The Archæologia Cambrensis; Chambers's Book of Days ;* &c. &c. I am also the 'Monkbarns' and 'Jonathan Oldbuck' of *Country Words"* (30*th January* 1867).

Mr Boulter was then collecting materials for his Bibliography of Hull, and hence the necessity of the preceding enumeration and list, which includes a pamphlet entitled

"Ten Days in Paris," privately printed by Mr Harland in 1854.

"Being only twenty-three when I left Hull altogether, I had not made much progress in local antiquities. I had acquired a smattering of Anglo-Saxon, and had copied and corrected the translation in Tickell of a monumental inscription, in short-hand, to a lady, on a marble tablet in Sculcotes Church. Also one or two Anglo-Saxon, or early English, inscriptions in churches in the Holderness; one, I think, at or near Swine. I have somewhere the copy of an old deed of Myton, which I could send you some day, if you are at all interested in old deeds. I have one or two silver pennies of Hull (temp. Edward I.), and a few copper tokens of the last and present century. These constitute my Hull reliques" (5*th February* 1867.)

"Between 1820 and 1830 there was a low comedian at the Theatre in Humber Street, named George Bailey, who used to sing comic songs; perhaps of his own writing; one of which I remember was called 'Hull is a wonderful town, oh!' Its burden was—

> 'And Geordie Bailey, singing gaily,
> Hey down, ho down, derry, derry down,
> Oh! this Hull is a wonderful town oh!'

I know Peter Arnull and Gawtrees best of the Hull editors" (28*th February* 1867).

"With one apprentice between us in time I was a successor of Etty in apprenticeship at the *Hull Packet* office. Etty gave a book containing some of his early chalk sketches to George Walker, who is, or was, lately in one of the Leeds printing offices" (25*th May* 1867).

"Your last letter of 25th November is before me, unanswered; another proof of the uncertainty of all earthly things. Since I received it you have lost your beloved father, my dear old friend. Amongst my papers, I found the other day a copy of some verses written in a volume of Burns's *Poems*, which I gave him in 1826. If the volume is still in the house you will find the verses on the first blank leaf. If not, and you wish to see a copy, I will make one for you" (*2d January*, 1868).

The volume of Burns's *Poems*, however, could not be found, and on this being made known to Mr Harland, he copied the verses and enclosed them in his next letter. They are well worthy of preservation.

" *To B. B.*

In thoughts of joyous scenes,
In memory's pleasing dreams,
In Friendship's brightest gleams,
   Remember me!

By all our hours of gladness,
Of reason, mirth, and sadness,
Unmixed with aught of madness,
   Remember me!

Through hours, and days, and years,
Through Fortune's smiles and tears,
Through all Life's hopes and fears,
   Remember me!

Whate'er of good or ill
May yet befall me, till
The clutch of Death, I'll still
   Remember thee!
       J. H."

November 1826.

Mr Harland always retained a fondness for poetry; and not unfrequently indulged in that species of composition. He had studied Shakespeare critically, and was well acquainted with the works of our leading authors, both ancient and modern. He proved his familiarity with our great dramatist in his contribution to our joint " Essay on Songs and Ballads," which appeared in the *Transactions of the Historic Society of Lancashire and Cheshire*, and in 1843 he published a few of his own compositions as " Stray Leaves," under the signature

"Iota." Five other fugitive pieces were printed in the volume of "Lancashire Lyrics" which he edited in 1866; one more appeared in *Country Words;* and only a few weeks before his death he read the following simnel song to a meeting of the Manchester Literary Club, of which he was long a valued member.

"*A SYMNELLE SONGE.*

Ye Lovers of oure olde Folk-lore,
Come listen to ane Balade more,
And chorusse synge from youre hearte's core—
To 'The Goode olde Burye Symnelle!'

Mid-lenten faste yt makes ryche feaste,
For olde and yonge, lyttelle and leaste;
For waterynge mouthes, sure, ne'er have ceaste;
For 'The Goode olde Burye Symnelle!'

Confeccion's hyghest arte yt makes
This huge, rounde, sugarye Kynge of Cakes,
To figure for three F's yt takes,
This 'Goode olde Burye Symnelle!'

It speakes of deareste *Familye* tyes;
From *Friend* to *Friend* in Lent yt hyes;
To alle goode *Felloweshippe* yt cryes;
'I'm a ryghte trewe Burye Symnelle!'

Longe maye symbolique Symnelles send
Friende's everye lovynge wyshe to friend;
From 'Auld Lang Syne,' till tyme shalle ende,
The 'Goode olde Burye Symnelle!'

J. H."

CHETHAM HILL, *March* 16, 1868.

When Mr Harland penned the preceding lines he had engaged to accompany the Literary Club in an excursion to Stratford-upon-Avon, on the anniversary of Shakespeare's birth and death. As the time drew near he felt unwell, and wrote to the President playfully requesting that he might "be *scratched* for that day." As will be seen his name was indeed withdrawn to join that "of the great shade" on the very day of the celebration.

Mr Harland continued as reporter and contributor to the Hull newspapers for several years after the expiration of his apprenticeship. During this period his reports were so remarkable for their fullness and accuracy, that they attracted the attention of every public speaker who visited the town. On one occasion he presented the Rev. Dr Beard with so accurate a report of his address in Bond Alley Lane Chapel, that "he mentioned the circumstance to the late John Edward Taylor, who was then conducting the *Manchester Guardian* with that energy and ability which placed it at the head of the provincial press. The consequence was an offer which induced Mr Harland to remove to Manchester in November 1830," in which city and its vicinity he resided till his death. He had here ample opportunities of proving the superiority of his method of writing shorthand; and so verbally accurate were his reports of trials, public meetings, &c., that they were even cited in courts of law as proof that certain expressions had been used. A gentleman connected with the *Manchester Guardian*, in an obituary notice, gives an interesting anecdote of this extreme accuracy. He says:—"A man was being tried at Lancaster for making a seditious speech, and Mr Harland had to produce and read his notes as evidence against him. These notes were read slowly to allow the Judge to write down the evidence. While this was going on, the counsel for the defence turned to a gentleman who sat near him, and said, 'I'll turn this fellow inside out.' The cross-examination for the defence began. 'You profess to give the exact words?' 'Yes.' 'You say the prisoner said so and so; now read what immediately follows.' Mr Harland turned to the place in his notes, and read off without hesitation, and without waiting for his evidence to be taken down, a passage of one hundred words or more. Again he was required to turn to another part of the speech, and the second passage then read agreed perfectly with what the counsel knew the prisoner had said. The learned counsel desisted, and remarked to the gentleman to whom he had previously spoken, ' I don't think there is another man in England who could do that.' "

At first the *Guardian* was only a weekly paper; but it began to be published on Wednesdays and Saturdays in 1836; and became a daily paper in 1855. Mr Harland continued to occupy an important position on the staff through all these changes; conducting the literary department of the journal with rare skill and industry, until July 1, 1839, when he was admitted to a partnership in the paper, which he retained till his retirement in December 1860. "While thus busied with his own professional work, however, he found time for the cultivation of literary tastes in other and higher directions. Possessing a keen sense of humour; endowed with considerable poetic powers; skilled in mediæval Latin; and a loving student of early English history, he speedily made himself a reputation among local literary men, and, as his pursuits took more decidedly the direction of archæology, gradually became widely known as an antiquary." He published many of his early dissertations in the columns of the *Guardian*; some of which were afterwards included in the "Collectanea," issued by the Chetham Society, and other works. In December 1854 he was elected a Fellow of the Society of Antiquaries, and was placed upon the Council of the Chetham Society in 1855; an office which he only vacated by death. He was also a member of the Historic Society of Lancashire and Cheshire; to whose *Transactions* he contributed some interesting papers, and presented to their library a valuable series of antiquarian cuttings from the *Manchester Guardian.* The Rosicrucians also enrolled him as one of their earliest members. For several years he acted as Secretary to the order, and edited for this society Edmonde Dudlay's "Tree of the Commonwealth," written by the author when under sentence of death for high treason. In a scrap-book entitled *The Manchester Olio*, now in the Chetham Library, Mr Harland included the transactions of this useful body, amongst a vast mass of other matter, but he has unfortunately omitted to particularise his own contributions. He was never a member of the Manchester Literary and Philosophical Society, although he contributed an excellent biographical notice of his friend, the late John Just, of Bury, to volume xi. of their *Memoirs.* To *Notes and Queries* Mr Harland was an occasional contributor; he supplied most of the articles relating to Lancashire to Chambers's "Book of Days;" of which his accounts of "John Shaw's Club," and the "Rev. Joshua Brookes," may be particularised. He supplied an account of the "Find of six thousand silver pennies at Eccles" to the *Reliquary*; and amongst other papers contributed to that journal may be noticed "an admirable contribution under the signature 'Crux' on 'Local and other Names and Words.'" When *Country Words* was established he was ready with his help; he contributed several curious papers under the *nom de plume* of "Monkbarns," and his essays on our Folk-speech, under the signature "Jonathan Oldbuck," attest both the fluency of his pen, and the extent and accuracy of his information. In 1851 he published a series of "Ancient Charters and other Muniments of the

Borough of Clithero;" several of which were afterwards included in his " Mamecestre," and in the same year he printed the " Autobiography of William Stout, of Lancaster, Wholesale and Retail Grocer and Ironmonger, a member of the Society of Friends, A.D. 1665–1732." This quaint and characteristic work was dedicated to his friend A. B. Rowley, Esq., the owner of the manuscript, and several curious notes were added by Mr Harland in illustration of portions of the text. Mr Harland published "An Historical Account of Salley Abbey," in Yorkshire, during 1853, illustrated by a series of lithographic sketches of the existing remains. This work was appropriately dedicated to Dixon Robinson, Esq., of Clitheroe Castle, who largely promoted the publication. It contains by far the most accurate and complete account of these interesting ruins; and the writer of this notice had the pleasure of re-examining all the principal details on the spot, in company with Mr Harland, when the Literary Club visited that locality. He had also the gratification of being present at a similar examination of the ruins or Whalley Abbey, on a later visit of the same club, when Mr Harland not only exhibited an amended plan of this Cistercian House, but read an exhaustive paper on the subject within the walls, which, in a condensed form, has since been issued as a guide-book to Whalley and the neighbourhood, under the editorship of the Rev. Brooke Herford, his literary executor.

During 1853 Sir James Kay-Shuttleworth, Bart., mentioned to the president of the Chetham Society that there were several books of accounts in the muniment chest at Gawthorpe Hall, which might furnish much useful information respecting the prices of labour, &c., between the years 1582 and 1621. These were examined in March 1854, and as the Council considered the information valuable, it was decided to publish the more important portions. They selected Mr Harland as the most competent person to edit and illustrate the accounts. The result was that during 1856-7-8 four volumes were issued, which are probably unequalled for the variety and importance of the information they contain. The first volume includes the House and Farm Accounts up to September 1618. These are continued in the second volume up to October 1621, when they close; and then follows "Appendix I.," containing a genealogical and biographical account of the Shuttleworth family, and descriptions of their several residences. "Appendix II." contains an exhaustive comparison of prices, wages, &c., of great value and interest; and this is followed by "Notes," occupying 740 closely printed quarto pages, illustrating the productions, manufactures, weights, measures, manners, customs, persons, and families mentioned in the accounts. Mr Harland put forth his whole strength in this work; and these four volumes will ever remain a standing monument of his extensive acquirements, his unwearied industry, and patient research.

Besides the documents relating to the house and farm accounts, the muniment chest at Gawthorpe contained three other series of documents relating to the "Lancashire Lieutenancy" under the Tudors and Stuarts. These seventy-eight papers were published by the Chetham Society, under the editorship of Mr Harland, as two of their volumes for 1853. He prefaced the documents by an introduction occupying one hundred and eleven pages, illustrating military and other matters during the Tudor and Stuart periods. The genealogical, and other matter, contained in numerous notes scattered throughout the two volumes, is extremely valuable, and fully sustain the credit of the editor. Mr Mayer of Liverpool contributed seven plates illustrative of ancient armour to these volumes at Mr Harland's special request. One of the most valuable of his contributions to the Chetham Society is the "Mamecestre," in three volumes, issued during 1861-2. The first volume contains twelve chapters on the early history of Manchester, and including the Lancashire town charters. The second volume continues the charters, and enters fully into the transfer, survey, and extent of the manor; and in the third volume we have an account of the rental of the manor, its various owners, &c., with special notice of the Mosleys, commencing with Sir Nicholas Mosley, who was Lord Mayor of London in 1599. At the close of the work we have a most valuable "Glossarial Gazetter," in which the derivations of a vast number of local names are very ably and satisfactorily explained. This chapter is of the utmost value to every student of local history.

"The Songs of the Wilsons" have long been popular in Lancashire. Mr Harland drew attention to their merits in a series of articles published in the *Manchester Guardian*, and in 1865 he was induced by Mr Gent "to edit a new revised and enlarged edition of the songs, with a brief memoir of the Wilson family." In the same year he issued a collection of the "Ballads and Songs of Lancashire," in which he included several which until then had only existed in broadsides. Each ballad or song is illustrated by judicious notes explaining its origin and connection with local family history. The edition was soon exhausted, and he next published the "Lancashire Lyrics;" a series of modern songs and ballads of the County Palatine. This work contains some of the best compositions of our local poets, arranged under six heads; and the selection bears ample testimony to the good taste and nice appreciation of the compiler. In 1862 Mr Harland assisted Mr William Dobson in compiling a "History of Preston Guilds;" to which he added a new translation of the "Custumal" of the ancient borough. He also contributed a paper containing the names of eight hundred inhabitants of Manchester, who took the oath of allegiance to Charles II. in 1679, to the second volume of the Chetham "Miscellanies;" and edited, for private circulation, an edition of Prestwick's "Respublica," to which he added a carefully prepared explanatory preface. On February 7, 1865, Mr Harland proposed to join the writer of the present notice in preparing and publishing a work on the "Folklore of Lancashire." In a letter dated April 30, 1866, he acknowledged the receipt of my "manuscript notes on twenty-six subjects" to be included in the volume; and on May 1st he wrote to say that "another packet of manuscript" had reached him that morning. The work was published in January 1867, when he congratulated me on our work being ended. Our intercourse during the whole of this period was cordial in the extreme; and at the close of every interview I was more and more deeply impressed with his upright manly worth, and his varied attainments. As the matter we had collected more than sufficed for the "Folk-lore," we re-arranged the remainder and began to prepare for a volume of "Lancashire Legends, Pageants, &c.;" but when he undertook the new edition of Baines's "Lancashire" this project was laid aside for a time, and on his lamented decease the manuscript was placed in my possession by his literary executor. It formed the germ of the present work.

In 1863 Mr Harland reprinted from "The Church of the People" a series of essays entitled "Some Account of Seats and Pews in old Parish Churches of the County Palatine of Lancaster." It is a small pamphlet of sixteen pages, and contains much curious information respecting seats and pews in the Churches of Ashton-under-Lyne, Eccles and Whalley. During this and the early part of the following year he published several " Church Notes" in the *Eccles Advertiser*, which were afterwards issued in an octavo pamphlet of eighty-two pages, and entitled "The Ancient Parish Church of Eccles ; its antiquity, alterations, and improvements. By Crux." Why he adopted this signature when publishing this very meritorious and exhaustive account of an ancient parish church is not known, but he also adopted the same *nom de plume* when writing to the *Reliquary*.

In 1864–5 he edited two volumes of "Court Leet Records" of the manor of Manchester. They contain many valuable accounts of the social and civil life of the inhabitants of that city during the sixteenth century. His introduction, preparatory chapter, notes and appendices, are especially curious and interesting. He closed his extracts at the date of the death of Queen Elizabeth ; and expressed a hope that other extracts would be made commencing with the reign of James I. This hope was not realised. During Mr Harland's connection with the *Manchester Guardian* he published in that journal, and in the *Weekly Express*, a vast number of antiquarian articles of much local interest. A selection from these was issued in two volumes as "Collectanea relating to Manchester and its neighbourhood at various periods." We have here descriptions of Manchester from British to Saxon times ; these are followed by accounts of Roman remains, relics, maps, plans, directories, local events, notices of notables, &c., of the highest importance to local history. The second volume more especially deals with places and institutions, genealogy and biography; and concludes with recollections of Manchester persons and places. The life-pictures in these volumes are sketched with a master-hand. The last work which Mr Harland edited for the Chetham Society was issued after his death. It contains "Three Lancashire Documents" of much interest. The first of these is the De Lacy Inquisition of 1311; the second is the survey of West Derby, Amounderness, and Lonsdale, 1330 to 1346; and the third is the Custom Roll and Rental of Ashton-under-Lyne for 1422. To all these he added introductions, indexes, and "after-words," explaining obscure points and giving the meaning of many personal and local names. In February 1868 he finished the third edition of Gregson's "Fragments," which had been revised, enlarged, and indexed by him when confined to bed by the affection in his knee. This edition is a great improvement upon the second issued by Gregson in 1824. The indexes alone occupy thirty-eight folio pages; and he added considerably from the Duchy Records.

The last and greatest work he undertook was a new edition of Baines's "History of Lancashire." It was originally issued in four volumes, and had long been out of print. When it was decided to republish the work it was deemed advisable to issue it in two volumes; and although the labour of verification and completion approached at times to a re-writing of large portions of the book, Mr Harland did not shrink from the task, and he did his work well. The writer visited him towards the close of 1867, and found him hard at work with the last sheets of the first volume. He was then looking haggard and careworn—the heavy work was evidently telling on his constitution; and yet both in conversation with myself, and in his letters to Mr Gent, joint publisher of this and several of his other works, he spoke and wrote hopefully of completing his labours within a reasonable time. On my next visit I found he was seriously ill. His medical attendant durst not risk the excitement of an interview, and I left without seeing him. In two days more he had passed to his rest. He died on the 23d April 1868, and his remains were interred in Rusholme Road Cemetery the Tuesday following. Although the funeral was strictly private, the carriages of many private friends joined the procession. The Chetham Society, the Geological Society, the Literary Club, and several other public bodies were represented; and the venerable Samuel Bamford, although blind and upwards of eighty years of age, was also present to do honour to the memory of his old and valued friend. During the week, Mr Harland's career was sketched with appreciative and kindly hands in all the local journals, as also in the *Reliquary*; and the son of one of his early friends bore testimony to his worth in one of the Hull papers to which he had contributed in early life. He there states that Mr Harland "was a member of the Hull Mechanics' Institute in its early existence, and took considerable trouble to forward its success. He was also a musician of no mean ability, and in the summer season, before the business of the day commenced, he was wont, with one or two of his friends, and with an ordinary hedge, tree, or bush, for a music stool, they would execute a duet, or a trio of some favourite theme, and return home with a sharpened appetite for breakfast." At the time of his death he was under engagements to edit Dr Whitaker's "Richmondshire," "Craven," and the "Whalley," the last of which has since been so ably accomplished by J. G. Nichols, Esq., F.S.A., for issue in two volumes.

Mr Harland "was twice married; first in 1833 to

Mary, daughter of the late Samuel Whitfield of Birmingham, who died in 1849; secondly, in 1852, to Eliza, daughter of the late Joseph Pilkington of Manchester, who, together with four children by the first marriage, and five by the second, survives him. By a wide circle of friends he was warmly esteemed as a kind and genial friend; a sincere and single-minded Christian. Born a Churchman he became a Unitarian by conviction in 1828. In the busiest years of his newspaper life, when he might have claimed exemption from extra work, he found time to be teacher and superintendent in a Sunday-school; and throughout his life was as active as he was unobtrusive in doing good." Such is the just and well-deserved tribute paid to his memory by the Rev. Brooke Herford, who carried on and completed the "History of Lancashire" with competent ability and in the spirit of his predecessor. Mr Harland's collection of works on Shorthand was very extensive, ranging from the sixteenth century downwards. They are now in the Chetham Library as a permanent memorial of one whose literary life was so intimately associated with the varied stores contained in those quaint old rooms. It may be added that the frontispiece to this volume is engraved from a photograph taken by C. A. Du Val & Co., of Manchester, and is an excellent likeness of Mr Harland as he appeared just before he was seized with his fatal illness.

T. T. W.

LANCASHIRE LEGENDS, &c.

PART I.

LEGENDS AND TRADITIONS.

INTRODUCTION.

In any endeavour to bring together the legends and traditions which form so striking a feature in the folk-lore of Lancashire, it is impossible to pass over unnoticed that collection which bears the name of the late Mr John Roby of Rochdale. In 1829 he published "The Traditions of Lancashire," in two volumes, containing twenty tales, more or less founded upon traditions current in their respective localities. During 1831 he published a second series of so-called "Traditions," likewise in two volumes, and also containing a score of tales. A posthumous volume, which appeared in 1854, contained three legends, but only one of these—"Mother Red Cap"—has its scene in Lancashire.

In the preface to the first series of his "Traditions of Lancashire," Mr Roby has the following passage:—"A native of Lancashire, and residing there during the greater part of his life, he has been enabled to collect a mass of local traditions, now fast dying from the memories of the inhabitants. It is his object to perpetuate these interesting relics of the past, and to present them in a form that may be generally acceptable, divested of the dust and dross in which the originals are but too often disfigured, so as to appear worthless and uninviting. . . . The tales are arranged chronologically, forming a somewhat irregular series from the earliest records to those of a comparatively modern date." This passage sufficiently indicates that the original legend was simply taken as the basis of a story of pure fiction. In short, the real character of the work would be better described by such a title as "Romantic Tales, suggested by Lancashire Traditions." Three of Mr Roby's traditions have no local habitation assigned to them, and are apparently pure fictions. A fourth, "The Luck of Muncaster," is not a Lancashire, but a Cumberland tradition. In the traditions to be found in the present volume, the popular legend in every case has been sought to be preserved, without any attempt to add the slightest embellishment, much less to rear a superstructure of invented fiction upon the crumbling foundations of a genuine tradition. In short, it is Lancashire folk-lore, and not the product of an editor's inventive imagination, that is recorded in the following pages. Where it is practicable, the traditions are arranged alphabetically, according to the names of their localities.

ASHTON-UNDER-LYNE CHURCH AND THE ACE OF SPADES.

SIR JOHN ASSHETON, in the 5th Henry VI. (1426–27) became possessed of the manor of Ashton-under-Lyne, on payment of the nominal rent of one penny yearly. He is generally supposed to have founded the church about the year 1420. We find him assigning the forms or benches to his tenants: the names for whose use they are appropriated are all female. From this, and from Sir John Towneley's fixing that the greater part of the seats in Whalley Church should be occupied "first come first served," and his adding, that this would make "the proud wives of Whalley come early to church"—it would seem that seats in our churches were first put up for women. Eighteen forms or benches are mentioned for the occupation in Ashton Church of a hundred wives and widows, who are named, besides their daughters and servant wenches. Their husbands had not this privilege, being forced to stand or kneel in the aisles as the service required. In the windows there yet remains a considerable quantity of stained glass, but very much mutilated. Three or four figures on the north side represent a king, saints, &c. In the chancel are the coats and effigies of the Asshetons in armour, kneeling. In one part seems to have been portrayed the Invention of the Holy Cross by St Helen. At whatever period the church was built, the steeple must either have been erected afterwards, or have undergone considerable repairs in the time of the last Sir Thomas Assheton; for upon the south side are the arms of Assheton impaling Stayley. There is a tradition that while the workmen were one day amusing themselves at cards, a female unexpectedly presented herself. She asked them to turn up an ace, promising, in case of compliance, that she would build several yards of the steeple; upon which they fortunately turned up the ace of spades. This tale, says Mr Roby, in his "Traditions," may owe its origin to the following circumstances:—Upon the marriage of Sir Thomas Assheton with the daughter of Ralph Stayley, a considerable accumulation of property was the consequence. This might induce him to repair the church and perform sundry other acts of charity and beneficence. Whilst the work was going on, Lady Elizabeth Assheton, it is not improbable, surprised the workmen at their pastime, and might desire that her arms should be fixed in the steeple, impaled with those of her husband. The shape of an escutcheon having a considerable resemblance to a spade-ace, in all likelihood, gave origin to the fable.

BARCROFT HALL AND THE IDIOT'S CURSE.

THE Barcrofts of Barcroft were for many generations a most respectable Lancashire family. The Hall is not more than a mile from Townley, and the fine estate by which it is surrounded must have been often coveted by their more ancient and wealthy neighbours. Barcroft is still a good specimen of the later Tudor style, and its ample cellarage not only conveys an idea of the liberal hospitality of its former owners, but has given occasion for a tradition which is not to the credit of one of the last possessors. The tradition states that one of the heirs to Barcroft was either an idiot or imbecile; that he was fastened by a younger brother with a chain in one of the cellars, and that he was there starved to death. This younger brother reported the heir as dead long before he was released from his sufferings, and thus obtained possession of the property. It is added, that during one of his lucid intervals, the prisoner pronounced a curse upon the family of the Barcrofts, to the effect that the name should perish for ever, and that the property should pass into other hands. Some rude scribblings on one of the walls of the cellars are still pointed out as the work of the captive; and his curse is said to have been fulfilled in the person of Thomas Barcroft, who died in 1688 without male issue.* After passing through the hands of the Bradshaws, the Pimlots, and the Isherwoods, the property was finally sold to Charles Towneley, Esq., the celebrated antiquary, in 1795.

BERNSHAW TOWER AND LADY SYBIL.

BERNSHAW TOWER, formerly a small fortified house, is now in ruins, little else than the foundations being visible above the surface. It stood in one of the many beautiful ravines branching off from the great gorge of Cliviger, about five miles from Burnley, and not far from the noted Eagle's Crag. Its last owner, and heiress, was celebrated for her wealth and beauty: she was intellectual beyond most of her sex, and frequently visited the Eagle's Crag in order to study nature and admire the varied aspects of the surrounding country. On these occasions she often felt a strong desire to possess super-

* In Dr Whitaker's pedigree of this family, William Barcroft, a *lunatic*, is stated to have died in 1641. His elder brother, Robert, died in 1647. His younger brother, Thomas, had one son, who died in 1642, and five daughters.

natural powers; and, in an unguarded moment, was induced to sell her soul to the devil in order that she might be able to join in the nightly revelries of the then famous Lancashire Witches. The bond was duly attested with her blood, and her utmost wishes were at all times fulfilled.

Hapton Tower was then occupied by a junior branch of the Towneley family, and "Lord William" had long been a suitor for the hand of "Lady Sybil" of Bernshaw Tower, but his proposals were constantly rejected. In despair he had recourse to a famous Lancashire witch, one Mother Helston, and after using many spells and incantations, she promised him success on the next All-Hallow's Eve. On that day he went out hunting, according to her directions, when, on nearing Eagle's Crag, he started a milk-white doe, and his dogs immediately gave chase. They scoured the country for many miles, and, at last, when the hounds were nearly exhausted, they again approached the Crag. A strange hound then joined them, which Lord William knew full well. It was the familiar of Mother Helston, which had been sent to capture Lady Sybil, who had assumed the disguise of the white doe. On passing the Crag, Lord William's horse had well-nigh thrown its rider down the fearful abyss; but just as the doe was making for the next precipice, the strange hound seized her by the throat and held her fast, until Lord William threw an enchanted silken leash around her neck, and led her in triumph to Hapton Tower. During the night the Tower was shaken as by an earthquake, and in the morning the captured doe appeared as the fair heiress of Bernshaw. Counter-spells were adopted—her powers of witchcraft were suspended—and soon Lord William had the happiness to lead his newly-wedded bride to his ancestral home. Within a year, however, she had renewed her diabolical practices, and whilst enjoying a frolic in Cliviger Mill, under the form of a beautiful white cat, she had one paw cut off by the man-servant, Robin, who had been set to watch by Giles Robinson, the miller. Next morning Lady Sybil was found at home in bed, pale and exhausted; but Robin's presence at the Tower, with a lady's hand, soon dispelled the mystery of her sudden indisposition. The owner of the hand, with its costly signet ring, was soon detected, and many angry expostulations from her husband followed. By means of some diabolical process the hand was restored to Lady Sybil's arm; but a red mark round the wrist bore witness to the sharpness of Robin's whittle. A reconciliation with her offended husband was afterwards effected; but her bodily strength gave way, and her health rapidly declined. On the approach of death the services of the neighbouring clergy were requested, and by their assistance the devil's bond was cancelled. Lady Sybil soon died in peace, but Bernshaw Tower was ever after deserted. As Mr Roby truly observes, popular tradition " still alleges that her grave was dug where the dark Eagle Crag shoots out its cold, bare peak into the sky; and on the eve of All-Hallows, the hound and the milk-white doe meet on the crag a spectre huntsman in full chase. The belated peasant crosses himself at the sound, as he remembers the fate of the Witch of Bernshaw Tower."

BURNLEY CROSS AND THE DEMON PIGS.

GODLY LANE CROSS, stands in a small plantation a few hundred yards from the Old Market Place of Burnley. It is evidently of great antiquity, and most probably has been removed from the churchyard to its present site. Like those at Whalley and Dewsbury, this Saxon relic is supposed to commemorate the preaching of Paulinus, the first Christian missionary in these parts, about the year 597. The cross has been of large size, and from what remains, it may be inferred that it has been bound by simple fillets, terminating at the apex in a spiral form. Dr Whitaker is inclined to attach considerable weight to the above supposition, from the fact, that a neighbouring field retains the name of "Bishop Leap." The tradition is, that prior to the foundation of any church in Burnley, religious rites were celebrated on the spot where this ancient cross now stands, and that Paulinus baptized his converts in the River Brun. Upon the attempt being made to erect an oratory, the materials were nightly removed by supernatural agents, in the form of pigs, to where St Peter's Church now stands. This popular opinion probably owes its origin to an ancient mural tablet, or escutcheon, yet remaining on the south side of the steeple. Its principal charge bears some resemblance to a pig; but was probably originally intended to represent the Paschal Lamb, since it appears to be surrounded by rude representations of the instruments of the Passion. A similar charge is also sculptured on the old font.

CLAYTON HALL AND KERSAL CELL.

FURTHER down the same by-lane (from the moor) that contains Kersal Hall, stands Kersal Cell, the retreat of "Dr." Byrom in the middle of the last century. It is a snug substantial residence, reminding us of Hawthorne's "House of Seven Gables." In the "Doctor's" time, it would be all that a poet could desire. In fixing here his hermitage, hundreds of years ago, its original recluse, Sir Hugh le Biron, showed taste as well as sanctity. He was no " friar of orders grey," no monk of the fraternity of Black Penitents; but a stalwart knight, once owner of Clayton Hall and Kersal Cell; both of which mansions have since become linked with nobler though untitled names. Tradition asserts that Sir Hugh left Clayton Hall for the Holy Land, with an esquire bearing his shield, and a hundred stout followers in his train. As the knight and retainers marched away, his lady prettily waved her handkerchief from the tower or turret of Clayton Hall. Arrived at the Holy Land, Le Biron dealt out his deadly blows with no niggardly measure, spreading dismay through the ranks of the enemy. Wherever an infidel's head was visible, there also was the arm of Sir Hugh, ready to cleave it in twain. At length his conscience became troubled, and he began to doubt the righteousness of his righteous cause. The ghosts of those slain by his valour rose in vast numbers before his distempered vision; the wailing of widows and the weeping of orphans, seemed to haunt him wheresoever he went, until he was glad to escape from the land thus rendered unholy, and turn his steps towards the English home from which he had been too long estranged. As he passed slowly up his own avenue he met a funeral train, bearing the remains of his lady to her final resting-place, there, as the tomb-stone sweetly expresses it, to "sleep in Jesus." Year after year she had pined for her absent lord, gradually sinking, the victim of "hope deferred." This blow severed the last link that bound Le Biron to the world, and he retreated from its turmoil to that solitude of Kersal Cell. Here, a "hermit lone," he alternately prayed and wandered,—climbing the picturesque heights of Kersal, or the wooded ways of Prestwich—until death, remembering the repentant warrior, removed him to the peaceful grave.—*Procter's " Our Turf, Stage, and Ring."*

THE CLEGG HALL TRAGEDY.

CLEGG HALL, about two miles N.E. from Rochdale, stands on the only estate within the parish of Whalley which still continues in the local family name. On this site was the old house built by Bernulf de Clegg and Quenilda his wife as early as the reign of Stephen. Not a vestige of it remains. The present comparatively modern erection was built by Theophilus Ashton, of Rochdale, a lawyer, and one of the Ashtons of Little Clegg, about the year 1620. After many changes of occupants, it is now in part used as a country alehouse; other portions are inhabited by the labouring classes, who find employment in that populous manufacturing district. It is the property of the Fentons, by purchase from the late John Entwisle, Esq., of Foxholes. To Clegg Hall, or rather what was once the site of that ancient house, tradition points through the dim vista of past ages as the scene of an unnatural and cruel tragedy. It was in the square, low, dark mansion, built in the reign of Stephen, that this crime is said to have been perpetrated,—one of those half-timbered houses, called post-and-petrel, having huge main timbers, crooks, &c., the interstices being wattled and filled with a compost of clay and chopped straw. Of this rude and primitive architecture were the houses of the English gentry in former ages. Here, then, was that horrible deed perpetrated

The Clegg Hall Tragedy.

which gave rise to the stories yet extant relating to the " Clegg Hall boggarts." The prevailing tradition is not exact as to the date of its occurrence ; but it is said that some time about the thirteenth or fourteenth century, a tragedy resembling that of the babes in the wood was perpetrated here. A wicked uncle destroyed the lawful heirs of Clegg Hall and estates—two orphan children that were left to his care—by throwing them over a balcony into the moat, in order that he might seize on their inheritance. Ever afterwards—so the story goes—the house was the reputed haunt of a troubled and angry spirit, until means were taken for its removal, or rather expulsion. Of course, this " boggart" could not be the manes of the murdered children, or it would have been seen as a plurality of spirits ; but was, in all likelihood, the wretched ghost of the ruffianly relative, whose double crime would not let him rest in the peace of the grave. Even after the original house was almost wholly pulled down, and that of A.D. 1620 erected on its site, the " boggart" still haunted the ancient spot, and its occasional visitations were the source of the great alarm and annoyance to which the inmates were subjected. From these slight materials, Mr Roby has woven one of those fictions, full of romantic incident, which have rendered his " Traditions of Lancashire" * so famous. We have taken such

* It is only just to state that the story of "Clegg Hall Boggart" was communicated to Mr Roby by Mr William Nuttall, of Rochdale, author of "Le Voyageur," and the composer of a ballad on the tradition. In this ballad, entitled " Sir Roland and Clegg Hall Boggart," Mr Nuttall makes Sir Roland murder the children in bed with a dagger. Remorse eventually drove him mad, and he died raving during a violent storm. The Hall was ever after haunted by the children's ghosts, and also by demons, till St Antonea (St Anthony), with a relic from the Virgin's shrine, exorcised and laid the evil spirits.

facts only as seem really traditionary, recommending the lovers of the marvellous to the work just cited for a very entertaining tale on this subject.

In a curious MS. volume, now the property of Charles Clay, Esq., M.D., of Manchester, Mr Nuttall states that "many ridiculous tales were told of 'the two boggarts [so that they were the ghosts of the children] of Clegg Hall,' by the country people. At one time, they unceasingly importuned a pious monk in the neighbourhood to exorcise or 'lay the ghosts,' to which request he consented. Having provided himself with a variety of charms and spells, he boldly entered on his undertaking, and in a few hours brought the ghosts to a parley. They demanded, as the condition of future quiet [the sacrifice of] a body and a soul. The spectators (who could not see the ghosts), on being informed of their desire, were petrified, none being willing to become the victim. The cunning monk told the tremblers, 'Bring me the body of a cock and the sole of a shoe.' This being done, the spirits were forbidden to 'revisit the pale glimpses of the moon' till the whole of the sacrifice was consumed. Thus ended the first laying of the Clegg Hall boggarts. But, in later times, it was conceived that the sacrifice must have been wholly consumed, and, consequently, that the two boggarts had full liberty to walk again; and hence the revival of the tradition and superstition." Another ballad by Mr Nuttall, entitled, "Rolfe and Quenilda," has Clegg Hall for its scene.

DILDRUM, KING OF THE CATS.

THE following tradition is often heard in South Lancashire:—A gentleman was one evening sitting cosily in his parlour, reading or meditating, when he was interrupted by the appearance of a cat, which came down the chimney, and called out, "Tell Dildrum, Doldrum's dead!" He was naturally startled by the occurrence; and when, shortly afterwards, his wife entered, he related to her what had happened, and their own cat, which had accompanied her, exclaimed, "Is Doldrum dead?" and immediately rushed up the chimney, and was heard or no more. Of course there were numberless conjectures upon such a remarkable event, but the general opinion appears to be that Doldrum had been king of cat-land, and that Dildrum was the next heir.—*N. and Q.*, 2d ser. x. 464.

THE "WRITTEN STONE" IN DILWORTH.

THE anonymous author of "The New Clock" mentions, in his "Curious Corners round Preston," that, having heard of a farm called "Written Stone," from an ancient stone bearing an inscription which stands near it, and that the place was reputed to be the haunt of boggarts, he determined to visit it. It is in the township of Dilworth, and parish of Ribchester, about two miles from the village of Longridge, and seven miles N.E. of Preston. Turning down a narrow lane, or old bridle-road, it soon plunged the searcher into a deep ravine, with a rapid mountain rivulet coursing through it, and a tall hedge of holly and hazel making the place a grove. For half a mile he walked and waded through mud and water, and on emerging from this long and tedious lane, turning to his right into a neat farmyard, he espied in a corner the object of his search. He describes it as a huge stone, a foot thick, nine feet long, two feet wide, and apparently from the adjacent rocks, placed like a gravestone on the cop. The inscription is on the side facing the road :—RAVFFE : RADCLIFFE : LAIDE : THIS : STONE : TO : LYE : FOR : EVER : A.D. 1655."*

The characters (he adds) are not the raised letters so prevalent in the seventeenth century, but deeply cut in the stone. He found the farmhouse tenanted by a young woman of very respectable appearance, the daughter of the owner of the estate, who, in this romantic spot, leads almost the life of a recluse. She had no dread of supernatural visitants, having never been disturbed by ghost or hobgoblin; and her theory on the subject was pithily summed up in the declaration, "that if folks only did what was right in this world, they would have nothing to fear." The date on the stone speaks of the days of sorcery and witchcraft, and of the troubled times of Cromwell's protectorate. Tradition declares this spot to have been the scene of a cruel and barbarous murder, and it is stated that this stone was put down in order to appease the restless spirit of the deceased, which played its nightly gambols long after the body had been "hearsed in earth." A story is told of one of the former occupants of Written Stone farm, who, thinking that the stone would make a capital "buttery stone," removed it into the house and applied it to that use. The result was, that the indignant or liberated spirit would never suffer his family to rest. Whatever pots, pans, kettles, or articles of crockery were placed on the stone, were tilted

---

* In Baines's "Lancashire" (vol. iii. p. 383), there is a somewhat different version of this inscription :—" Rafe Ratcliffe laid this stone here to lie for ever. A.D. 1607." He adds, that this Rafe was owner of the estate. It will be seen that neither christian name nor surname nor date agrees with the text, which latter, however, we believe to be correct.

over, their contents spilled, and the vessels themselves kept up a clattering dance the live-long night, at the beck of the unseen spirit. Thus worried out of his night's rest, the farmer soon found himself compelled to have the stone carefully conveyed back to its original resting-place, where it has remained ever since, and the good man's family have not again been disturbed by inexplicable nocturnal noises. Well may they say with Hamlet, " Rest, perturbed spirit !"

THE DULE UPO' DUN.

THE tradition upon which Mr Roby has founded one of his stories appeared many years ago in the *Kaleidoscope*, a Liverpool weekly literary publication. Barely three miles from Clitheroe, as you enter a small village on the right of the high road to Gisburne, stood a public-house, having for its sign the above title, which, being translated into plain English, is " The Devil upon Dun" (horse) The story runs that a poor tailor sold himself to Satan for seven years, after which term, according to the contract, signed, as is customary, with the victim's own blood, his soul was to become "the devil's own." He was to have three wishes, and these were expended in a wish for a collop of bacon ; in a second, that his wife were " far enough ;" and then that she were back home again. At the end of the seven years the Father of Lies appeared and claimed his victim, who tremblingly contended that the contract was won from him by fraud and dishonest pretences, and had not been fulfilled. He ventured to hint at the other party's lack of power to bestow riches or any great gift ; on which Satan was goaded into granting him another wish. " Then," said the trembling tailor,

"I wish thou wert riding back again to thy quarters, on yonder dun horse, and never able to plague me again, or any other poor wretch whom thou hast gotten into thy clutches!" The demon, with a roar, went away riveted to the back of this dun horse, and the tailor watched his departure almost beside himself for joy. He lived happy to a good old age, leaving behind him at his death good store of this world's gear, which was divided amongst his poorer relatives. One of them, having bought the house where the tailor dwelt, set up the trade of a tapster therein, having for his sign, "The Dule upo' Dun." On it is depicted "Old Hornie," mounted upon a scraggy dun horse, without saddle, bridle, or any sort of equipments whatever—the terrified steed being "off and away" at full gallop from the door, where a small hilarious tailor, with shears and measures, appears to view the departure of him of the cloven foot with anything but grief or disapprobation. The house itself is one of those ancient gabled black-and-white edifices, now fast disappearing under the march of improvement. Many windows of little lozenge-shaped panes set in lead, might be seen here in all the various stages of renovation and decay. Over the door, till lately, swung the old and quaint sign, attesting the truth of the tradition and the excellence of mine host's beer.

THE DUN COW AND THE OLD RIB.

THE anonymous writer of "Curious Corners round Preston," states that the "Old Rib" is the name given to an old farm in the township of Whittingham, in the parish of Kirkham, five miles north of Preston. The name, he says, is derived from an extraordinary rib, which was taken from an extraordinary old dun cow; which rib is placed over the door of the farmhouse, as a monument to the excellence of the defunct animal. About a quarter of a mile below the Towneley Arms Inn, in Longridge, about seven miles north-east of Preston, the seeker diverged from the main road into one of those old lanes or pack-horse roads so common in England, a short distance down which lane he came to the house bearing the name of "The Old Rib." It is a somewhat lofty, square building, with four turrets, like elongated sugar-loaves. The windows are of various forms and sizes, some of elaborate workmanship; and altogether the place has the aspect of having once been a mansion of some importance. On the doorway, at one end of the house, the architect and sculptor appear to have bestowed the greatest labour. The door is of oak, thick and strong, and studded with large square-headed nails; and there is a ponderous iron ring, serving at once for latch and knocker. Some armorial bearings are seen above, and over these again the "Old Rib." The doorway has the date of 1615, so that the place was in existence two years before the visit of King James I. to Hoghton Tower. The remains of a moat may be traced around the Old Rib House; but the moat has been filled up, and the surface is nearly level with its old banks. The few out-buildings standing near are ruins, notwithstanding that they had been built at a much later period, in all probability, than the house itself. As to the tradition of the "Old Dun Cow," it is related that "once upon a time" there wandered over the elevated and dark moors of Parlick, Bleasdale, Bowland, and Browsholme, a dun cow of stupendous size, and withal of most generous and extraordinary nature; and it is supposed in its daily pasturings to have been in the habit of quenching its thirst at "Nick's Water-Pot,"—a well on the summit of Parlick. The great merit of this wonderful cow was, that to all comers she gave an abundant supply of milk. Hence her fame spread; and from the heights of Browsholme, the brows of Leagrim, the valley of Chipping—from lofty Bleasdale and lowly Thornley, from haughty Parlick and humble Goosnargh, came milk-seekers in plenty, and none went empty-handed away. No matter how large the pail, it was always filled to the brim. But judging from the size of the rib, the cow must have been of gigantic size—a very Brobdignagian beast! The rib is still about a yard in length, and several inches in thickness; but within the memory of many residing in the district, it was more than twice its present size. Besides the decay consequent on time and exposure to the elements, the rib has suffered greatly from the ruthless hands of relic lovers or despoilers, who have cut and carried off portions of the rib as memorials of the Old Dun Cow. In short, the rib in its pristine proportions must have been "very like a whale," as Polonius says—at least, a whale's jaw-bone. Can this have been the origin of the quaint ballad which runs thus?—

"Did you ever, ever, ever, ever, ever, ever, ever, ever, ever, ever, ever, ever see a whale?"
"No I never, never, never, never, never, never, never, never, never, never, never, never, never saw a whale;
But I've often, often, often, often, often, often, often, often, often, often, often, often, often seen a cow,
Yes, I've often, often, often, often, often, often, often, often, often, often, often, often, often seen a cow."

To return to the legend of the Old Dun Cow; it may be conjectured that, with such ribs, and giving an ever-flowing, never-failing supply of milk, it must have needed a ladder to milk old Cushy. But alas! "much would have more." We know how the goose was served that laid golden eggs. It is conjectured that one of the far-famed Pendle witches (perhaps bribed and instigated by some envious milk-seller who had lost his custom, and wished to destroy the opposition shop) took, instead of a milk-pail, a large riddle or sieve, and went up to milk the old dun cow. At work she kept all day; the milk flowed in rich and copious streams; but at night the riddle was still empty. In vain the bountiful milk-giver taxed her powers to fill the old hag's strange milk-pail; the effort was too much; the fountain that had never failed before at last became dry; and either through the exhaustion of nature, or from vexation and disappointment at being outwitted by an old woman, the old cow gave up the ghost, and those dreary moors ceased for ever to be "a land flowing with milk." The rib hangs over the door, a sad memento of the Old Dun Cow, and by its size challenges the attention of the passer-by—a sort of "Ex pede Herculem."

THE EAGLE AND CHILD.

THE fabulous tradition of the Eagle and Child, the crest of the Stanleys, Earls of Derby, associates itself with the family of Lathom, and is thus gravely related: —Sir Thomas Lathom, the father of Isabel, having this only child, and cherishing an ardent desire for a son to inherit his name and fortune, had an intrigue with a young gentlewoman, the fruit of which was a son. This infant he contrived to have conveyed by a confidential servant to the foot of a tree in his park frequented by an eagle; and Sir Thomas and his lady, taking their usual walk, found the infant as if by accident. The old lady, considering it a gift from Heaven brought thither by the bird of prey and miraculously preserved, consented to adopt the boy as their heir.

> "That their content was such to see the hap,
> The ancient lady hugs it in her lap;
> Smothers it in kisses, bathes it in her tears,
> And unto Lathom House the babe she bears."

The name of Oskatel was given to the little foundling, Mary Oskatel being the name of his mother. From this time the crest of the eagle and child was assumed; but as the old knight approached near the grave, his conscience smote him, and on his death-bed he bequeathed the principal part of his fortune to Isabel, his daughter, now become the lady of Sir John Stanley, leaving poor Oskatel, on whom the king had conferred the honour of knighthood, only the manors of Islam and Urmston, near Manchester, and some possessions in the county of Chester, in which county he settled, and became the founder of the family of Latham of Astbury. This story is an after-thought, adapted to that which had previously existed. In the Harleian MS. (cod. 2151, fol. 4) is an account of some painted windows in Astbury Church, near Congleton, on which a figure is represented, with a sword and spurs, habited in a white tabard, the hands clasped, over the head a shield placed angle-wise under a helmet and mantle, emblazoned or, on a chief indented, azure, three bezants, over all a bondlet, gules; crest, an eagle standing on an empty cradle, with wings displayed, regardant or, with the inscription, "Orate pro anima Philippi Dom. Roberti Lathom militis"—(Pray for the soul of Philip, son of Sir Robert Lathom, knight). This Philip Lathom

The Eagle and Child.

of Astbury was uncle of Sir Thomas, *alias* Oskatel, the father of Isabella; and it would be a strange circumstance if an uncle should have assumed a crest bearing allusion to the adoption of an illegitimate child. Supposing Sir Oskatel to have been the son of Sir Thomas, instead of Sir Thomas himself, the fact of Philip bearing the crest would be still more extraordinary. That there was an Oskel or Oskatel Lathom, who bore as his crest an eagle standing on a child, is proved by the painting formerly in the windows of Northenden Church, 1580, —viz., an eagle sinister, regardant, rising, standing on a child, swaddled, placed on a nest; inscribed, "Oskell Lathum" (Harl. MS. 2151, fol. 10). But this may have been because it was the old Lathom crest; and the eagle seems to have been from a remote period a favourite cognisance of the family. The Torbocks, the younger branch of the Lathoms, took an eagle's claw for a difference on the family shield; and the grant of Witherington by Sir Thomas Lathom, sen., reputed further of Sir Oskatel, was sealed with the Lathom arms on an eagle's breast. But a legend of the eagle and child is as old as the time of King Alfred— several centuries earlier than the time of the De Lathoms :
—" One day as Alfred was hunting in a wood, he heard the cry of a little infant in a tree, and ordered his huntsmen to examine the place. They ascended the branches, and found at the top, in an eagle's nest, a beautiful child dressed in purple, with golden bracelets (the marks of nobility) on his arms. The King had him brought down and baptized and well educated. From the accident he named the foundling Nestingum. His grandson's daughter is said to have been one of the ladies for whom Edgar indulged an improper passion." If for Edgar we read Oscital, the Danish prince, this would complete

the parallel with the Lancashire tradition, as given by Baines in his history of the county.

Mr Roby, who expands this tradition into an interesting little romance, states that Sir Oskatel, the Earl of Derby's illegitimate child, palmed upon the Countess, and for a time adopted as heir to the Stanleys, had reserved to him and his descendants the manors of Islam and Urmston near Manchester, with other valuable estates. At the same time was given to him the signet of his arms, with the crest assumed for his sake, "an eagle regardant, proper." It was only subsequent to the supplanting of Sir Oskatel (continues our author) that his rivals took the present crest of the eagle and child, where the eagle is represented as having secured his prey, in token of their triumph over the foundling, whom he is preparing to devour. This crest the descendants of Sir John Stanley, the present Earls of Derby, continue to hold.—*See Appendix.*

"OLD MADAM" OF EGERTON HALL.

EGERTON HALL, in the township of Turton, was a quaint old residence some two centuries ago; but most of it has been pulled down, and the rest converted into a plain modern cottage. There was a curious legend connected with the old house, which still clings to the site, respecting the occasional appearance of the form of an old lady, dressed in white silk, and who is known by the name of the "Old Madam" to the residents in the district. This tradition is a very common one in most parts of Lancashire, as well as in other counties, and answers to the "Lady in White," who has become the common property of the folk-lore of nearly every country in Europe.

SIR BERTINE ENTWISEL.

IN Roby's "Traditions of Lancashire" is given "the ballad of Sir Bertine, the famous Lancashire knight, who was killed at St Alban's, fighting for the glorious Red Rose of Lancashire." A marble tablet to his memory, erected by a descendant in the parish church of St Chad, Rochdale, states that he was Viscount and Baron of Brybeke in Normandy, and sometime bailiff of Constantin; that he distinguished himself in arms in the service of his sovereigns Henry V. and Henry VI., more particularly at Agincourt; and that he was killed at the first battle of St Alban's, "fighting on King Henry VI. party, 28th May 1455. On whose sowl Jesu have mercy." The story goes, that being summoned by Henry VI., to aid him against his foes, he went at the head of a body of his retainers, men-at-arms, spears and lances, to join the King, notwithstanding the entreaties of his wife and daughter that he would stay at home. In his absence the ladies were startled by various evil omens; the great bell of the hall tolled without human hands; fingers tapped outside the casements; heavy footsteps, as of an armed man, were heard upon the stairs and in the chambers; and these evil auguries received their solution in an aged man appearing at the hall on the third day, bearing the bloody signet ring of Sir Bertine, and telling his wretched widow that he was slain in battle, and buried in the Priory of St Alban's.

"The brave Sir Bertine Entwisel
    Hath donned his coat of steel,
And left his hall, his stately home,
    To fight for England's weal.

"To fight for England's weal, I trow,
　　And good King Harry's right;
His loyal heart was warm and true,
　　His sword and buckler bright.

"That sword, once felt the craven foe,
　　Its hilt was black with gore;
And many a mother's son did rue
　　His might at Agincourt.

"And now he stately steps his hall—
　　'A summons from the King?
My armour bright, my casque and plume,
　　My sword and buckler bring.

"'Blow, warder, blow; thy horn is shrill;
　　My liegemen hither call;
For I must away to the south countrie,
　　And spears and lances all.'

"'Oh, go not to the south countrie!'
　　His lady weeping said;
'Oh, go not to the battle-field,
　　For I dreamed of the waters red!'

"'Oh, go not to the south countrie,'
　　Cried out his daughter dear;
'Oh, go not to the bloody fight,
　　For I dreamed of the waters clear!'

"Sir Bertine raised his dark vizor,
　　And he kissed his fond lady;
'I must away to the wars and fight,
　　For our King in jeopardy!'

"The lady gat her to the tower,
　　She clomb the battlement;
She watched and greet, while thro' the woods
　　The glittering falchions went.

"The wind was high, the storm grew loud,
　　Fierce rose the billowy sea;
When from Sir Bertine's lordly tower
　　The bell boomed heavily.

"'O mother dear! what bodes that speech
    From yonder iron-tongue?'
'Tis but the rude, rude blast, my love,
    That idle bell hath swung.'

"Upon the rattling casement still
    The beating rain fell fast,
When creeping fingers, wandering thrice,
    Across that window passed.

"'O mother dear! what means that sound
    Upon the lattice nigh?'
''Tis but the cold, cold arrowy sleet
    That hurtles in the sky.'

"The blast was still—a pause more dread
    Ne'er terror felt—when, lo!
An armed footstep on the stair
    Clanked heavily and slow.

"Up flew the latch and tirling pin;
    Wide swung the grated door;
Then came a solemn, stately tread
    Upon the quaking floor!

"A shudder through the building ran,
    A chill and icy blast;
A moan, as tho' in agony
    Some viewless spirit passed.

"'O mother dear, my heart is froze,
    My limbs are stark and cold:'
Her mother spake not, for again
    That turret-bell hath tolled.

"Three days passed by; at eventide
    There came an aged man;
He bent him low before the dame,
    His wrinkled cheek was wan,

"'Now speak, thou evil messenger,
    Thy biddings show to me.'
That aged man nor look vouchsafed,
    Nor ever a word spake he.

> "'What bringest thou?' the lady said,
> 'I charge thee by the rood.'
> He drew a signet from his hand;
> 'Twas speckled o'er with blood.
>
> "'Thy husband's grave is wide and deep;
> In St Alban's Priory
> His body lies; but on his soul
> Christ Jesu have mercy!'"

GENERAL FAIRFAX BURIED IN ASHTON CHURCH.

In one of his MS. vols. in Chetham's Library, Thomas Barrett, the Manchester antiquary, says:—"They have long had a tradition at Ashton-under-Lyne, that in the chancel of the church, the famous General Fairfax lies buried. How this came about I am at a loss to account for, unless done through privacy, to preserve his corpse from the ill-usage of his enemies, and that it was thus secreted through the means of Colonel Dukinfield, who served in the same cause with Fairfax in the Parliamentary army. Dukinfield Hall lies very near Ashton."

GORTON, REDDISH, AND THE NICKER DITCH.

According to a tradition noted in Greswell's MS. collections for a history of Manchester—"The inhabitants of Manchester are said to have behaved themselves valiantly against the Danes when they landed about A.D. 869." Whitaker says, "The house upon the Gore Brook challenged the denomination of Gore-ton." An old MS. formerly in the possession of the Rev. Joshua Brookes, A.M., chaplain of the College Church, Manchester, gives the following tradition:—"There is now to be seen in Denton, Gorton, Birch, &c., a ditch called Nicko or Micko, which (tradition says) was made in one night, from Ashton Moss to Ouse [Hough's] Moss; such a number of men being appointed as to cast up each the length of himself, in order to entrench themselves from the Danes, then invading England. The land on one side the ditch is called 'Danes' to this day, and the place in Gorton called 'Winding Hill' is said to take its name from the Briton's winding or going round to drive off the Danes. The township of Reddish (anciently written and still locally pronounced by the peasantry, Red-ditch), adjoining to Gorton and Denton, is said to take its name from the water in this ditch after the engagement being red." Such are the older traditions. Mr John Higson, of Droylsden, who has given considerable attention to the subject, supplies us with the existing traditions of the neighbourhood. He says that the above appears substantially correct (*i.e.*, to agree with current tradition), except as to the hill in Gorton, which old residents call "Winning Hill," and the name is so written in old title-deeds. The tradition is, that the great battle was "won" here, and that the name was given to commemorate the happy event, which unbound the necks of the Saxons from the thraldom of the Danes. During the battle the brook running through Gorton (by traditional etymology Goretown or the Blood-town) is said to have been filled with human gore, and was thence styled "Gore Brook," which name it has certainly borne five centuries and a half. The vale running from Gorton to Audenshaw is "the Dane Wood." There are also "the Danes" in Gorton; "Dane Head" and "Dane Shut" in Audenshaw. The two former are supposed to have been occupied by these invaders prior to the final conflict; and, after that engagement was over, a fugitive is said to have been decapitated at the third, and another to have been shot at the latter. The probable etymology, however (adds Mr Higson), is "dane, dene, or den," a valley with a stream running through the midst of it. The formation of the Nicker Ditch was apparently anterior to the general cultivation of the land through which it passes, as it forms the meare or boundary of various townships. He says this is known in the locality as "Th' Nickoditch," and thinks its etymology is of Danish origin; for according to Scandinavian mythology Odin assumes the name of Nickar, or Hnickar, when he acts as the destroying or evil principle. In this character, and under this name, he inhabits the lakes and rivers of Scandinavia.

[The editor has felt bound to give the ancient traditions and those still current in the neighbourhood, with the interpretation suggested by an intelligent resident well acquainted with the localities and their present names. But he must add that he sees no sufficient authority or reason for these traditional etymologies of the local names at the head of this parish. As to Gorton, Whitaker is probably right in deriving its name from the brook; but *Gor* (Anglo-Saxon) not only means gore or blood, but also, and with more probable significance here, dirt or mud. It also denotes a triangular plot of land; and either of these meanings is more likely to be the true one than that of a supposed bloody battle with the Danes. Mr Higson has correctly given the more probable etymology for the places pronounced Dane and Danes; for in Lancashire generally, *dean* or *dene* is pronounced *dane*, and these places are *denes* or hollow places, some of which are to be found in Worsley (the Deans or Danes Brow, &c.) The wood, the head, and the shut or shoot (A.S. *sceot*, pronounced *sheot*), are all applicable to a little dene, hollow, or valley. And so the invading Danes may disappear from these etymologies; and without them, what becomes of the battle? So as to Reddish, so far from being the red ditch, the etymologies of the thirteenth and fourteenth centuries are Re-dich or dyche, *i.e.*, the reed or reedy ditch. As to the Nicko or Nicker ditch, the old MS. quoted above gives us an alternative, " Micko," which we think guides to the true etymology. In deeds of the fourteenth century this was always called the Michel, Mikel, or Muchil Diche (from the Anglo-Saxon *micel, mucel*, pronounced mickle, muckle), and, of course, meaning the great ditch. There was an estate in the neighbourhood called the Milk Wall Slade, and this name may have been a corruption of Mickle, or Muckle, into Milk-wall; but there is not the slightest warrant in old deeds and charters for the Nicker or Nicko Ditch; so that the Scandinavian myth must depart with the Danes themselves.]

HABERGHAM HALL AND THE LADY'S LAMENT.

HABERGHAM HALL, near Burnley, was long the residence of a respectable family of the same name. In the year 1201 Alina and Sabina de Habringham litigated the possession of four bovates of land, about eighty acres, against their sister Eugenia. Roger de Lacy was on good terms with this family, and, in 1204, gave to Matthew de Hambringham two bovates of land in Hambringham. The last heir-male was John Habergham, Esq., who was born in the year 1650, and died without legitimate issue in the beginning of the last century. Where he died, and where he was buried, are not known; for during the latter portion of his life he wandered about as a vagabond, without a home, and deserted by those friends who had assisted in wasting his family estates. He married Fleetwood, daughter of Nicholas Towneley, Esq., of Royle Hall, but their union was not a happy one. She bore with her husband's misconduct as long as possible; and on being deprived of her home, by the forfeiture of the Habergham estate, she went to reside with her friends, and dying in 1703, was buried at Padiham. Tradition states that Mrs Habergham soothed her sorrow by composing and singing the following stanzas, which are still held in remembrance, not only in the neighbourhood, but throughout Lancashire. They are here reprinted, with some verbal alterations, from Harland's "Lancashire Ballads:"—

LOVE'S EVIL CHOICE.

I sowed the seeds of love;
  It was all in the spring,
In April, May, and June likewise,
  When small birds they do sing.

My garden planted was with care,
  With blooming wild-flowers everywhere;
Yet had I not the leave to choose
  The flower I loved most dear.

The gardener standing by
  Proffered to choose for me
The pink, the primrose, and the rose,
  But I refused all three.

The primrose I forsook
  Because it came too soon;
The violet I o'erlooked,
  And vowed to wait till June.

In June the red rose sprang,
  But 'twas no flower for me;
I plucked it up, lo! by the stalk,
  And planted the willow-tree.

The willow I now must wear,
  With sorrows twined among,

That all the world may know
  I falsehood loved too long.
The willow-tree will twist,
  The willow-tree will twine,
I wish I was in that dear youth's arms
  That once had this heart of mine.

The gardener he stood by,
  And warned me to take care ;
For in the midst of a red rosebud
  There grows a sharp thorn there.

I said I'd take no care,
  Till I did feel the smart ;
And when I plucked the red rosebud,
  It pierced me to the heart.

Now I'll make a hyssop posy,
  No other can I touch ;
For all the world do plainly see
  I loved one flower too much.

My garden is now run wild ;
  Where shall I plant anew?
My bed, that once was thick with thyme,
  Is now o'errun with rue.

THE "CHYLDE OF HALE."

JOHN MIDDLETON, the "Chylde of Hale," was born at the village of Hale, in the parish of Childwall, during 1578, and was buried in the churchyard of Hale in 1623. His gravestone is yet shown about the centre of the south aisle, with the following inscription upon it in letters run in with lead :—" Here lyeth the bodye of John Middleton, the Chylde of Hale. Born A.D. 1578. Dyed A.D. 1623." He is said to have been nine feet three inches in height ; his hand measured seventeen inches from the carpus to the end of the middle finger ; and the breadth of his palm was eight inches and a half.

Sir Gilbert Ireland took him to the court of James I., on which occasion some Lancashire gentlemen dressed him " with large ruffs about his neck and hands ; a striped doublet of crimson and white round his waist ; a blue girdle embroidered with gold ; large white plush breeches powdered with blue flowers ; green stockings ; broad shoes of a light colour, having red heels, and tied with large bows of red ribbon ; just below his knees bandages of the same colour, with large bows ; by his side a sword, suspended by a broad belt over his shoulder, and embroidered, as his girdle, with blue and gold, with the addition of gold fringe upon the edge." In this costume he is said to have wrestled with the king's wrestler, whom he overcame and put out his thumb. This displeased some of the courtiers, and hence the King dismissed him with a present of £20. He returned home by Brazenose College, Oxford, which was then full of Lancashire students. While resident at Oxford his portrait was taken of full life size, and is now to be seen in the College Library. There is also another likeness of him preserved at High Leigh; and an original painting of the " Chylde " is kept in the gallery at Hale Hall, bearing the following inscription :—" This is the true portraiture of John Middleton, the ' Chylde of Hale,' who was born at Hale 1578, and was buried at Hale, 1623." About eighty years ago, the body is said to have been taken up, and the principal bones were for some time preserved at Hale Hall. The thigh-bone reached from the hip of a common man to his feet, and the rest measured in proportion. After some time, the bones were reburied in the churchyard, but whereabouts is not known. He could only stand upright in the centre of the cottage in which he resided ; and tradition states that he attained his wonderful stature in one night, in consequence of some spells and incantations that were practised against him. The Rev. William Stewart, in his "Memorials of Hale, 1848," says that "the cottage is now inhabited by Mr Thomas Johnson, and is situated near the south-west corner of the Parsonage Green. A descendant of his family, Charles Chadwick, was living in 1804, and was more than six feet high. Some descendants of Charles Chadwick are now living of the name of Blundell, very similar in bulk to the 'Chylde,' but only of common size as to height." Another writer states, what is well known in the neighbourhood, that—"There exists a cavity in the sands near Hale, in Lancashire, where tradition asserts that, on one occasion the famous 'Chylde' fell asleep, and on awaking found all his clothes had burst; and so much had he grown during this short nap, that he doubted his own identity. On his way homewards, he was attacked by a furious bull; but so strong had he become, that he caught it by the horns and threw it to an immense distance. The bull did not approve of such tossing, and, consequently, suffered him to proceed without further molestation." A still more extravagant tradition relates that "he was so strong in one of his illnesses that his friends had to chain him in bed. When he recovered, two of the chains were given away; one was sent to Chester in order to keep the Dee Mills from floating down the river; the second was sent to Boston to prevent the Stump from being blown into the sea; and the third was lent in order to chain down his infernal majesty, who had been captured when suffering from an internal complaint! On another occasion, some robbers attempted to break into his mother's house; and had removed a window for that purpose; but, on being confronted by the "Chylde," they took to their heels, and never looked behind them till they reached the shores of the Mersey, at Liverpool. The bed said to have been used by this modern giant was exhibited at Hale until within these few years; and, if a genuine relic, proves him to have been of vast size.

HANGING DITCH, MANCHESTER.

LOCAL tradition declares that it derived this ominous name from having been the scene of the execution of several Romish clergy and recusants in the reign of Queen Elizabeth. But there are two very strong reasons against this being the fact :—First, there is no record of any execution in Manchester on the ground of recusancy or treason during the whole of that reign; second, there was formerly a "hanging bridge" over the stream, which has left its name and some portion of one of the piers remaining. Now, Hanging Bridge needs no search for a derivation; and we can hardly doubt that the ditch below the Hanging Bridge soon took the name of the Hanging Ditch.

HORNBY CHAPEL AND SIR EDWARD STANLEY.

SIR EDWARD STANLEY, fifth son of Thomas, first Earl of Derby, early received the notice and favour of Henry VIII. It is said of him that "the camp was his school, and his learning the pike and sword." The King's greeting when they met was, "Ho! my soldier." Honour floated in his veins, and valour danced in his spirit. At the battle of Flodden he commanded the rear of the English army, and through his great bravery and skill, he mainly contributed to that memorable victory. A sudden feint inducing the Scots to descend a hill, their stronghold, an opening was caused in their ranks, which Sir Edward Stanley espying, he attacked them on a sudden with his Lancashire bowmen. So unexpected an assault put them into great disorder, which gave the first hopes of success, and kindled fresh courage through the English ranks, ending in the complete overthrow and discomfiture of their enemies. Upon this signal achievement, Sir Edward received from the hand of his royal master a letter of thanks, with an assurance of some future reward. Accordingly, the following year, the King keeping Whitsuntide at Eltham, in Kent, and Sir Edward being in his train, his majesty commanded that, for his valiant acts against the Scots at Flodden—an achievement worthy of his ancestors, who bore an eagle on their crest—he should be created Lord Monteagle; and he had a special summons to Parliament in the same year by the title of Baron Stanley, Lord Monteagle. On various occasions in France, and also in the northern rebellions headed by Aske and Captain Cobbler, he rendered great service both by his bravery and his craft. Marrying into the family of the Harringtons, he resided the latter part of his life at Hornby Castle, engaged in schemes for the most part tending to his own wealth and aggrandisement. Foul surmises prevailed, especially during his later years, as to the means by which he possessed himself of the estates which he then held in right of his lady, and those, too, that he enjoyed through the attainder of her uncle, Sir James Harrington. Stanley acknowledged himself a free-thinker and a materialist—a character of rare occurrence in that age, showing him to be as daring in his opinions as in his pursuits. Amongst his recorded expressions are—"That the soul of man was like the winding-up of a watch; and that when the spring was run down, the man died, and the soul was extinct." He displayed a thorough contempt for the maxims and opinions of the world, and an utter recklessness of its censure or esteem. Dr Whitaker says of him, "From several hints obliquely thrown out by friends as well as enemies, this man appears to have been a very wicked person, of a cast and character very uncommon in those unreflecting times . . . There certainly was something very extraordinary about the man, which, amidst the feudal and knightly habits in which young persons of his high rank were then bred, prompted him to speculate, however unhappily, on any metaphysical subject. Now whether this abominable persuasion [of atheism] were the cause or effect of his actual guilt—whether he had reasoned himself into materialism in order to drown the voice of conscience, or fell into the sin of murder because he had previously reasoned himself out of all ideas of responsibility, does not appear; but his practice, as might have been expected, was suited to his principles, and Hornby was too rich a bait to a man who hoped for no enjoyment but in the present life, and feared no retribution in another. Accordingly we find him loudly accused of having poisoned his brother-in-law, John Harrington, by the agency of a servant; and he is suspected also of having, through subornation of perjury, proved, or attempted to prove, himself tenant of the Honour of Hornby." Mr Roby has written a pleasant fiction, based on the character and imputed crimes of Lord Monteagle, in which he represents him as occupying midnight vigils in the castle-turret, in "wizard spells and rites unholy." He sends for the parson of Slaidburn, that he may put him to shame in an argument on the authenticity of the Christian religion; but the parson has the better of the argument, and does not fear to taunt the ruthless baron with the mur-

der of John Harrington, whom he styles "my lady's cousin." The dispute with the parson ends with an apparition of the murdered man, in the form of a thick white cloud, and the unbelieving baron becomes an altered man. Under the ministrations of the worthy parson, he became gradually more enlightened; his terrors were calmed, and he at length accepted Christianity as truth. Soon afterwards arose that noble structure the chapel of Hornby, bearing on its front the following legend:—
"Edwardus Stanley, Miles, Dñs Monteagle, me fieri fecit"
—(Edward Stanley, Knight, Lord Monteagle, caused me to be erected). Its foundation was generally ascribed to some vow made at Flodden; but at that time the bold soldier was not a vower of vows; and Mr Roby thinks that his conversion from infidelity is the more probable cause of his chapel-building. It is recorded that Edward Stanley, Baron Monteagle, died in the faith he had once despised.

THE HULME HALL TREASURE.

BURIED treasure and its unearthly guardians attach themselves to many of our ancient mansions; and they cease to be haunted as soon as the cause is removed. There is a tradition of this kind relating to Hulme Hall, formerly the seat of a branch of the Prestwich family. During the civil wars its then owner, Sir Thomas Prestwich, was very much impoverished by fines and sequestrations; so that in 1660 he sold the mansion and estate to Sir Oswald Mosley. His mother had, on many occasions, induced him to advance large sums of money to Charles I. and his adherents, under the assurance that she had hidden treasures which would amply repay him. This hoard was supposed to have been hidden either in the Hall itself or in the grounds adjoining; and it was said to be protected by spells and incantations known only to the Lady Dowager herself. Time passed on, and the old lady became infirm; and at last she was struck down by apoplexy before she could either practise the requisite incantations or inform her son where the treasure was secreted. After her burial diligent search was made, but without result; and he too went down to the grave in comparative poverty. Since that period fortune-tellers and astrologers have frequently tried their powers in order to discover this hidden wealth; but they have not yet been successful. It is still believed, however, that on some future occasion they will be more fortunate, and that the demons who guard the hoard will be overcome and forced to give up their charge. The Hall and estate passed from the hands of the Mosleys into the possession of other proprietors, and were ultimately sold to the late Duke of Bridgewater. Some years ago the site was required for other purposes, and the Hall was pulled down; but although considerable care was taken, no money was discovered.

INCE HALL AND THE DEAD HAND.

INCE HALL is one of those curious half-timbered mansions which are now becoming rare in this county. Its six sharply-pointed gables, and its long ranges of mullioned windows, give it an imposing appearance from a distance; and on a nearer approach the remains of a moat are visible, which proves that it has once possessed means of defence. The estate connected with the Hall belonged to the Gerards for upwards of seven hundred years; the owners being descended from Walter Fitzother,

Ince Hall and the Dead Hand.

castellan of Windsor at the time when Domesday Book was compiled. William, son of Walter, adopted De Windsor for his family name; but his brother Gerard was content with his ordinary patronymic, and became the ancestor of the Gerards of Bryn, now represented by Sir Robert Gerard of Garswood Hall.

The family of Ince is also very ancient, dating nearly, if not quite, from the conquest. Private documents show that Richard de Ince, in 1322, held one-sixteenth of a knight's fee in Aspull; and a grandson of this Richard left, as sole heiress, a daughter Ellen, who married John the third son of Sir Peter Gerard, of Bryn, about the year 1368. The township of Ince was conveyed to him by this marriage, and the family resided at the old Hall for many generations. Maurice Fitz-Gerald, or Gerard, was a younger son of this family, and was one of the adventurers who accompanied Strongbow, Earl of Pembroke, on his expedition to conquer Ireland in 1170. The present Earls of Macclesfield are also lineally descended from the same John Gerard of Ince. This portion of the property subsequently belonged to a branch of the Walmsleys, whose parent stock resided at Showley, near Blackburn, and is now owned by Richard Walmsley, Esq., of Bath.

The mansion which has obtained the name of Ince Hall, without the designation of "old," was built by Roger Browne during the reign of James I. He was descended from Roger Browne de Ince, who is designated as a "gentleman," and held some lands here in the 14 Richard II., or 1390. A descendant named William resided here in 2 Elizabeth, or 1559, and was succeeded by his son Roger, who mortgaged his estates in order to defray the expenses of this costly erection. He died comparatively poor, but the mortgages were redeemed by his brother Ralph, his heir and successor, during 12 James I, or 1614.

There is a story of wrong attaching to Ince Hall which has given rise to the legend of the Dead Hand. One of its early possessors lay on his death-bed, and a lawyer was sent for at the last moment to make his will; but before he reached the man was dead. In this dilemma it was determined to try the effect of a dead man's hand on the corpse, and the attorney's clerk was sent for one to Bryn Hall in all haste. The body of the dead man was rubbed with the holy hand, and it was asserted that he revived sufficiently to sign his will. After the funeral a daughter of the deceased produced a will which was not signed, leaving the property to his son and daughter; but the lawyer soon produced another will signed by the dead hand, which conveyed all the property to himself. The son quarrelled with the attorney, and after wounding him, as he supposed mortally, he left the country and was never heard of more. The daughter also disappeared, but no one knew how or when. After many years the gardener turned up a skull in the garden with his spade, and the secret was revealed. When this took place the Hall had long been uninhabited; for the murdered daughter's ghost hung suspended in the air before the dishonest lawyer wherever he went. It is said that he spent the remainder of his days in Wigan, the victim of remorse and despair. There is a room in the Hall which is said to be haunted by the ghost of a young lady, and her shadowy form is frequently seen by the passers by hovering over the spot where her remains were buried.

The Holy Hand alluded to in the preceding legend is now kept in the Catholic chapel at Ashton-in-Mackerfield. It is known to have belonged to Father Arrowsmith, who was executed at Lancaster on the 28th August 1628. As the crime for which he suffered has been variously stated, we may add that—Father Edmund Arrowsmith, of the Society of Jesus, was born at Haydock, in the parish of Winwick, during 1585. In 1605 he entered the college at Douay, and in 1612 was ordained priest. In the next year he was sent on the mission to England; and in 1628 he was apprehended and brought to Lancaster on a charge of being a Romish priest, contrary to the laws "in that case made and provided." He was tried and sentenced to death at the August assizes of that year. After he was cut down one of his friends cut off his right hand, which was kept for many years at Bryn Hall. On the demolition of that ancient structure it was removed to Garswood, and afterwards to Ashton, where it still remains in the custody of the priest.

The virtues of this "Dead Hand" are said to be manifold. It is believed to remove tumours when rubbed over the parts affected; and persons come from long distances to be cured by it of various diseases. In August 1872, a paralytic walked from Salford to Mackerfield, in order that she might be cured by the holy hand. She was found exhausted on a door-step by the way, not being able to reach her destination, and this brought the matter under the parish authorities. It is preserved with great care in a white silken bag, and many wonderful cures are said to have been wrought by this saintly relic.

KERSAL HALL TRADITIONS.

THOUGH many of the antiquated mansions of Lancashire can boast of a ghostly legend, or a half-historical tradition, few are so rich in boggart-lore as Kersal Hall (now a dependency of Kersal Cell), two or three hobgoblin stories being attached to its name. When Richard Peveril, the last Saxon inheritor of Kersal, in defending his home against Norman intruders, was overpowered by numbers, his body was thrown into the Irwell opposite to his own door. The knight who slew Peveril took immediate possession of the envied domain by right of conquest; but his triumph was of short duration. While he slumbered at midnight, the gnomes of the lower earth and the spirits of the upper air united their forces to effect his destruction. When daylight appeared, the Norman was found extended upon the spacious threshold—a notice or caution, written with his own crimson fluid, being visible on his brow, to the effect that all trespassers would be prosecuted to the utmost rigour of fairy law. The night thus made hideous must have been especially dreary to the retainers of Kersal Hall; the rhyming history of Anthony de Irwell averring that they could not sleep in their beds:—

> "Terror o'er each hind would creep,
> As, starting from his dreamy sleep,
> He listened to the echoing shout
> Which told him that the fiends were out."

Bold Avaranches was the next victim, and then came Eustace Dauntesey as chief of the fated mansion. Dauntesey wooed a maiden—no doubt a beautiful young lady, with a handsome fortune—who was ultimately won by a rival suitor. The wedding-day was fixed, and the prospect of their coming happiness was utter misery to Eustace. Having in his studious youth perfected himself in the black art—a genteel accomplishment in the dark ages—he drew a magic circle, even at the witching hour, and summoned the evil one to a consultation. The usual bargain was soon struck, the soul of Eustace being bartered for the coveted body of the maid; the compact to close at the lady's death, and the demon to remain meanwhile by the side of Dauntesey in the form of an elegant "self," or genteel companion. Eustace and his dear one (in a double sense) stood before the altar in due course, and the marriage ceremony was completed. On stepping out of the sacred edifice the elements were found to be unfavourable. The flowers strewed before their feet stuck to their wet shoes, and the torch of Hymen refused to burn brightly in a soaking shower. Arrived within his festive hall, the ill-fortune of Eustace took another shape. His bride began to melt away before his eyes. Familiar as he was with magic, here was a mystery beyond his comprehension. Something is recorded about a holy prayer, a sunny beam, and an angel train, bearing her slowly to a fleecy cloud, in whose bosom she became lost to earth. Taken altogether, the affair was a perfect swindle in its bearings upon Eustace. Awakened to consciousness by a touch from his sinister companion, Dauntesey saw a yawning gulf at his feet, and felt himself gradually going in a direction exactly the reverse of that taken by his bride of an hour.—*Procter's* "*Our Turf, Stage, and Ring.*"

LOSTOCK TOWER—"TOO LATE."

Lostock Tower lies about four miles to the west of Bolton. It was formerly an imposing structure, formed mainly of wood and plaster, and surrounded by a moat. There is now little left except the gateway, which occupies the site of a much more ancient building. This is mostly built of brick and stone, interspersed with string-courses and mouldings. The windows are very large, and are divided into compartments by strong mullions. Over one of the upper windows there is a deep panel containing a coat of arms, now almost obliterated. On the front of the house there is the date "A.D. 1591;" and a panel over the doorway, on which is the inscription "S. F. A. 1702," obviously marks the period when this portion of the Hall was either enlarged or repaired. This characteristic residence was not very judiciously situated, according to modern ideas. There is much low ground in the neighbourhood, which contains several rather picturesque sheets of water, and it is, besides, in the immediate vicinity of the boggy tract known as Red Moss. The river Croal rises from this marshy ground, which, after passing through Bolton, falls into the Irwell; the far-famed Douglas, also, has its origin in the same Moss, and, after flowing through Wigan, falls into the Ribble near Hesketh.

Lostock Tower formerly belonged to the Andertons, but has since merged into the hands of the Blundells of Ince. There is a story of wrong connected with one of the early Andertons, which has passed into a tradition, and is even yet a source of heart-burning to a family named Heaton resident in a neighbouring township of the same name. This tradition states that one of the Heatons was an improvident man, and wasted much of his patrimony. He became deeply involved in debt, and mortgaged his township to Anderton of the Tower. The day for payment duly arrived, but the Heatons had not raised the money. The evening passed on, and at a somewhat early hour the Andertons retired to bed. They had not lain long before the Heatons were thundering at the doors; for they had raised the amount at the last moment, and were ready to pay. The owner of the

Tower, however, coveted the property, and refused to let them in because they ought to have been ready before the going down of the sun. On the morrow he said they were too late, and declared that the mortgage was foreclosed. The wrong done to the Heatons was never forgiven, for the family was utterly ruined; and it is stated that the soul of the wrongdoer is doomed to revisit the scene of his crime until the property is restored. It is also affirmed that no horse from the Tower, so long as it was occupied by an Anderton, could ever be forced to cross the stream into the manor of Heaton. Sir Francis Anderton took part in the Rebellion of 1745, and soon after lost his estates. In 1750 he was reported to be over sixty years of age, and childless; his property was held by the crown under trustees, and eventually passed to the Blundells, he living in retirement until his death. This gentleman's fate is considered to be an act of retributive justice for the wrong done to the Heaton family by his ancestor of the Tower.

MAB'S CROSS

IN the Church of Wigan near one of the four gates called Standish Gate, stands a ruined stone cross, connected with an ancient tradition, which the late Mr Roby, *more suo*, has expanded and embellished into a long and interesting story; but the principal source he draws from is the genealogical roll of the Bradshaighs, from which we take the old tradition, in the quaint terms of the original:
—" Sir William Bradshaigh, second son to Sir John, was a great traveller and a soldier, and married to Mabel, daughter and sole heiress of Hugh Norres de Haghe

[Haigh] and Blackrode, and had issue, &c. Of this Mabel is a story by tradition of undoubted verity, that in Sir William Bradshaigh's absence (being ten years away in the holy wars) she married a Welsh knight. Sir William, returning from the wars, came in a palmer's habit amongst the poor to Haghe; who when she saw and congetringe [conjecturing] that he favoured [resembled] her former husband, wept—for which the knight [her second husband] chastised her; at which Sir William went and made himself known to his tenants; in which space the knight fled, but near to Newton Park, Sir William overtook and slew him. The said Dame Mabel was enjoined by her confessor to do penance by going once every week, barefooted and barelegged, to a cross near Wigan from the Haghe, whilst she lived, and [it is] called Mabb's to this day; and their monument lies in Wigan Church, as you see them there pourtrayed." Sir William Bradshaigh was outlawed during the space of a year and a day for killing the Welsh knight; but he and his lady, it is said, lived happily together afterwards until their death. The remains of the effigies on their tomb have been decayed by time, perhaps further injured by iconoclasts, and finally have suffered from the embellishing hands of whitewashing churchwardens. The tradition trips in stating that Sir William was in the Holy Wars, as he was not born till about ten years after the sixth and last of the Crusades. It is probable that he was in the disastrous campaign of Edward II. against the Scots; and his long absence from home is accounted for by the supposition that he was for the greater part of the time a captive.

The most ancient and interesting monument in Wigan parish church is placed under the stairs leading to the east gallery, where two mangled figures of whitewashed stone preserve the remembrance of Sir William Bradshaigh, of Haigh, and his lady Mabel—he in an antique coat of mail, cross-legged, with his sword partly drawn from the scabbard by his left side, and on his shoulder his shield, charged with two bends; and she in a long robe, veiled, her hands elevated and conjoined in the attitude of fervent prayer. The history of this valorous knight and his lady is preserved in the family pedigree of the Bradshaighs in the terms already given. In 1664, when Sir William Dugdale made his visitation, he sketched a drawing of the monument, as it then stood, upon the family pedigree, now in the possession of the Earl of Balcarres. Sir William was not only outlawed for slaying the Welsh knight, but in the *Inquisitiones ad quod damnum* of 11 Edward II. (1317-18), he is designated "a felon." Mab's Cross stands at the top of Standish Gate, Wigan, at the entrance to the town from the Standish road, and consists of the base of a pillar and half a shaft of four sides, rounded off by time, to which the lady made her weekly pilgrimages, in penitential attire, from the chapel at Haigh Hall, a distance of two miles, in an age when ten years' widowhood was not thought a sufficient expiation of the crime of taking a second husband.

ORMSKIRK CHURCH.

THIS church is a large massive structure, on a slightly rising ground, north-west of the town, and has a tower commanding a fine view of the Irish Sea, Liverpool, Preston, &c., and also a spire at the south-east corner, which is partly modern, but resting on an ancient octagonal base. The church was probably built soon after the Conquest by Orm, the proprietor of Hatton. A local tradition, of no well-ascertained authority, represents it as having been erected at the cost of two maiden ladies [? sisters] named Orm, who, being unable to decide whether it should have a tower or a spire, accommodated their differences by giving it both. A more probable tradition states that the spire was attached to the original edifice, and that, on the suppression of Burscough Priory, the tower was built for the reception of eight of the bells taken thence, the remainder of the priory bells being removed to Croston Church. The tenor bell at Ormskirk, which is said to have been the third at Burscough, has a Latin inscription in old English letters, "J. S. de Burscough, Esq., and E. my wife, made [this bell] in honour of the Trinity. R.B. 1497."

Roby observes that this tradition is an idle and impertinent invention, as the old ladies might each have had her way by building a tower and surmounting it by a spire. But who can say whether, in self-will, one lady would like to see her tower capped, surmounted, and so to speak, extinguished, by the spire of her sister? He suggests as a more probable solution that at the dissolution of the Priory of Burscough, temp. Henry VIII., the bells of its conventual church were removed to Ormskirk; and, as the small tower beneath the spire was not sufficiently capacious to receive them, the present square steeple was added. This suggestion receives some confirmation in the fact that the tenor bell of Ormskirk church, said to have been previously the third bell at Burscough Priory, bears some apparent proof of its translation. Round the circle below the ear is the following inscription, all, except the founder's initials, in black letter:—"J. S. * de Burscough, * Armig. * et * E. * vr. me fecerunt in honoris Trinitatis. * R.B. 1497." That is, "J. S. of Burscough, Esq., and E. his wife, made me in honour of the Trinity." Where each asterisk is marked are the rose, portcullis, and fleur-de-lis. The Lancashire rose and the portcullis (borne by the Countess of Richmond and Derby, as a daughter of the Duke of Somerset) were favourite badges of Henry VII., who, besides the fleur-de-lis of France, being usually quartered at that time in the royal arms of England, had some claim to that bearing as the grandson of Sir Owen Tudor and Catherine of France, relict of Henry V. Henry VII. visited the neighbourhood, at Lathom House, the year before this bell was cast; and hence it was probably presented to the Priory in honour of his visit.

RHODES AND PILKINGTON.

In Watson's MSS. the following traditional story relating to the estate called Rhodes, in the manor of Pilkington, is preserved:—"Rhodes of Rhodes, having his estate, and it being land of inheritance, and lying within the manor of Pilkington, then belonging to Sir John [? Sir Thomas] Pilkington, the knight, desirous of purchasing the estate, applied to Rhodes; but he, being unwilling to part with it, refused to sell. The estate is of considerable length, and is bounded by the river Irwell for more than a mile, and at the extremity of the land stood a cowhouse, of which Rhodes made use as a shelter for young cattle during winter, but at other times it was disused. Into this building, it is said, Sir John ordered some of his own cattle to be put, and locked them up there, giving out that they were stolen, and a reward was offered accordingly. Some time passed before the cattle were found; at length, as had been concerted, some of Sir John's people found them in the above cowhouse; and proceedings in law were immediately commenced against Rhodes for this pretended robbery, against which Rhodes defended himself; but the fact of the cattle being locked up in his building being notorious, and the presumption of his being privy to, if not a principal in, the concealment, was evidence so strong against Rhodes, that he was obliged to come upon terms with Sir John, which caused the loss of his inheritance. Sir John afterwards forfeited the manor of Pilkington: this, in those days, was called a just judgment, and believed to have been inflicted upon him for the above treachery. The manor was given to the Derby family by the crown. The mansion-house was formerly encompassed by a moat, part of which still remains."

The late Mr Thomas Barritt, the antiquary, gives the following very different account of the matter:—" In Prestwich parish is a place called the Rhodes, where there is an old hall nearly surrounded with a moat. This appears to have been long ago the seat of some old family of note, but of what name I cannot learn. There is, however, a tradition in that neighbourhood that the first Earl of Derby had lands given him in Lancashire by his stepson, Henry VII., that belonged to gentry in this county; particularly in Broughton, Pilkington, Prestwich, Bury, and Chetham. The owners of these estates not taking the part of Henry, were by him outlawed, and were driven from their homes by the Earl of Derby. Amongst them was Sir John Chetham of Chetham, whose seat was at what is now called Peel, a little beyond Scotland Bridge, Manchester. His house was razed. Quere, whether the site of a Roman *castrum* at this place, mentioned by the Rev. John Whitaker, was not the old situation of Sir John Chetham's house? This land is now owned by the present Earl of Derby (1780), who likewise now owns one half of Rhodes estate, and one half of the old hall, which is now divided into two dwellings. On a chimneypiece in one of the parlours I observed the letters 'H.P.,' which recalled to memory that this house was once the residence of the Prestwich family of Prestwich, one of which family founded Prestwich church. All or great part of this estate was sold by the sequestrators in the time of the civil war in the reign of Charles I., and one half was bought by a Mr Fox, whose family hath lived there till very lately. But after the Restoration, Charles, Earl of Derby, son of that Earl who was beheaded at Bolton, laid claim to the share that Mr Fox had bought, who was determined to keep his purchase. The Earl, on finding this, had recourse to the following stratagem:— It was pretended that two oxen had been stolen from Knowsley; but they were privily conveyed one night into the shippon of Mr Fox. Persons were immediately dispatched all over the country in search of the beasts, which were found in the shippon of Mr Fox, who was seized on as the thief, and threatened with being sent to prison. Mr Fox, knowing his innocence, and that the charge was a juggle, was willing to go to prison; but the persons sent by the Earl, and instructed how to proceed, finding this, offered him the Earl's pardon on condition he would deliver up the land, which Mr Fox still refused, and persisted in going to prison. But when he had got a little distance from the house, his wife and children followed, and persuaded him to hearken to the terms proposed by the Earl's servants; who then offered him his release upon these terms,—that the Earl should receive again the estate, and Mr Fox still continue thereon, and become the Earl's tenant, and, on paying rent for the same, continue, he and his heirs, tenants for ever; which place they now enjoy."

THE SITE OF ST CHAD'S CHURCH, ROCHDALE.

TOWARDS the close of the reign of William the Conqueror, Gamel, the Saxon thane, Lord of Recedham or Rochdale, being left in the quiet possession of his lands and privileges, was "minded, for the fear of God and the salvation of his immortal soul, to build a chapel unto St Chadde," nigh to the banks of the Rache or Roach. According to Mr Roby, in his "Traditions," a place was set apart on the north bank of the river, in a low and sheltered spot now called "The Newgate." Piles of timber and huge stones were gathered in profusion; the foundations were laid; stakes having been driven; and several courses of rubble stone laid ready to receive the grouting or cement. In one night, the whole mass was conveyed, without the loss of a single stone, to the summit of a steep hill on the opposite bank, and apparently without any visible signs of the mode of removal. The Saxon thane was greatly incensed at what he supposed to be a trick of some of his own vassals, and threatened punishment; to obviate which, a number of the villeins and bordarii with great difficulty and labour conveyed the building materials back to the site for the church; but again were they all removed in the night to the top of the hill. Gamel having learned the truth, sought counsel from Holy Church, and it was thereon resolved that the chapel should be built on the hill-top, as the unknown persons would not permit it to be erected on the site originally selected. This explains the chapel or church of St Chadde, still standing on a hill so high that one hundred and twenty-four steps were cut to accomplish the ascent, and enable the good people to go to prayers. Such are the outlines of the tradition as dramatically told by Roby in his popular work under the title of "The Goblin Builders." We find no vestige of the tradition in Baines's "Lancashire" or Dr Whitaker's "Whalley." There is a belief and a saying in Rochdale, which Roby connects with his tradition, but which seems to have no natural relation to it, that "in Rochdale strangers prosper and natives fail."

STRETFORD ROAD GREAT STONE.

Not far from the "Great Stone Farm," and lying on the footpath, is the "Plague Stone," whence the farm takes its name. It is an oblong coarse gritstone, foreign to the locality, and quite different from the stone quarried at Collyhurst. Some term it a "travelled stone." It was probably brought hither during the glacial period by iceberg agency, and deposited in a manner similar to the huge boulder now exhibited in Peel Park, Manchester. The Stretford stone measures five feet four inches in length; and the breadth and height are two and three feet respectively. On the upper surface are two cavities, or small rock basins, divided by a ridge, or moulding, the cavities measuring thirteen inches in length, eight inches in breadth, and seven inches in depth. There are, of course, various traditions to account for the origin and use of this curious relic of the olden time. One of these states that the stone was hurled from the Castle Field, and that the two cavities are the prints of Giant Tarquin's finger and thumb. Another alleges that it was thrown from the Old Bridge at Manchester; that it is gradually sinking into the earth, like Nixon's stone in Delamere Forest, and that on its final disappearance, the destruction of the world will ensue. A third tradition is recorded by Baines in his "History of Lancashire" (vol. ii. p. 257), and was also noticed in a paper read before the Rosicrucian Brotherhood of Manchester. The latter account, as obtained from two old residents near the memorial, is somewhat as follows:—During a malignant plague visitation (one of which took place in A.D. 1351, three near the close of the sixteenth, and six or seven during the seventeenth century), in order to prevent the infection from spreading, the inhabitants, like those of Eyam, Derbyshire, during a similar epidemic, were confined within specified limits, marked on the highways leading to the town by certain stones like the one now under notice. A similar stone once existed at Cheetham Hill, according to the statement of an old person still living; and Rochdale had also, till within these few years, its plague stones, locally called "milk stones," evidently a corruption of "mickle" or great stones. The Stretford tradition goes on to assert that a market was held there, and the townspeople, after washing the money in one of the basins, filled with water or vinegar, as a disinfectant, deposited it in the other, filled in like manner, and then retired to a short distance. The country folks then advanced for the corn, vegetables, and other produce, and left their money in one of the cavities. There yet remain two other traditions respecting this stone. The first is, that the stone was formerly on the opposite side of the road, and about fifty or sixty yards nearer to Manchester; secondly, that before the plague visitation, the stone bore a cross and bells, and was used as a mass stone or altar—the custom being for travellers and other passers-by there to stop and perform their devotions. The late Mr John Higson has given some further particulars in the *Ashton Reporter* newspaper, but they do not affect the tradition.

OLD SYKES'S WIFE.

IN a secluded dell, on the banks of Mellor Brook, not far from the famous Old Hall of Samlesbury, stands a lonely farmhouse which was occupied for many generations by a family named Sykes. They gave their name to the homestead, or *vice versâ*, on its being cleared from the forest; and from the fact of the pastures lying at a short distance from a broad and deep portion of the brook, it became generally known by the name of Sykes Lumb Farm. The Sykes, however, have long since become extinct; but the doings of one of the race have passed into tradition, and will, no doubt, be handed down to many future generations.

It is said that one of the latest occupiers of the farm had become very rich, partly by the constant hoarding of his ancestors, partly by the thrift of his too covetous wife, but much more by having discovered the hidden treasures of some former possessor. Be this as it may, civil troubles arose, and the Wars of the Roses exhausted not only the wealth but the population of Lancashire. Old Sykes's wife had neither son nor daughter. Her husband was too old to be called off to the wars; and hence her only anxiety was lest some lawless marauders should seize upon their stores. She had, besides, no notion of becoming dependent upon the bounty of the Southworths of the Hall, nor did she relish the idea of soliciting charity at the gates of the lordly Abbot of Whalley. The treasure was therefore carefully secured in earthenware jars, and was then buried deep beneath the roots of an apple-tree in the orchard. Years passed away, and the troubles of the country did not cease. The Yorkists at length lost the ascendancy, and the reins of government passed into the hands of the Lancastrians ;— until at last the northern feud was healed by the mingling of the White Rose with the Red. Henry VII. sat upon the throne with Elizabeth of York as Queen ;— but, ere peace thus blessed the land, Old Sykes had paid the debt of nature, and left his widow the sole possessor of their buried wealth. She, too, soon passed away ; and, as the legend asserts, so suddenly that she had no opportunity to disclose the place where she had deposited her treasure. Rumour had not failed to give her the credit of being possessed of considerable wealth ; but, although her relatives made diligent search, they were unsuccessful in discovering the place of the hidden jars. The farm passed into other hands, and Old Sykes's wife might have been forgotten had not her ghost, unable to find rest, continued occasionally to visit the old farmhouse. Many a time, in the dusk of the evening, have the neighbouring peasants met an old wrinkled woman dressed in ancient garb, passing along the gloomy road which leads across the Lumb, but fear always prevented them from speaking. She never lifted her head, but helped herself noiselessly along, by means of a crooked stick, which bore no resemblance to those then in use. At times she was seen in the old barn, on other occasions in the house, but more frequently in the orchard, standing by an apple-tree which still flourished over the place where the buried treasure was afterwards said to have been found. Generations passed away, and still her visits continued. One informant minutely described her withered visage, her short quaintly-cut gown, her striped petticoat, and her stick. He was so much alarmed that he ran away from the place, notwithstanding that he had engaged to perform some urgent work. "She was not there," he gravely said, "when I went to pluck an apple, but no sooner did I raise my hand towards the fruit, than she made her appearance just before me." At last, it is said, an occupier of the farm, when somewhat elated by liquor, ventured to question her as to the reasons of her visits. She returned no answer, but after moving slowly towards the stump of an old apple-tree, she pointed significantly towards a portion of the orchard which had never been disturbed. On search being made, the treasure was found deep down in the earth, and as the soil was being removed, the venerable looking shade was seen standing on the edge of the trench. When the last jar was lifted out, an unearthly smile passed over her withered features; her bodily form became less and less distinct, until at last it disappeared altogether. Since then the old farmhouse has ceased to be haunted. Old Sykes's wife is believed to have found eternal rest;—but there are yet many, both old and young, who walk with quickened pace past the Lumb whenever they are belated, fearful lest they should be once more confronted with the dreaded form of its unearthly visitor.

TOWNELEY HALL.

THE license for enclosing the old park of Towneley, which lay west from the house, is dated 6th Henry VII. (1490-

91). The malice and the superstition of the common people have doomed the spirit of some former and hitherto forgotten possessor of this estate to wander in restless and long unappeased solicitude, crying—

> "Lay out, lay out
> Horelaw and Hollinhey Clough."

"Lay out" means the reverse of "take in,"—*i.e.*, to throw open, or disappropriate land previously enclosed. To show at once the foundation and the antiquity of this story, as well as to illustrate a remark that traditions, when stripped of the marvellous, have generally their basis in truth, Dr Whitaker quotes the following record: —"By letters patent dated February 28, 1 James I. (1604), the said King grants unto Charles, Lord Mountjoy, Earl of Devon, in consideration of the good services done by him in the time of Queen Elizabeth and since, *inter alia*, all that parcel of land called Horelaw Pasture, containing by estimation 194 acres, of 24 feet to every perch, abutting on the north upon a pasture called Hollinhey, parcel of the possession of the Duchy of Lancashire, and formerly enclosed in severalty by John Towneley, knight." This was evidently an encroachment, which had been seized by the officers of the Duchy, and granted out afresh. But the offence was remembered long after it had been redressed, and even when the name of the offending party was forgotten. Enclosures were always unpopular among the common people, who uniformly inflicted upon enclosers that punishment after death which they were unable to do in their lifetime. It is also said that this spirit requires *one* life every *seven* years, and that some fatal accident happens at the end of each period.

TURTON TOWER.

TURTON TOWER is now one of the most interesting structures in the neighbourhood of Bolton. The manor is said to have been granted by William the Conqueror to De Orrell, one of his followers, for military services rendered to him in the conquest of England. De Orrell, having fixed upon the place of his residence, erected a strong house of defence, which was afterwards known as Turton Tower; and it is said that the wages of the workmen were then only one penny a day. Even at this low rate of payment the Tower is said to have been built in such a style of magnificence that the family never recovered from the difficulties created by the immense outlay. The principal portions of the Tower, as it now exists, were built of stone by William, son of John Orrell, Esq., in 1596; but the older portions still retain their gabled wood-and-plaster decorations, so characteristic of the many ancient mansions of the early Tudor period still or lately existing in Lancashire. The Orrells disposed of their estates to the noted Humphrey Chetham; and subsequently, through Mr Hoare, it became the property of James Kay, Esq., of Pendleton, who has made it his principal residence, and has restored the decayed portions of the house with strict regard to their original design. Some years ago the writer spent several pleasant hours in and around this imposing feudal structure, and heard the tradition that the tower is haunted by a lady who can occasionally be heard passing along the lobbies and into the rooms, as if dressed in very stiff rustling silk, but is never able to be seen. It is said that the sound is most distinct as she sweeps along the broad massive oaken staircase which leads from the hall into the upper rooms. Many traditions also prevail in the neighbourhood respecting the wealth and expenditure of Sir Humphrey Chetham during his residence at the Tower; and certainly they are quite justified by those portions of the structure which bear his name.

At a short distance from the Tower there is a farmhouse, known by the name of Timberbottom, or the Skull House. It is so called from the circumstance that two skulls are or were kept here, one of which was much decayed, and the other appeared to have been cut through by a blow from some sharp instrument. Tradition says that these skulls must be kept in the house, or the inmates will never cease to be disturbed. They are said to have been buried many times in the graveyard at Bradshaw Chapel, but they have always had to be exhumed and brought back to the farmhouse. They have even been thrown into the adjacent river, but to no purpose; for they had to be fished up and restored to their old quarters before the ghosts of their owners could once more rest in peace.

TYRONE'S BED.

IN a bend of the Roach, to the north of Morland or Merland, is Tyrone's Bed, a woody glen, admired for its picturesque scenery, which is said to have been the retreat of one of the Earls of Tyrone in the reign of Elizabeth. The craggy rocks on the one side of this lovely valley, and the steep wooded slopes on the other, with the rivulet in the channel below, are not inappropriately termed "the bed;" but the chief interest of this "romantic dell" centred in the ancient home of the Holts of Grizelhurst, but of which not a vestige now remains. At the period of the legend it was surrounded " by dark and almost trackless woods," which would furnish a refuge for the wanderer, "secure from hostility or alarm." The Earl of Tyrone who claimed to be a King in Ireland, by his rebellions harassed Queen Elizabeth and her armies for years during the latter period of her reign. His history would fill a volume. Hugh O'Neale was nephew to Shan (John) O'Neale, or "the great O'Neale," as he was more commonly called. He was well known for his great courage, a virtue much prized by the half-civilised hordes he commanded. He was created Earl of Tyrone by Queen Elizabeth; but disliking the allegiance this implied, and desirous to liberate his country from the English yoke, he entered into a correspondence with Spain, procured from thence a supply of arms and ammunition; and having united many of the Irish chiefs in a dependence upon himself, he soon proved himself a formidable enemy of English rule in Ireland. The first English commander that opposed him, Sir John Norris, after a war, and purposely protracted negotiations with Tyrone, died at length, it was said, of vexation and discontent. He was succeeded by Sir Henry Bagnall, who, going to the relief of Blackwater, was surrounded; fifteen hundred men and the general himself were slain on the spot, and the rest put to flight. This victory raised the renown of Tyrone, who was hailed as the deliverer of his country, and the restorer of Irish liberty. The unfortunate Earl of Essex was afterwards appointed to take command of the English army; but his troops were so terrified at the reputation of Tyrone, that many of them counterfeited sickness, and others deserted. Tyrone asked a conference, and Essex received from him a proposal of peace, in which Tyrone had inserted many unreasonable and exorbitant conditions. Essex, anxious to return to England, nevertheless accepted the proposal, which led to a suspicion that he had betrayed his high trust. From this time the beam of his royal mistress's favour was obscured, and the result was his disgrace and death. Meanwhile Tyrone broke the truce, and overran almost the whole of Ireland. Essex being recalled, the Queen appointed Mountjoy as Lord Deputy of Ireland. He defeated Tyrone in Ulster. Four thousand Spaniards, under Don Juan d'Aguila, landed and took Kinsale; Mountjoy besieged it; and on Tyrone and many other Irish chieftains marching to its relief, he intercepted them, and attacked and put them to flight, slaughtering twelve hundred men. Tyrone and other chiefs fled, and the Spaniards capitulated. It is supposed that at this period the outlawed Earl crossed the sea into England, and remained for some time concealed in the neighbourhood of Rochdale. The site of a few cottages in a romantic dell by the river Roach is still associated with the memory of the unfortunate Earl, and yet bears the name of "Tyrone's Bed." Upon this fact Mr Roby has based a fictitious love story,* there being a prediction that—

----"Woman's breast
Thou shalt darken o'er with woe;
None thou lookest on or lovest
Joy or hope hereafter know.
Many a maid thy glance shall rue:
Where it smites it shall subdue."

Tyrone is made to save from drowning Constance the daughter of Holt of Grizelhurst; they love; she conceals

* It would be more correct to state that the tradition in Mr Roby's work is really derived from a ballad by Mr William Nuttall, of Rochdale, entitled "Tyrone and Constance, or the Outlaw in the Dell of Grizelhurst." The story was first told to Mr Nuttall, as he states, by a Mr Ralph Holt, formerly steward to the late William Bamford of Bamford, Esq. In his "notes" to the ballad, Mr Nuttall relates the story at considerable length.

him from pursuit by the sheriff and posse in a hidden chamber, the entrance to which is from her own bedroom. He escapes, and she wastes away and dies, the victim of the prophecy. Tyrone eventually secured a pardon from Queen Elizabeth. One incident is related, illustrative of his character. Appearing in person to execute a treaty, immediately on the issue of some sanguinary engagement, Tyrone was requested to sign the terms. " Here is my signature," said he, laying his bloody hand on the deed; "'tis the mark of the Kings of Ulster." Hence, tradition gravely asserts, was the origin of "the bloody hand," the arms of Ulster, and, in heraldic shields, the badge of knighthood. It is scarcely necessary to add that this derivation for the arms is altogether a fable.

THE DRAGON OF UNSWORTH.

TRADITIONS respecting the ravages formerly made by the so-called dragons occur in many counties. Yorkshire has claimed the legend of the Dragon of Wantley, and the Lambton Worm has rendered the county of Durham famous. One of the most noted dragon stories of Lancashire has its locality assigned to Unsworth, a small village or hamlet about three miles from Bury. The principal mansion in this village is occupied by a lineal descendant of the ancient family of Unsworth, who probably derived their name from the homestead they have so long occupied. The house contains little worthy of notice; but it has long been famous for containing an ancient carved oak table and panel connected with a legend attaching to the family. It is said that Thomas Unsworth was the owner of this property when the district was devastated by an enormous dragon, which was not content with its ordinary fare but proceeded to swallow up the women and children. The scales of this dragon were so hard and firmly set, that bullets shot by the guns of those days took no effect upon the monster; and the owner of Unsworth, finding this the case, loaded his gun with his dagger and mortally wounded the dragon under the throat, as it was raising its head to rush at its assailant. The table is said to have been constructed after this event, and was partly carved by the dagger which had destroyed the reptile. The carvings on the table and panel are somewhat curious. One is a representation of St George and the Dragon, another contains rude figures of the eagle and child, a third the lion and unicorn, and a fourth of the Dragon of Unsworth. The crest of the family consists of a man in black armour holding a battle axe in one hand; and tradition states that this is a portrait of Thomas Unsworth in the dress he wore at the time of the conflict. What may have given rise to the legend it is quite impossible to determine; but an estate was once granted to a member of this family for some important military service, and this may have had something to do with its origin. There are several carvings of the dragon in the possession of the family. One of these resembles a long serpent with the head and wings of a sphinx; another represents the monster as a serpent with the head of an old man; and a third resembles a serpent in folds with stings at the ends of the tongue and tail. The initials "C.V.," under the head of one of the figures, serve to indicate that the carvings have been executed for one of the owners of the mansion.

There is a singular circumstance connected with most of these dragon stories which is worthy of special notice. It is that of the frequent use of *sacred* and *mystic* numbers in the narratives, and this in some degree supports the conjecture that they are allegorical in their nature. In the case of the Dragon of Wantley (Wharncliffe) there are *seven* heads mentioned, and twice *seven* eyes; the monster itself ate up *three* children, the fight lasted *two* days and *one* night, and he turned twice *three* times round when he received his fatal wound. The Lambton Worm had *nine* holes on each side of his mouth, he encircled Worm hill *three* times, he drank the milk of *nine* cows; the reckless heir of Lambton returned a true knight at the end of *seven* years, and for *nine* generations the sybil's curse remained on his house in consequence of the non-performance of his vow. His mail was also studded all over with spear heads, just the same expedient which was adopted by More of More Hall.

WARDLEY HALL SKULL.

In the township of Worsley, about seven miles west of Manchester, and to the east of Kempnall Hall, is the ancient pile of Wardley Hall, erected in the reign of Edward VI. It is situated in the midst of a small woody glade, and was originally surrounded by a moat, except on the east side, which was protected by natural defences. This black-and-white half-timbered edifice is of a quadrangular form, consisting of ornamented wood and plaster frames, interlined with bricks (plastered and whitewashed, the wood-work being painted black), and entered by a covered archway, opening into a courtyard in the centre, like so many of the manor houses of the same age in Lancashire. About 1830 it was in a ruinous condition, one part being occupied as a farmhouse, and the other formed into a cluster of nine cottages. The hall has since been thoroughly renovated, and has been occupied for many years, under the Earl of Ellesmere, by a gentleman farmer and colliery-owner. In the room called the hall is a coat-of-arms, in a frame, belonging to the Downes family : a stag couchant within the shield ; crest, a stag's head. The room has an ornamented wainscot, and a fluted roof of oak. The stairs have an air of noble antiquity about them, which has been somewhat diminished by the daubings of a modern painter. The chimneys are clustered. The Tildesleys became lords of Wardley by marriage with the Worsleys in the reign of Henry IV., and settled here before they occupied Morley. On the eve of the civil wars, Wardley was quitted by the Tildesleys, and became the residence of Roger Downes, Esq., whose son John, married Penelope, daughter of Sir Cecil Trafford, knight, who, endeavouring to convert Mr Downes [a Catholic] to Protestantism, became himself a Catholic. The issue of that marriage was Roger Downes, son and heir, and an only daughter, named Penelope, after her mother. She married Richard, Earl Rivers, a rake, a warrior, and a statesman. There is a human skull kept at the Hall, which tradition says once belonged to Roger Downes, the last male representative of his family, and who was one of the most abandoned courtiers of Charles II.

Roby, in his " Traditions," has represented him as rushing forth " hot from the stews "—drawing his sword as he staggered along—and swearing that he would kill the first man he met. His victim was a poor tailor, whom he ran through with his weapon, and killed him on the spot. He was apprehended for the crime ; but his interest at court soon procured him a free pardon, and he immediately began to pursue his usual reckless course. At length " Heaven avenged the innocent blood he had shed ; " for " in the lusty vigour," continues Roby, " of a drunken debauch, passing over London Bridge, he encountered another brawl, wherein, having run at the watchman with his rapier, one blow of the bill which they carried severed his head from his trunk. The latter was cast over the parapet into the Thames, and the head was carefully packed up in a box and sent to his sisters at Wardley. It was Maria who ventured to open the package and read the sad fate of her brother from a paper which was enclosed. The skull was removed, secretly at first, but invariably it returned to the Hall, and no human power could drive it thence. It hath been riven to pieces, burnt, and otherwise destroyed; but on the subsequent day it was seen filling its wonted place. This wilful piece of mortality will not allow the little aperture in which it rests to be walled up—it remains there—whitened and bleached by the weather, looking forth from those rayless sockets upon the scenes which, when living, they had once beheld." This curious legend exists under various forms, and has been noticed by several writers, but all agree in the main facts. One account varies the place of his death, stating, in short, that Roger Downes, in the licentious spirit of the age, having abandoned himself to vicious courses, was killed by a watchman in a fray at Epsom Wells, in June 1676, and dying without issue, the family quitted Wardley. It is of this Roger Downes that Lucas speaks, when he says that, according to tradition, "while in London, in a drunken frolic, he vowed to his companions that he would kill the first man he met; then, sallying forth, he ran his sword through a poor tailor. Soon after this, being in a riot, a watchman made a stroke at him with his bill, which severed his head from his body. The head was enclosed in a box and sent to his sister, who lived at Wardley Hall. "The skull," adds the narrator, "has been kept at Wardley ever since, and many superstitious notions are entertained concerning it, not worth repeating." After the Downeses ceased to reside there, Wardley Hall was occupied for a time by Lord Barrymore. Towards the end of the eighteenth century, Thomas Barritt, the Manchester antiquary, visited the Hall, where he says there is "a human skull, which, time out of mind, hath had a superstitious veneration paid to it, by [the occupiers of the hall] not permitting it to be removed from its situation, which is on the topmost step of a staircase. There is a tradition that, if removed, or ill-used, some uncommon noise and disturbance always follows, to the terror of the whole house; yet I cannot persuade myself this is always the case. But some few years ago, I and three of my acquaintances went to view this surprising piece of household furniture, and found it as above mentioned, and bleached white with the weather, that beats in upon it from a four-square window in the hall, which the tenants never permit to be glazed or filled up, thus to oblige the skull, which, they say, is unruly and disturbed at the hole not being always open. However, one of us, who was last in company with the skull, removed it from its place into a dark part of the room, and there left it, and returned home; but the night but one following, such a storm arose about the house, of wind and lightning, as tore down some trees, and unthatched outhousing. We hearing of this, my father went over in a few days after to see his mother, who lived near the Hall, and was witness to the wreck the storm had made. Yet all this might have happened had the skull never been removed; but withal it keeps alive the credibility of the tradition (or the credulity of its believers). But what I can learn of the above affair from old people in the neighbourhood is, that a young man of the Downes family, being in London, one night in his frolics vowed to his companions that he would kill the first man he met; and accordingly he ran his sword through a man immediately, a tailor by trade. However, justice overtook him in his career of wickedness; for in some while after, he being in a riot upon London Bridge, a watchman made a stroke at him with his bill, and severed his head from his body, which head was enclosed in a box, and sent to his sister, who then lived at Wardley, where it hath continued ever since." Barritt adds— "There is likewise a skull near Wigan of this surprising sort, of which I have heard stories too ridiculous to relate." In the "Traditions," the substance of this legend is given with graphic effect under the appellation of the "Skull House." It is there remarked of Wardley that,—"A human skull is still shown here, which is usually kept in a little locked recess in the staircase wall, and which the occupiers of the Hall would never permit to be removed. This grim *caput mortuum* being, it is said, much averse to any change of place or position, never failed to punish the individual severely which should dare to lay hands upon it with any such purpose. If removed, drowned in the neighbouring pond (which is in fact a part of the old moat which formerly surrounded the house), or buried, it was sure to return; so that, in the end, each succeeding tenant was fain to endure its presence rather than be subject to the terrors and annoyances consequent upon its removal. Even the square aperture in the wall was not permitted to be glazed without the skull or its long-defunct owner creating some disturbance. It was almost bleached white by exposure to the weather, and many curious persons have made a pilgrimage there, even of late years." Mr Roby then relates the freak of Barritt and his companions, and gives the story of the skull from Barritt's MS. The editor of the present volume visited the Hall some years ago, and found that a locked door concealed at once the square aperture and its fearful tenant. Of this "place of a skull," two keys were provided; one being kept by the tenant of the Hall, who farms some of the adjacent land, and the other being in the possession of the late (and first) Countess of Ellesmere, the lady of the lamented "Lord Francis Egerton." The Countess occasionally accompanied visitors from the neighbouring Worsley Hall, and herself unlocked the door and revealed to her friends the grinning skull of Wardley Hall. The writer paid another visit to this quaint old Hall in October 1861, and again held the old skull in his hands. The bone of the lower jaw had become detached; but there is no sign of violence about the skull itself. If the tradition as to the violent death of its owner be correct, that result has been effected without any fracture of the bone. The keystone of an arched entrance into the courtyard has on its outer face, "R. H. D. 1625," and beneath this, "1818." On its inner face, "1846." These dates doubtless indicate the times of rebuilding or repairing a portion of the old place.

WARDLEY HALL.

WARDLEY Hall was originally the property of the Worsleys or Workedleys, who were settled at Worsley about the time of the Norman Conquest. They retained possession of Wardley till about the reign of Edward II., when Thurston de Tyldesley marrying Margaret, daughter and heiress of Jordan de Workesley, it passed to the Tyldesleys; and, prior to the herald's visitation of 1567, became the residence of the elder branch of the family; a younger branch being settled at Morley Hall in Astley, which had come to the family by the marriage of Edmund, second son of Thurstan Tyldesley, of Tyldesley and Wardley, with Anne, daughter and sole heiress of Thomas Leyland, of Morley; and from that line descended the unfortunate and gallant royalist Sir Thomas Tyldesley. Wardley continued the property of the Tyldesleys until the beginning of the seventeenth century, when Thurston, son of Thomas Tyldesley, of Gray's Inn, Attorney-General for the Duchy of Lancaster, sold the estate in parcels, and Wardley passed to the Cheshire family of Downes. Roger Downes, the first of the name settled at Wardley, was Vice-Chamberlain of Chester to William Earl of Derby, and James Lord Strange, his son. He died about 1638, leaving by his wife, a daughter of John Calvert, of Cockerham, three sons and one daughter. Francis and Lawrence both died young; John succeeded to the estates on the death of his father; and Jane married Robert Snede, Esq., of Keele, Staffordshire. John Downes, a zealous Roman Catholic and supporter of the Royalist cause, accompanied Lord Strange (afterwards the unfortunate Earl of Derby) to the siege of Manchester in September 1642. He married Penelope, daughter of Sir Cecil Trafford, knight, the only issue being Roger, son and heir (who was unfortunately killed by a watchman at Epsom Wells in June 1676), and a daughter named Penelope. How the story of the skull arose, it is impossible to say; but it seems to have been to a great extent true; at least, as regards Roger Downes, who is represented as being one of the wildest and most licentious of the courtiers of

Charles II. Upon the wall of Wigan Church is a tablet to the memory of this same Roger Downes, with the inscription :—" Rogerus Downes de Wardley, armiger, filius Johannis Downes, hujus comitatis, armigeri, obiit 27 Junii 1676, ætatis suæ 28"—(Roger Downes of Wardley, Esq., son of John Downes of this county, Esq., died 27th June 1676, aged twenty-eight years).

Thomas Barritt, the antiquary, besides the story he has given relating to the skull in his " MS. Pedigrees," offers the following explanation :—" Thomas Stockport told me that the skull belonged to a Romish priest, who was executed at Lancaster for seditious practices in the time of William III. He was most likely the priest at Wardley, to which place his head being sent, might be preserved as a relic of his martyrdom. . . . The late Rev. Mr Kenyon of Peel, and librarian at the College in this town [Chetham's Library, Manchester], told me, about the year 1779, that the family vault of the Downeses in Wigan Church had been opened about that time, and a coffin discovered, on which was an inscription to the memory of the above young Downes. Curiosity led to the opening of it, and the skeleton, *head* and all, was there; but, whatever was the cause of his death, the upper part of the skull had been sawed off, a little above the eyes, by a surgeon, perhaps by order of his friends, to be satisfied of the nature of his disease. His shroud was in tolerable preservation; and Mr Kenyon showed me some of the ribbon that tied his suit at the arms, wrists, and ankles; it was of a brown colour—what it was at first could not be ascertained." Penelope, sister and heiress of Roger Downes, conveyed the estate by marriage to Richard Savage, fourth Earl Rivers, who died in 1712, leaving an only daughter, Elizabeth, married to James, fourth Earl of Barrymore, the representative of an ancient Irish family. The only issue by this marriage was a daughter named Penelope, wife of James, second surviving son of George, Earl of Cholmondeley, who died without issue in 1775. Wardley is now the property of the Earl of Ellesmere. The hall itself is an interesting structure, of the time of Edward VI.; partially surrounded by a moat, and constructed of ornamental timber and plaster, the interstices of the framework being filled with bricks. It is quadrangular in form, with a courtyard in the centre, the entrance being by a covered archway. The principal room has an ornamented wainscot, and a ceiling of fluted oak; in this room is also preserved a coat of arms of the Downes family—sable a hart lodged argent. Wardley Hall has been engraved in Philips's "Old Halls of Lancashire," and in other works.

THE CROSSES IN WHALLEY CHURCHYARD.

THE parish church at Whalley is one of the most interesting structures in the county. Its foundation dates from the earlier Saxon times, when Northumbria was an independent kingdom, and when York, the ancient Eboracum, still retained its importance as the metropolis of the North. The curious old document entitled the *Status de Blackburnshire*, preserves an ancient traditional account that the parish of Whalley was little more than a wilderness at the close of the sixth century; that it was remote from the usual centres of population, and almost inaccessible, and that it was "entangled with woods, and overrun with wild beasts." Notwithstanding these difficulties, St Augustine is represented as penetrating into these wilds and converting the inhabitants to Christianity.

This record further states that he preached at Whalley, and, as a consequence of his ministry, a parish church was erected, which was dedicated to All Saints, and denominated the "White Church under the Leigh." It was then, also, that the three tall crosses were formed and erected at Whalley in honour of Augustine's mission; and that "after seven centuries these continued to be called the crosses of Augustine." After quoting the *Status*, Dr Whitaker very justly requires his readers to suspend their assent to "this ancient ecclesiastical story," since the "account is merely abstracted from a monkish manuscript of the fourteenth century." In his opinion there is no evidence whatever, nor even a probability, that St Augustine ever visited Whalley; whilst there is much to show that Paulinus is really the person intended.

We know, from the authority of the venerable Bede, that Paulinus, under the auspices of Edwin of Northumbria, his illustrious convert, passed through Deira and Bernicia, preaching the gospel to the inhabitants, and baptizing great numbers of them in the rivers which intersect these provinces. His presence at Dewsbury was attested by an inscription on one of these stately and beautiful Saxon crosses. There is another of these relics at Burnley; and tradition "assigns with one voice" that the three crosses now standing in the churchyard at Whalley were erected to commemorate the same events. The writer of the *Status*, or some transcriber, must therefore have transferred the labours of Paulinus to Augustine, and thus in some degree has done injustice to the zealous missionary. The "obeliscal form and ornaments of fretwork," which distinguish these crosses, are characteristic of the state of art among the Saxons, Norwegians, and Danes; and the period of their erection may therefore be placed with much probability about the middle of the seventh century, since Paulinus was banished Northumbria in A.D. 631, "on the death of his royal convert."

Bede tells the story of Edwin's conversion with dramatic effect. There is the doubt as to the truth of the Christian doctrines—the hope that the power of the true God will aid him in his troubles, and the resolve that, if he be successful, then he would cast away his idols. Paulinus took advantage of this hesitation, and by confirming the sign of the hand upon Edwin's head, he brought the king to his knees in full determination that he and his should embrace Christianity. Coifi, his chief priest, was the next important convert; and after he had resolved to abandon the worship of Thor and Woden, he encouraged the people to imitate his example and learn from Paulinus. He then mounted the king's war-horse, and defiled the heathen temple at York by casting a spear into the sacred enclosure. He and "all the nobility of the nation, with a large number of the common sort," then "received the faith" and were baptized. Paulinus was appointed Archbishop of York, and soon after set out into the most distant parts of the kingdom, preaching, converting, and baptizing the crowds who flocked to hear him. When we look upon these weather-worn crosses, we may imagine that we see the venerable Archbishop standing on the banks of the Calder, or at Bishop Leap on the Brun, surrounded by the rude inhabitants of the district, eager to be instructed in the doctrines of the new religion. He is said by Bede to have been "tall of stature, a little stooping, his hair black, his visage meagre, his nose slender and aquiline, his aspect both venerable and majestic." No wonder, then, that his fervid exhortations produced converts by the thousand—they were awed by his presence as well as convinced by his arguments; and he was powerfully assisted by "James the deacon, a man of zeal and great fame in Christ's Church." It was fortunate that the mistake in the *Status* should have been investigated by such a competent authority as the historian of Whalley; and there is satisfaction in the thought that tradition has restored to the great "Apostle of the North" the honour of having banished the Paganism of the kingdom of Northumbria, and planted Christianity in its stead.

WINWICK CHURCH.

The parish church of Winwick stands near that miracle-working spot where St Oswald, King of the Northumbrians, was killed. The founder had destined a different site for it, but his intention was overruled. Winwick had not then even received its name, the church being one of the earliest erections in the parish. The foundation of the church was laid where the founder had directed; and the close of the first day's labour showed that the workmen had not been idle by the progress made in the building. But the approach of night brought to pass an event which utterly destroyed the repose of the few inhabitants around the spot. A pig was seen running hastily to the site of the new church; and as he ran he was heard to cry or scream aloud, "We-ee-wick, we-ee-wick, we-ee-wick." Then, taking up a stone in his mouth, he carried it up to the spot sanctified by the death of St Oswald, and thus employing himself through the whole night, succeeded in removing all the stones which had been laid by the builders. The founder, feeling himself justly reproved for not having chosen that sacred spot for the site of his church, unhesitatingly yielded to the wise counsel of the pig. Thus the pig not only decided the site of the church, but gave a name to the parish. In support of this tradition, there is the figure of a pig sculptured on the tower of the church, just above the western entrance; and also the following Latin doggrel:—

> " Hic locus Oswalde, quondam placint tibi valde;
> Northanhumbrorum fueras Rex, nunc que Polorum
> Regna tenes, loco papus Marcelde vocato."

"This place, O Oswald, formerly pleased thee greatly;
Thou wert King of the Northumbrians, and now of the Poles (?);
Thou holdest the kingdom in the place called Marcelde" [Macer or Mackerfield].

There are other churches in Lancashire besides Winwick whose sites have been changed by the devil, and he has also built some bridges; that at Kirkby Lonsdale owes much of its beauty to the string of his apron giving way when he was carrying stones in it. The stones may be seen yet in the picturesque groups of rock below the bridge. According to some a priest, according to others the devil, stamped his foot into the church wall at Brindle, to prove the truth of Popery; and George Marsh the martyr did the same at Smithell's Hall, to prove the truth of Protestantism. The footmarks still remain on the wall and the flag. There is great sameness in these traditions, one story doing for several places, except that at Winwick it was as a pig, at Leyland as a cat, and somewhere else as a fish, that Satan played his pranks.—*N. ana Q.*, vi. 71.

THE GIANT OF WORSLEY.

WORSLEY HALL and manor are said to date their foundation from about the time of the Conquest. At that time the owner was an eminent hero, whose deeds are recorded in ancient romance. Eliseus de Workesley or Worsley was one of the first Norman barons who raised his vassals and joined in the first crusade. His personal acquaintance with Robert, Duke of Normandy, is said to have induced him to accompany his friend and patron in attempting to rescue the Holy Land from the hands of the Saracens. It was for this too that Robert relinquished his claims to the English crown, and mortgaged the revenues of his Norman duchy. Eliseus de Worsley met with numerous enemies in the forms of giants, Saracens, and dragons, all of which he conquered and slew. On arriving at Rhodes, he emulated "More of More Hall," by encountering a venomous serpent which was devastating the district. In this combat, however, he was unsuccessful; for the serpent is said to have stung him so severely that he died and was buried on the spot. In Hopkinson's MS. "Pedigrees of the North Riding of Yorkshire" (fol. 483), is a notice of him which states that "he was of such strength and valour that he was a reputed giant, and in old scrips [writings,] is often called 'Elias Gigas.' He fought many duels, combats, &c., for the love of our Lord and Saviour Jesus Christ, and obtained many victories." These undoubtedly gave rise to the legend; the serpent being probably selected to typify the crafty dealings by which some rapacious landowner sought to enrich himself at the expense of others.

WYECOLLER HALL AND ITS SPECTRE HORSEMAN.

WYECOLLER HALL, near Colne, was long the seat of the Cunliffes of Billington. They were noted persons in their day, and the names of successive members of the family are attached to documents relating to the property of the Abbots of Whalley. But evil days came, and their ancestral estates passed out of their hands. In the days of the Commonwealth their loyalty cost them dear; and ultimately they retired to Wyecoller with a remnant only of their once extensive estates. About 1819 the last of the family passed away, and the Hall is now a mass of ruins. Little but the antique fireplace remains entire; and even the room alluded to in the following legend cannot now be identified. Tradition says that once every year a spectre horseman visits Wyecoller Hall. He is attired in the costume of the early Stuart period, and the trappings of his horse are of a most uncouth description. On the evening of his visit the weather is always wild and tempestuous. There is no moon to light the lonely roads, and the residents of the district do not venture out of their cottages. When the wind howls the loudest the horseman can be heard dashing up the road at full speed, and after crossing the narrow bridge, he suddenly stops at the door of the hall. The rider then dismounts and makes his way up the broad oaken stairs into one of the rooms of the house. Dreadful screams, as from a woman, are then heard, which soon subside into groans. The horseman then makes his appearance at the door—at once mounts his steed—and gallops off the road he came. His body can be seen through by those who may chance to be present; his horse appears to be wild with rage, and its nostrils stream with fire. The tradition is that one of the Cunliffes murdered his wife in that room, and that the spectre horseman is the ghost of the murderer, who is doomed to pay an annual visit to the home of his victim. She is said to have predicted the extinction of the family, which has literally been fulfilled.

PART II.

PAGEANTS, MASKINGS, AND MUMMINGS.

PAGEANTS, MASKINGS, AND MUMMINGS.

INTRODUCTION.

THESE formed a very imposing if not important part of the festal celebrations of old Lancashire. The only one of them which retains anything of its ancient splendour and reputation is the Preston Guild, held every twenty years, during which that town is the scene of great rejoicings and festivities, with various pageants and processions during several days, together with dinners, balls, concerts, and various kinds of outdoor games and sports. The "ale-gysts" and the "guisings" are fast passing away, and the "rush-bearings" are only now to be seen at a few places in the county, though formerly almost every parish had its rush-cart and rush-bearing festival.

ACA'S, OR ACRES, OR ST MATTHEW'S FAIR, MANCHESTER.

ROBERT GRESLET, the fifth Baron of Manchester of that name, granted a portion of land to one Aca, a clerk, for the sum of three shillings yearly. In the *Testa de Nevill* it is stated that:—" The Robert Grelle, that now is," gave this oxgang belonging to his " demense of Mamecestre," and that the same Aca now holds this land. Some hold that Acres Fields derived their name from Aca, their early proprietor; but in the "Mamecestre" a suggestion is offered that their derivation may probably merely be from *acer*, plural *acres*, fields, lands, anything sown, acres. Aca was probably the chantry priest of an ancient chapel dedicated to St Matthew, which was afterwards known as " Grelle's Chantry," and the land is supposed to have included the "Four Acres" upon which the ancient fair was long held. The first charter for a fair in Manchester appears to have been granted by Henry III., when a minor, to Robert Greslet, in 1222, for the consideration of a palfrey for a licence until the king came of age. A more extensive charter was obtained in 1227, and the fair was held in accordance therewith on the eve feast of St Matthew the Apostle, and the days following, *i.e.*, on the 20th, 21st, and 22d of September.

Owing to the enterprise of the inhabitants of Manchester this fair attained considerable importance. Many merchants from distant parts attended this central mart, and the proceedings were originally commenced by a formal opening of the fair by the Baron of Manchester in person. During the three days no person was permitted to wear arms, and each adult inhabitant was bound to assist the "*grith*-sergeant," or principal *peace*-officer in putting down any riot or disorder which might arise. The authority of the lord was not acceptable to some of the inhabitants, and consequently on the first day of the fair they used to assemble in large crowds, many being armed with whips, and others with large quantities of acorns which they had procured from the neighbouring woods. This was intended as a protest against the claims of the lord of the manor for the time being; and on the first horses, cows, sheep, or pigs, making their appearance on the ground, some of the men cracked their whips, others pelted the cattle with the acorns, and the rest shouted with a deafening noise, "First horse," "First cow," "First sheep," "First pig." At a later period this rough commencement degenerated into mere juvenile sport, and was finally discontinued long before the fair was removed to Knot Mill.

GYST-ALES, GUISINGS, OR MARLINGS—
THE ASHTON GYST-ALE.

THE gyst-ale, or guising feast, was an annual festival of the town of Ashton-under-Lyne. It appears from the rental of Sir John de Assheton, compiled A.D. 1422, that a sum of twenty shillings was paid to him as lord of the manor for the privilege of holding this feast by its then conductors. The persons named in the roll as having paid three shillings and fourpence each are :—" Margret, that was the wife of Hobbe the Kynges (of Misrule); Hobbe Adamson; Roger the Baxter; Robert Somayster, Jenkyn of the Wode; and Thomas of Curtnal." The meaning of the term *gyst-ale* is involved in some obscurity, and the custom itself is not mentioned by either Brand or Ellis in their collections of popular antiquities. Most probably the payments mentioned above were for the *gyst*, or hire, for the privilege of selling ale and other refreshments during the festivals held on the payment of the rents of the manor. These *guisings* were frequently held in the spring, most probably about Lady Day, when manorial rents were usually paid ; and as the fields were manured with *marl* about the same period, the term *marlings* has been supposed to indicate the rough play, or *marlocking* which was then practised. This, however, must be a mistake, since the term relates to merry pranks, or pleasure gambols only, and has no connection with marl as a manure.

These gyst-ales, or guisings, once ranked amongst the principal festivals of Lancashire, and large sums of money were subscribed by all ranks of society in order that they might be celebrated with becoming splendour. The lord of the manor, the vicar of the parish, the farmer, and the operative, severally announced the sums they intended to give, and when the treasurer exclaimed "A largesse !" the crowd demanded " From whom ? " and then due proclamation was made of the sum subscribed. The real amount, however, was seldom named, but it was announced that "Lord Johnson," or some other equally distinguished person had contributed " a portion of ten thousand pounds " towards the expenses of the feast.

After the subscription lists were closed an immense garland was prepared, which contained abundance of every flower in season, interspersed with a profusion of evergreens and ribbons of every shade and pattern. The framework of this garland was made of wood, to which hooks were affixed, and on these were suspended a large collection of watches, jewels, and silver articles borrowed from the richer residents in the town. On the day of the gyst this garland was borne through the principal streets and thoroughfares, attended by crowds of townspeople

Gyst-Ales, Guisings, or Marlings. 87

dressed in their best attire. These were formed into a procession by a master of the ceremonies, locally termed the King. Another principal attendant was the Fool, dressed in a grotesque cap, a hideous grinning mask, a long tail hanging behind, and a bell with which he commanded attention when announcements were to be made. In an early period of these guisings the fool was usually mounted on a hobby-horse, and indulged in grotesque pranks at he passed along. Hence we obtained the term "hob-riding," and more recently the proverbial expression of "riding one's hobby to death."

In the manor roll from which we have previously quoted, " Jack the mercer" is inserted as having paid the lord of the manor the annual sum of 6s. 8d. for the privilege of hob-riding; and the office appears to have become a lucrative one, when rivalry between towns and villages was excited. On such occasions the residents spared neither time nor expense to outshine their neighbours, and it will be seen in a subsequent article that a single village has been known to expend several thousand pounds on this unmeaning pageant.

WAITS AT BURNLEY.

For about three weeks before Christmas the inhabitants of Burnley and the neighbourhood are almost nightly roused from their slumbers by the "Christmas waits." Two men generally go together. They parade the streets and lanes, playing Christmas tunes on fiddles, or any other instruments they prefer. On stopping at any person's door they generally play some favourite air, and then wish the family a "Merry Christmas when it comes," and "hope that all are well within." These good wishes are followed up by the following ditty, chanted to a quaint old air by both performers :—

> "Good master and mistress,
> We wish you good cheer;
> For this is Old Christmas,
> A merry time of the year,
> When Christ did come to save us
> From all our worldly sin.
> We wish you a happy Christmas,
> And all good health within."

There are several variations of this ditty; but all are much to the same purport. After Christmas Day the "waits" go round to their friends and collect money. The last "wait" in Burnley was unfortunately burnt to death some years ago in a warehouse which took fire during the night. He had been his usual rounds, and had gone to sleep amongst the waste just before the fire broke out.

DOWNHAM KING AND QUEEN.

In the parish of Whalley the ancient annual amusements of rush-bearings and village-wakes are very general, and it is only within a very few years that the practice of adorning a man and woman in the costume of the king and queen was observed yearly at Downham wakes, when a crown was carried before them, "by prescriptive right" as they maintained, founded on a grant from some king at a period too early to form the subject of record. This innocent delusion has been discarded; but the practice still prevails of parties of eight or ten women running after and "lifting" or "heaving" men on Easter Tuesday, in allusion, it is said, to the resurrection of the Saviour. The last "Downham Queen" died in Burnley about six years ago; "lifting" frequently causes much amusement, and sometimes dissatisfaction. The men lift the women on Monday, and *vice versâ* on the Tuesday.

ECCLES GUISING.

THE *gyst-ale* or *guising* was celebrated in Eccles and the neighbouring townships with much rustic splendour, at the termination of the marling season, when the villagers, with a king at their head, walked in procession with garlands, to which silver-plate was attached, which was contributed by the principal gentry in the neighbourhood. The object of ambition was to excel in the splendour of their procession, which was conducted with the personages and the circumstances described in the account of *gyst-ales*. We have, however, a still more curious record of the *guisings* of Eccles and of the adjacent township of Barton-upon-Irwell in a quaint and exceedingly rare octavo pamphlet of nineteen pages, printed in 1778, and of which Mr William Ford, the Manchester bookseller and antiquary, never saw but one copy. Its title-page runs thus :—" The History of Eccles and Barton's Contentious Guising War. 1. An account of the heathens and ancient Christians observing the first of May having some resemblance to guising. 2. Some fictitious debates bordering within the matter of truth; with an account of these guisings, from the first rise to the present time, between Eccles and Barton, with several entertaining remarks. By F. H**R**G**N." [? Harrington.]

> Barton and Eccles they will not agree,
> For envy and pride is the reason, you 'll see.
> France and Spain with England are the same,
> And a great many more compose the ill-natured train.
> You, neighbours, over each other do crow,
> And now and then turn out to make a great show,
> Like England and America do make a great noise :
> Be wise, for it only diverts our girls and boys.

Price threepence." In his preface, the writer, who speaks of having visited other countries, and being now at a low ebb, says, "Having lived in the parish of Eccles for the last eight months (1777), I have had some opportunity of making some remarks of the customs, manners, and behaviour of the inhabitants of the said parish, not only to strangers, but to each other, which behaviour I shall treat upon, together with some remarks upon the folly of *guising*." In some doggrel lines he reproves the local folly of guising, stigmatises a recent song as "base scurrility" and "lies," and adds—

"If Eccles has faults, Barton has the same;
Wisdom it will be not each other to blame."

The origin of Eccles guisings he understands to be, that "Mr Chorlton, of Monks Hall, had some men getting marl, and it being a custom for the general part of the neighbours to give some little to these men to drink, which enables them to go through that hard labour with cheerfulness, was a sort of foundation for the above custom. Some few young people of Catch Inn [a locality near the village, but within the township of Barton; there is still a Catch Inn or Catching Lane] made a small garland, by some called a *posey*, and on Friday, June 13th, 1777, carried the garland to the marl pit, and made the marlers a present of it, with 3s. 6d. The marlers in the evening bringing the garland into Eccles, it excited the curiosity of the young people to know by what means they got it, and being informed they had it from some young people of Catch Inn, it was then thought by the young people of Eccles an insult upon them for Catch Inn people to bring a garland to Mr Chorlton's marl-pit, as they belonged to the township of Barton, and Monks Hall and the pit belonged to the township [village] of Eccles." The pamphlet continues the story in an inflated style, as describing a war between two great nations; but it may suffice to say that the marl-pit was alternately taken possession of by parties of guisers from Eccles and from Barton, and that the rivalry was displayed chiefly in the amount of subscriptions these places could respectively collect, and in the splendour of the display of flowers, ribbons, and especially of silver-plate, in the processions of each party. These "guisings" were continued throughout the summer and autumn of 1777, and the following brief account of the respective sums collected in succession from the two places will suffice to show the extent of the extravagance and folly of this "guising war":—

1777.	BARTON.				1777.	ECCLES.			
June 13,	.	.	£0	3	6	June 16,	. .	£0	4	6
,, 30,	.	.	5	0	6	July 14,	. .	13	0	0
Aug. 4,	.	.	37	0	0	Sept. 1,	. .	347	11	6
Sept. 24,	.	.	644	17	0	Oct. 20,	. .	1881	5	6
Barton,	.	.	£687	1	0	Eccles, .	.	£2242	1	6

So that the two places contributed from motives of rivalry to pageants of idle display and folly, not to say disorder, *nearly three thousand pounds!* These sums, however, do not seem to have been *spent*, but only *exhibited*, or, as the writer says, "laid down on the drumhead," by way of vain display! They were probably lent for the hour, and returned to the pockets of the owners, except so much as may have been expended in horse-hire and other expenses, and in ale, &c., for the feast with which these pageants seem to have terminated. From the pamphlet, it appears that on the 14th July, the Eccles guisers (exceeding a hundred men and women), with spikes, swords, &c.;

some dressed as Robin Hood and Little John, others as Adam and Eve "in a single-horse chair, with an orange-tree fixed before them and oranges growing thereon," proceeded to Barton and various parts of the parish of Eccles, with drums beating, colours flying, trumpets sounding, music playing, and about sixteen couples of morris-dancers. The Barton subscription of £37 would seem to have included a communion-plate for the church. Their pageant of August 4 is not described in detail. The Eccles pageant of September 1 was the month of Eccles wakes, and their procession of more than a hundred and fifty men and women marched to Pendleton Pole, with a king and queen at their head. The £347, 11s. 6d. was "tendered" in vain pomp, by way of doubling the enemy's amount of cash. Barton next mustered about two hundred and twenty men and women, with about twenty-one guns, cannons, and muskets, which they began firing at five o'clock in the morning of the 24th of September, after which, with a bull at their head with bells about his neck, they marched to Eccles. The pamphlet describes the order of the procession, which consisted of many guisers on horseback. The queen had thirty-four maids of honour, and there were twenty couple of morris-dancers, several bands of music, many colours, and a "grand garland drawn by four good horses and proper attendance." In the evening, the treasurer exhibited his cash, £649, 17s. The last of these rival guisings was that of Eccles, on the 20th October, when their procession numbered two hundred and sixteen horsemen, and nearly a hundred footmen. They assembled at Pendleton. The queen had fifty-six maids of honour, every one handsomely dressed, and with a watch by her side. After marching as far as Salford, they returned to Eccles, and the cash displayed was £1881, 5s. 6d. Whether there was any further pageant after the issue of this pamphlet does not appear. The writer names a Mr L—— as "one of the most principal supporters of the guising on the side of Barton." He concludes by declaring his conviction that Barton was the first offender and assailant, by invading Eccles with guisers; and that the victory remained with Eccles, which had only sought to defend its own territory.

HOGHTON PAGEANT IN 1617.

THE following is given in Nichols's "Progresses of James I." as "A speech made to King James at his coming to Hoghton Tower [in August 1617] by two conceived to be the household gods. The first attired in a purple taffeta mantle, in one hand a palm-tree branch, on his head a garland of the same, and in the other hand a dog":—

First Tutelar God.

This day, great King, for government admired,
Which these thy subjects have so much desired,
Shall be kept holy in their heart's best treasure,
And vowed to James, as is this month to Cæsar.
And now the landlord of this ancient tower,
Thrice fortunate to see this happy hour,
Whose trembling heart thy presence sets on fire,
Unto this house (the heart of all the shire)
Does bid thee hearty welcome, and would speak it
In higher notes, but extreme joy doth break it.
He makes his guest most welcome, in whose eyes
Love-tears do sit,—not he that shouts and cries.
And we, the gods and guardians of this place,
I of this house—he of the fruitful chace—
Since the Hoghtons from this hill took name,
Who with the stiff unbridled Saxons came;

And so have flourished in this fairer clime
Successively from that to this our time,
Still offering up to our immortal powers
Sweet incense, wine, and odoriferous flowers,
While sacred Vesta, in her virgin tire,
With vows and wishes tends the hallowed fire.
Now seeing that thy majesty we see,
Greater than country gods, more good than we,
We render up to thy more powerful guard
This house. This knight is thine, he is thy ward;
For by thy helping and auspicious hand
He and his home shall ever, ever stand,
And flourish in despite of envious Fate,
And then live, like Augustus, fortunate.
And long, long mayest thou live ! To which both men,
God, saints, and angels, say, " Amen, Amen !"

The Second Tutelar God begins :—

Thou greatest of mortals ! [*He is nonplussed.*

The First God begins again :—

Dread Lord ! the splendour and the glorious ray
Of thy high majesty hath stricken dumb
His weaker godhead. If that himself he come
Unto thy service straight, he will commend
These foresters, and charge them to attend
Thy pleasure in this park, and show such sport
To the chief huntsman and thy princely court
As the small circuit of this round affords,
And be more ready than he was in 's words.

This is doubtless the same pageant thus recorded in *Nicholas Assheton's Journal :—*" Then, about ten or eleven o'clock, a mask of noblemen, knights, gentlemen, and courtiers, afore the King, in the middle round, in the garden. Some speeches ; of the rest, dancing the Huckler, Tom Bedlo, and the Coup Justice of Peace." The Rev. Canon Raines, who edited the journal for the Chetham Society, observes—" These ancient and fashionable Lancashire dances have passed away and are forgotten. The origin of the second name is obviously" (from the Tom o' Bedlams, released from that hospital, and licensed to beg, wearing tin badges. There was also a play or interlude of "Tom o' Bedlam, the Tinker"). The particular frolic here referred to seems to be described in the following passage from the "History of Preston," vol. ii. p. 358 :—" A grand masque took place, and a rush-bearing was introduced, in which a man was enclosed in a dendrological foliage of fronds, and was the admiration of the company. This spectacle was exhibited in that part of the garden called 'the middle circular.' Speeches were made in dialogue wittily pleasant, and all kinds of frolics were carried on to the highest pitch, by Robin Goodfellow, Will Huckler, Tom Bedloe, Old Crambo, Jem Tosspot, Dolly Wango, and the Cap Justice. These characters were played to the life; and the Justices Crooke, Houghton, and Doddridge, who were present, declared to the King that 'the Cap Justice was acted to the very life.' Sir John Finett, knight, and master of the ceremonies to the King, performed the part of Cap Justice." Crambo is named in Ben Jonson's masque of the "Fortunate Isles." Recent inquiry has thrown much doubt upon the strict accuracy of this passage.

CUSTOM AT LIVERPOOL FAIRS.

THE fair days are 25th July and 11th November. Ten days before and ten days after each fair day, a hand (or perhaps a glove) is exhibited in front of the town-hall, which denotes protection; during which time no person coming to or going from the town on business connected with the fair can be arrested for debt within its liberty. This custom is noticed in *Gore's Directory*, but it has long been discontinued, and no such exemption now exists.

LIVERPOOL MAY-DAY CELEBRATIONS.

THE first of May has lost many of its attractions since May-poles and May-queens passed out of fashion. Yet, in most country places and small towns it has become usual for each driver of a team to decorate his horses with gaudy ribbons and other ornaments on that day. In Liverpool and Birkenhead, where some thousands of men are employed as carters, this May-Day dressing has grown into a most imposing institution. Every driver of a team in and around the docks appears to enter into rivalry with his neighbours, and the consequence is that most of the horses are gaily dressed and expensively ornamented. The drivers put on new suits, covered with white linen slops, and sport new whips in honour of the occasion. Some of the embellishments for the horses are of a most costly character; not a few are disposed in admirable taste; and in several instances they amount to actual art exhibitions, since the carts are filled with the articles in which their owners deal. Real and artificial flowers are disposed in wreaths and other forms upon different portions of the harness—brilliant velvet cloths, worked in silver and gold, are thrown over the loins of the horses; and if their owners are of sufficient standing to bear coats of arms, these are emblazoned upon the cloths, surrounded with many curious and artistic devices. Not only are the men interested in these displays, but wives and daughters, mistresses and servants, vie with each other as to who shall produce the most gorgeous exhibition. A few years ago the Corporation of Liverpool exhibited no fewer than one hundred and sixty-six horses in the procession, the first cart containing all the implements used by the scavenging department most artistically arranged. The railway companies, the brewers, the spirit merchants, and all the principal dock-carriers, &c., send their teams with samples of produce to swell the procession. After parading the principal streets, headed by bands of music and banners, the horses are taken home to their respective stables, and public dinners are given to the carters by the Corporation, the railway companies, and other extensive firms. The Mayor and other members of the Corporation attend these annual feasts, and after the repasts are ended, the carters are usually addressed by some popular speaker, and much good advice is frequently given them from such quaint old sayings as—" The grey mare is the better horse;" " One man can lead a horse to the water, but ten cannot make him drink;" "Never put the cart before the horse," &c.

PRESTON GUILD MERCHANT—ITS CELEBRATION EVERY TWENTY YEARS.

ONE of the most ancient pageant festivals in the kingdom is held in the borough of Preston every twenty years, under the designation of the "Preston Guild Merchant." The guilds were of Anglo-Saxon origin, and Camden describes the *Gilda Mercatoria* as a liberty or privilege granted to merchants, whereby they were entitled to hold certain pleas of land and other possessions within their own precincts, and whereby neighbours enter into associations, and become bound to each other to bring forth him who commits any crime, or to make satisfaction to the injured party. At present, the Guild at Preston has for its object to receive and register the claims of persons having any right to the freedom or the franchises of the borough, whether by ancestry, prescription, or purchase, and to celebrate a periodical jubilee, rendered distinguished by the rarity of its recurrence. The first royal charter granted to Preston was in the reign of Henry II. It is without date, but held to be about 1179 or 1180. By it that king confirmed to the burgesses of Preston all the same liberties and free customs which he had granted to Newcastle-under-Lyne, the principal of which were a grant of Guild Merchant, exemption from tolls, soc, sac, &c., throughout the kingdom, &c. Dr Kuerden, in his MS. collections in the Heralds' College (vol. iv. p. 23), has preserved a paper entitled, "First Gild Merchant at Preston, second Edward III." (1328). It consists of thirteen rules or ordinances, the second of which ordains that "it shall be lawful to the mayor, bailiffs, and burgesses, their heirs and successors, to set a Guild Merchant at every twenty years' end or erer (earlier), if they have need, to confirm charters, or other distres that 'long to our franchises." From an examination of the Preston Guild roll in the time of Richard II., this festival appears to have been held before the mayor, three stewards or seneschals, nine aldermen, and a clerk of the Guild. From that time till the grant of the governing charter, the entries have been in the same form; but since the reign of Charles II., with one exception (in 1 Anne), all the guilds have been holden before the mayor, the three senior aldermen, who are called seneschals or stewards, four other aldermen, called aldermen of the Guild, and the clerk of the Guild. The officers or the guilds seem to have exercised at some of these celebrations the whole power of legislating for the body corporate and for the burgesses. The guilds form a kind of court of session of corporate legislation, held every twenty years, at which all the laws for the government of the corporation are passed, and at which all the privileges of the burgesses are first claimed. Including that called by Kuerden the first guild, there have been twenty-one guilds, and those of 1802 and 1822 were presided over by the same individual, the late Nicholas Grimshaw, Esq., who was seven times mayor of Preston, and is the only mayor who has twice, at an interval of twenty years, presided over this festival. These ceremonials and the attendant festivities attract a very large number of visitors of all classes. At that of 1822, from fifty to sixty thousand persons were present. On the first day, Monday, September 2, the companies or fraternities assembled at eight A.M., under their respective banners, and in their gayest attire. At 10.30 they were formed in order by the grand-marshal, and the mayor and corporation moved through their lines in procession to the parish church, accompanied by a large assemblage of nobility and gentry, amongst whom were the Lord-Lieutenant, and the High Sheriff of the county, the Earl of Wilton, the Earl of Stamford and Warrington, Lords Lindsay, Aylmer, Grey, &c. After divine service, the grand procession commenced, and the companies, decorated with the insignia of their trades, and headed by the bands of music, paraded the town in the following order:—1st, Tanners, skinners, curriers, and glovers; 2d, Cotton spinners and weavers, headed by their masters, and accompanied by machines in motion, mounted on stages, by which all the processes of the business were performed, from the steam-engine to the loom; 3d, cordwainers; 4th, carpenters; 5th, butchers; 6th, vintners; 7th, tailors; 8th, plasterers; 9th, smiths; 10th, gardeners; 11th, Oddfellows; 12th, printers and bookbinders: 13th, Freemasons; the rear of the procession being brought up by the corporation and the gentry. But the great attraction of the Guild was the procession of the lady-mayoress on the following day, when about 160 ladies, headed by the representative of the lady-mayoress, supported by the mayor, and the mayor's chaplain; the Countess of Derby, supported by the Earl; the Countess of Wilton, by the Hon. Mr Stanley; Lady Lindsay, Lady Hoghton, the Misses Stanley, and numerous other ladies of distinction, all decorated with towering plumes, and dressed in the full costume of the ball-room, passed in procession from the Guildhall along the principal street to the parish church, where divine service was performed, and afterwards round the market-place to the Guildhall. These splendid processions were only the forerunners of other entertainments. For a whole fortnight the town remained full of company; banquets, plays, balls, and races, each in their turn claimed the attention of the visitors. A fancy ball, at which from six to seven hundred of the gentry of the city were present, was given in the first week. The second week was ushered in by an ascent of Mr Livingston in his balloon, and a series of musical performances of the first order, consisting of oratorios and concerts, while a charity ball and a masquerade served to engage and delight the company during the remainder of the festival. It is erroneously supposed by some to be obligatory upon the corporation to celebrate a guild every twenty years; no such obligation exists. The guilds have, indeed, for upwards of two centuries and a half, been held at regular intervals, by virtue of a bye-law of the mayor, stewards, and aldermen of the Guild, and passed in the reign of Queen Elizabeth; but this is quite a matter of choice and arrangement; and should the entertainments and processions ever wholly cease, no privilege or franchise would be lost. The "ordinances" and "orders" may be found in *Baines's Lancashire*, and for the guilds of 1842 and 1862, see *Dobson's History of Preston Guild*.

THE PACE-EGG MUMMERS.

THOUGH from its title this piece of rustic pageantry and mumming apparently belongs to Easter, it is evident from the fourth, fifth, and sixth lines of the doggrel that it was a piece written for and enacted at Christmas. The writer has seen and heard it performed in the open air, before country houses, at both seasons, and some years ago a sort of dramatic entertainment of a similar kind was performed at the annual Christmas festive night of the Manchester Mechanics' Institute, in the old Free Trade Hall, Peter Street. The *dramatis personæ* are usually the *Fool*, whose byplay, antics, and buffeting of the spectators, especially women, with a bladder suspended to a stick, serve to sustain the action of the piece throughout ; *St George*, the champion of England ; *Slasher*, a soldier with sword and buckler ; the *Doctor*, a specimen of the old itinerant quack-salver; the *Prince of Paradine*, wherever that may be ; perhaps originally a misprint for Palestine. He is "a black Morocco dog," and the son of the *King of Egypt*, who, on finding his son slain, calls on *Hector* to slay *St George.* It is needless to say that the English champion defeats *Hector*, as he had before vanquished *Slasher* and the *Prince;* and here ends the heroic part of the piece. As is found in many of these relics of mediæval pageants, the play ends with the appearance of two devils, *Beelzebub* and *Little Devil Doubt.*

ACT I.

Enter Actors.

Fool.—Room, room, brave gallants! give us room to sport;
For in this room we wish for to resort—
Resort, and to repeat to you our merry rhyme,
For remember, good sirs, this is Christmas-time.
The time to cut up goose-pies now doth appear,
So we are come to act our merry Christmas here,
At the sound of the trumpet, and beat of the drum:
Make room, brave gentlemen, and let our actors come.
We are the merry actors that traverse the street;
We are the merry actors that fight for our meat;
We are the merry actors that show pleasant play:
Step in, St George, thou champion, and clear the way.

Enter St George.

I am St George, who from old England sprung;
My famous name throughout the world hath rung;
Many bloody deeds and wonders have I made known
And made the tyrants tremble on their throne.
I followed a fair lady to a giant's gate,
Confined in dungeon deep, to meet her fate;
Then I resolved, with true knight-errantry,
To burst the door, and set the prisoner free,
When a giant almost struck me dead,
But by my valour I cut off his head.
I've searched the world all round and round,
But a man to equal me I never found.

Enter Slasher to St George.

Slasher.—I am a valiant soldier, and Slasher is my name;

The Pace-Egg Mummers.

With sword and buckler by my side, I hope to win the game;
And for to fight with me I see thou art not able,
So with my trusty broad-sword I soon will thee disable.

St George.—Disable! disable! it lies not in thy power,
For with my glittering sword and spear I soon will thee devour.
Stand off! Slasher! let no more be said,
For if I draw my sword I'm sure to break thy head.

Slasher.—How canst thou break my head?
Since it is made of iron,
And my body's made of steel,
My hands and feet of knuckle-bone,
I challenge thee to the field.

(*They fight, and Slasher is wounded.—Exit St George.*)

Enter Fool to Slasher.

Fool.—Alas! alas! my chiefest son is slain;
What must I do to raise him up again?
Here he lies in the presence of you all;
I'll lovingly for a doctor call.
(*Aloud*) A doctor! a doctor! ten pounds for a doctor.
I'll go and fetch a doctor (*going*).

Enter Doctor.

Doctor.—Here am I.

Fool.—Are you the doctor?

Doctor.—Yes; that you may plainly see
By my art and activity.

Fool.—Well, what's your fee to cure this man?

Doctor.—Ten pounds is my fee:
But, Jack, if thou be an honest man,
I'll only take five off thee.

Fool.—You'll be wondrous cunning if you get any (*aside*).
Well, how far have you travelled in doctorship?
Doctor.—From Italy, Titaly [Sicily], High Germany, France, and Spain,
And now am returned to cure diseases in Old England again.
Fool.—So far, and no further?
Doctor.—O yes! a great deal further.
Fool.—How far?
Doctor.—From the fireside cupboard up-stairs and into bed.
Fool.—What diseases can you cure?
Doctor.—All sorts.
Fool.—What's all sorts?
Doctor.—The itch, the pitch, the palsy, and the gout,
If a man gets nineteen devils in his skull, I'll cast twenty of them out.
I have in my pockets crutches for lame ducks, spectacles for blind humble-bees, packsaddles and panniers for grasshoppers, and plaisters for broken-backed mice. I cured Sir Harry of a nang-nail, almost fifty yards long; surely I can cure this poor man.
Here, Jack; take a little out of my bottle,
And let it run down thy throttle;
If thou be not quite slain,
Rise, Jack, and fight again. (*Slasher rises.*)
Slasher.—O my back!
Fool.—What's amiss with thy back?
Slasher.—My back it is wounded,
And my heart is confounded,
To be struck out of seven senses into fourscore,
The like was never seen in old England before!

Enter St George.

O hark! St George, I hear the silver trumpet sound,
That summons us from off this bloody ground:
Down yonder is the way (*pointing*).
Farewell, St George! we can no longer stay.

Exeunt Slasher, Doctor, and Fool.

ACT II.

St George.—I am St George, that noble champion bold,
And with my trusty sword I won ten thousand pounds in gold;
'Twas I that fought the fiery dragon, and brought him to the slaughter,
And by those means I won the King of Egypt's daughter.

Enter Prince of Paradine [Palestine].

Prince.—I am Black Prince of Paradine, born of high renown.
Soon I will fetch St George's lofty courage down;
Before St George shall be received by me,
St George shall die to all eternity.

St George.—Stand off, thou black Morocco dog,
Or by my sword thou 'lt die,
I'll pierce thy body full of holes,
And make thy buttons fly.

Prince.—Draw out thy sword and slay,
Pull out thy purse and pay,
For I will have a recompense
Before I go away.

St George.—Now Prince Paradine, where have you been,

And what fine sights pray have you seen?
Dost think that no man of thy age
Dares such a black as thee engage?
Lay down thy sword, take to me a spear,
And then I'll fight thee without dread or fear.

(They fight, and the Prince of Paradine is slain.)

St George.—Now Prince of Paradine is dead,
And all his joys entirely fled,
Take him and give him to the flies,
And never more come near my eyes.

Enter King of Egypt.

King.—I am the King of Egypt, as plainly doth appear;
I'm come to seek my son, my son and only heir.
St George.—He is slain!
King.—Who did him slay, who did him kill,
And on the ground his precious blood did spill?
St George.—I did him slay, I did him kill,
And on the ground his precious blood did spill,
Please you, my liege, my honour to maintain;
Had you been there you might have fared the same.
King.—Cursed Christian! what is this thou'st done?
Thou hast ruined me, and slain my only son.
St George.—He gave me a challenge: why should I it deny?
How high he was, but see how low he lies!
King.—O Hector! Hector! help me with speed,
For in my life I never stood more need.

Enter Hector.

And stand not there with sword in hand,
But rise and fight at my command.
Hector.—Yes, yes, my liege, I will obey;
And by my sword I hope to win the day.

If that be he who doth stand there
That slew my master's son and heir,
If he be sprung from royal blood,
I'll make it run like Noah's flood.

St George.—Hold, Hector ! do not be so hot,
For here thou knowest not who thou 'st got;
For I can tame thee of thy pride,
And lay thine anger too aside,
Inch thee and cut thee as small as flies,
And send thee over sea to make mince-pies,
Mince-pies hot and mince-pies cold,
I'll send thee to Black Sam before thou'rt three days old!

Hector.— How canst thou tame me of my pride,
And lay mine anger too aside,
Inch me, and cut me as small as flies,
Send me over the sea to make mince-pies,
Mince-pies hot, mince-pies cold,
How canst thou send me to Black Sam before I'm three
　　days old ?
Since my head is made of iron,
My body's made of steel,
My hands and feet of knuckle-bone,
I challenge thee to the field.

(*They fight, and Hector is wounded.*)

I am a valiant knight, and Hector is my name,
Many bloody battles have I fought, and always won the
　　same.
But from St George I received this bloody wound,

(*A trumpet sounds.*)

Hark ! hark ! I hear the silver trumpet sound;
Down yonder is the way (*pointing*).
Farewell, St George ! I can no longer stay.　(*Exit.*)

Enter Fool to St George.

St George.—Here comes from post, Old Bold Ben.
Fool.—Why, master, did ever I take you to be my friend?
St George.—Why, Jack, did ever I do thee any harm?
Fool.—Thou proud saucy coxcomb, begone!
St George.—A coxcomb! I defy that name!
With a sword thou ought to be stabbed for the same.
Fool.—To be stabbed is the least I fear;
Appoint your time and place, I'll meet you there.
St George.—I'll cross the water at the hour of five,
And meet you there, sir, if I be alive. (*Exit.*)

Enter Beelzebub.

Here come I, Beelzebub,
And over my shoulders I carry my club,
And in my hand a dripping pan,
And I think myself a jolly old man;
And if you don't believe what I say,
Enter in Devil Doubt, and clear the way.

Enter Devil Doubt.

Here come I, little Devil Doubt,
If you do not give me money I'll sweep you all out.
Money I want, and money I crave;
If you do not give me money, I'll sweep you all to the grave.

MAY-DAY—ROBIN HOOD AND MAID MARION.

In the sixteenth century, or perhaps earlier, Robin Hood presided in the May-Day pageant as lord of the May, and Maid Marion was the lady of the May. Their companions were distinguished as " Robin Hood's men," and were all dressed in "Lincoln green." In Garrick's collection of old plays is one entitled, "A New Play of Robin Hood, for to be played in the May-games: very pleasant and full of pastime." These May-games seem to have been acted, before the Reformation, within the walls of the old parish and Collegiate Church of Manchester; for Hollinworth says that John Bradford, the martyr, "preaching in Manchester in King Edward [the VI.'s] days, told the people, as it were by a prophetical spirit, that because they did not readily embrace the Word of God, mass should be said again in that church, and the play of Robin Hood acted there; which accordingly came to pass in Queen Mary's reign."

RUSH-BEARINGS.

THE ancient custom of strewing church-floors with rushes, which were renewed every year on the day of the dedication of the church, seems to have been practised in times before the floors were flagged, to cover the soil or mud of the floors, and to give warmth in winter, and a sort of cleanliness in summer. In the parish register of Kirkham are entries to this effect:—"1604. Rushes to strew the church cost this year 9s. 6d." "1631. Paid for carrying the rushes out of the church in the sickness time, 5s." In Thomas Newton's "Herbal to the Bible," 1587, it is stated that "with sedge and rushes many in the country do use in summer-time to strew their parlours and churches, as well for coolness as for pleasant smell." Brand adds—"As our ancestors rarely washed their floors, disguises of uncleanliness became very necessary." It may be noted that disbursements for rushes never appear in the Kirkham register after 1634, when the church was flagged for the first time. The custom was, however, observed till of late years in Penwortham Church. The festival of rush-bearing does not always, however, coincide with the feast of the dedication. At Altcar the church is dedicated to St Michael (Sept. 29), yet the rush-bearing is celebrated in July. Mr Roby speaks of it as an unmeaning pageant still practised in the northern and eastern parts of Lancashire, for the purpose of levying contributions. The rush-cart, preceded by a large silk banner, and decorated with flowers, ribbons, &c., is drawn round to the dwellings of the principal inhabitants by morrice-dancers, who perform an uncouth dance, one of the mummers being a man in motley attire, a sort of compound of the ancient fool and of Maid Marion; who jingles a horse-collar hung with bells, and makes jokes with the bystanders. The rush-bearing is still kept up with much ceremony at Ambleside.

WAKES AND RUSH-BEARINGS ON THE LANCASHIRE AND YORKSHIRE BORDER.

THE village festival which, in most counties of England, takes place on the anniversary of the day when the parish church was consecrated, or on the day of the saint to whom it is dedicated, is kept here at a different time and in a different manner than in any other county I have lived in. At the approach of autumn, when rushes are in full length, certain days are set apart for the different towns and villages in the neighbourhood of Saddleworth, when all work is stopped, and everybody rejoices and makes merry. Some young men of the parish load a hand-cart with rushes, sometimes ten to twelve feet high; and with these carts, which are often most gorgeously decorated with flags, ribbons, &c., sometimes with plate borrowed for the purpose from the wealthier parishioners, and preceded by fife and drum, they march in procession through the parish, stopping at almost every house, and after three hearty cheers for the inhabitants, ask either for a present of money or for some refreshments. The money collected is divided among those who loaded and decorated the rush-cart. This custom of gathering rushes is very old, and dates its origin from times when such luxuries as carpeted pews, with cushions and curtains, hot-water or gas pipes, were not known in our country churches. In those days, at the approach of winter, the young people collected the rushes and took them to the parish church, and covered the floor with them, to keep warm the feet of the good Christians whom the cold winter's wind, and the long, dreary walk over the snow-covered Yorkshire moors, could not keep from attending matins or evensong. A good old neighbour of mine, seventy-eight years old, well remembers the time when six or eight rush-carts met at Saddleworth Church, and with their contents a warm (church) carpet was prepared for the coming winter.—*N. and Q.*, 2d ser. xii. 229.

RUSH-BEARING IN EAST LANCASHIRE.

THESE used to have a real significance. The rushes were cut, dried, and then carried in carts to the churchyard. The rushes were then strewn along the aisles of the church and in the bottoms of the pews in preparation for winter. Carpets and cushions (locally termed "wishons") were then unknown, except in the pews of the wealthy. Barrowford rush-bearing is always held on the first Sunday after the 19th August. This festival is still visited by vast numbers of persons from Burnley, Colne, Padiham, and elsewhere. Cheap trips are run on the East Lancashire line from Burnley and Colne to Nelson Station. Riot and drunkenness reign supreme. Rush-bearing Sundays are also observed at other places, as Holme, Worsthorn, Downham, &c., but usually not in so disreputable a manner. Most of the clergy take advantage of these Sundays, and fix their "charity sermons" for those days. They thus obtain contributions from many distant friends, who pay special visits to their relatives on these occasions. In Yorkshire these pastimes take the name of "feasts."

HAMBLETON FAIR.

HAMBLETON HILL is one of the most elevated points in East Lancashire. It ranks third to Pendle and Boulsworth. On the first Sunday in May vast numbers of persons are in the habit of climbing the hill; and this annual gathering has now taken the name of "the fair." The neighbouring Sunday-schools are almost emptied on that day, notwithstanding all the efforts of the superintendents and ministers.

ROCHDALE RUSH-BEARING.

THE annual ceremony of rush-bearing is celebrated in Rochdale and in many other parishes in Lancashire. This custom, partaking of the nature of a village-wake, is of high antiquity, probably as remote as the age of Pope Gregory IV. (A.D. 827), who, on the introduction of

Rochdale Rush-bearing.

Christianity into this country, recommended to Melletus, the coadjutor of St Augustine, that on the anniversary of the dedication of the Christian churches wrested from the pagans, the converts to Christianity should " build themselves huts of the boughs of trees about their churches, and celebrate the solemnities with religious feastings." On a fixed day in every year—in Rochdale on the 19th August—a kind of obtuse pyramid of rushes, erected on a cart, is highly ornamented in front, and surmounted by a splendid garland. To the vehicle so laden, from thirty to forty young men, wearing white jackets and ornamented with ribbons and flowers, are harnessed in pairs. A band of music is always in attendance, which strikes up on the cart moving on, and thousands of spectators, attracted from a distance of ten or even twenty miles around, hail with repeated cheers the showy pageant. The procession then advances to the town, and, on arriving in front of each of the inns, a kind of morrice-dance is performed by the men in harness, who jingle copper bells, and beat or rather stamp tune with their wooden shoes—the clown, who is dressed in female attire, all the while collecting money to refresh the actors in the grotesque exhibition. From the town, the procession passes to the neighbouring mansions, where the dance is again repeated, and where the performers are presented by the ladies with garlands and money. Till about the early part of the nineteenth century the rush-bearing usually terminated at the church, and the rushes were spread on the clay floor under the benches used as seats by the congregation, to serve as a winter carpet; while the garlands were hung up in the chancel and over the pews of the families by whom they had been presented, where they remained till their beauty had faded. But within the last half century the church is frequently the last place thought of in this festival, which has degenerated into mere rustic saturnalia. Formerly not fewer than a dozen of these processions from different parts of the parish entered Rochdale on the annual celebration; but they have now (1832) dwindled down to three or four, and are gradually dying away. This is in accordance with what Baines says in his "Lancashire," but a correspondent of Hone's "Year Book," signing "J. L." and dating from Rochdale, May 31, 1825, gives the following account of the custom of rush-bearing in that neighbourhood, illustrated by a woodcut (col. x. 1103). A few years ago, I was told by an old man now deceased, that he remembered the rushes to have been borne on the shoulders of the country people in bundles, some very plain and others ornamented with ribbons, garlands, &c., to the churchyard in Rochdale; that they were there dried previous to being put into the church, and that these rush-bearers received a small compensation from the churchwardens. This was before churches were floored with wood. The rushes were strewed for the purpose of rendering the congregation more comfortable, and saving their feet from being chilled by the stone pavements, and, in some instances, the clay floors. In many churches rushes are used in the same manner in the present day; but the old, homely method of rush-bearing on the shoulders has given place to the more luxurious and gorgeous display of the rush-cart and banner. The rushes are laid transversely on the rush-cart, and are cut by sharp knives to the form desired, in which no little art is required. The bolts, as they are termed, are formed of the largest rushes tied up in bundles of about two inches in diameter. These bolts, as the work of making proceeds, are affixed to rods fixed in the four corners of the cart, and carved to the form required. When the cart is finished, the load of rushes is decorated with carnations and other flowers, in different devices, and surmounted by branches of oak, and a person rides upon the top. The carts are sometimes drawn by horses gaily caparisoned, but more frequently by young men, to the number of twenty or thirty couples, profusely adorned with ribbons, tinsel, &c. They were generally preceded by men with horse-bells about them, grotesquely jumping from side to side, and jingling the bells. After these is a band of music, and sometimes a set of morris-dancers (but without the ancient appendage of bells) followed by young women bearing garlands; then comes the banner, made of silk of various colours, joined by narrow ribbon fretted, the whole profusely covered on both sides with roses, stars, &c., of tinsel (which in this part is called horse-gold), and which being viewed when the sun shines upon it, dazzles the eye. The banners are generally from four to five yards broad and six to eight yards long, having on either side in the centre a painting of Britannia, the king's arms, or some other device. The whole procession is flanked by men with long cart-whips, which they keep continually cracking to make a clear path On the front of some carts is a white cloth, to which is attached a number of silver spoons, tankards, cups, and watches, tastefully displayed. Great rivalry exists between the young men of the neighbouring villages which should produce the best-formed cart and banner, and it not unfrequently happens that when two of them meet in the street, a scuffle takes place and many bloody noses are the result. Six or seven rush-carts are frequently in the town of Rochdale on the third Monday in August, which is the day for strewing them. A collection is made by each party from the gentry and other inhabitants, which enables the rush-bearers to sacrifice very freely at the shrine of Sir John Barleycorn. The displays are very gay, and afford much gratification to a stranger who never before witnessed a rush-bearing. The practice is general in the months of July, August, and September, Those held round this place are at Ashworth, Littleborough, Milnrow, Shaw, Oldham, Royton, Middleton, Heywood, and Whitworth; the customs at each place being much alike. The person who has the forming of a rush-cart is called a *featherer*, and it was one of these men who unfortunately lost his life at the riots in this town on Easter Monday in April 1794 or 1795. He resided at Mereland, and for a number of years afterwards, in commemoration of his death, the young men who drew the rush-cart from Mereland wore a black scarf, but it is now discontinued. The author of "Scarsdale" has given a graphic account of rush-bearings as they were celebrated fifty years ago. He says: —On the bowling-green behind the house a booth had been built with ribs of timber covered with canvas, and a floor of rough boards to protect the smooth sward. Here, to the accompaniment of a couple of fiddles, flageolets and a fife, about fifty couple were in the full excitement of a country-dance, while many country lads and lasses were looking on. Through the garden behind the green wandered other groups. In front of the inn stood the rush-cart, which to our southern readers may require a more detailed description. One of the larger carts used in Lancashire either to carry manufactured goods or to bring harvest from the field had been heaped with rushes to the height of about twenty-four feet from the ground. The rushes were skilfully arranged into a perfectly smooth conical stack, rising to a sharp ridge at the top. From this centre four hedges, formed of rushes woven into a neat pattern, and each hedge about two feet high, descended to the four corners of the cart. On the summit was a bower in the form of a crown, made of holly, laurel, and other evergreens, round which were twined garlands. An immense wreath of large flowers encircled the base of the arbour, and a smaller one decorated its top. On each of the smooth sides of the cone, between the boundary of rush-hedges, were inscriptions in brilliantly coloured flowers, such as "Colliers and Weavers," "Fear God," "Honour the King," &c. Spangled flags of various bright hues hung from the sides of the crowning bower. A large silver salver from the Hall, with some silver tankards, hung on the front. About thirty young men, with white shirts down to the waist, profusely adorned with gay ribbons, and with wreaths of flowers on their heads, were yoked in couples between two strong new ropes. Each couple held a stave fastened on either side into a knot in the rope, and they were engaged in practising some dances, with which their entry into the principal streets of Rochdale was to be celebrated. A strong horse was in the shafts, and behind was a band of other gaily-dressed young men, similarly yoked between ropes, to hold the cart while descending any steep hill. A bugle sounded to summon the dancers from the booth, the revellers from the club-room, and the wandering groups and whispering lovers from the garden. Some miles of road had to be traversed, and all the rush-carts from the neighbouring villages were to meet in Rochdale at noon. There issued from behind the house the whole united band, with a big drum, two bugles, two trumpets, several other brass instruments, with fifes, flageolets, &c. They were the heralds of an immense banner, held in the air by four men, two on each side, who grasped long slender poles supporting a transverse piece, from which swung this mighty achievement of the art of Scarsdale. In the centre were the Scarsdale arms, which had never been so fiercely emblazoned before; on the top was a view of Scarsdale Hall, painted on paper mounted on cloth. There were masonic devices, emblematic monsters, wonderfully shaped spangles, roses, wreaths, and other caprices of the imagination of the Scarsdale artists. The result was one of barbaric splendour of colour and tinsel. This marvellous pomp was heralded by a deafening clamour of the band, which did its worst against rival sounds, even almost drowning the frantic shouts with which the phenomenon of the banner was greeted. Seth Diggle had been promoted to the post of honour on the top of the cart, where he held a banner on which the Scarsdale arms were emblazoned on the Union Jack. Before the cart started for Rochdale, however, a country-dance was formed on each side of the road, it being the privilege of the young men yoked in the cart to choose their partners from the prettiest country girls—nothing loath for such a distinction. The band struck up loudly, the banners stood grandly at one end of the two sets of thirty couples, and at the other the cart, with Seth in the bower at its crown. Half-an-hour was devoted to this dance, when the bugle again sounded, the dance at once ceased, the young men kissed their partners and took their places, and, amidst the shouts of the crowd, and the wildest efforts of the band, the Scarsdale rush-cart started for Rochdale. About the same time a similar fête was in progress at Hurstwood, at Martinmere, at Eastleton, at Milnrow, at Smallbridge, at Whitworth, at Spotland, and other villages; for it was the glory of Rochdale to assemble at its rush-bearing, forty years ago, at least eight, and sometimes a dozen, rush-carts from the neighbouring villages. Meanwhile, the gala of the rush-bearing was in the delirium of its frenzy, the rush-carts having assembled in the street opposite the Butts, each with its band in front, the order of procession extending over the bridge across the Roche, and a considerable distance up Yorkshire Street. Every band played with stentorian energy, "Rule Britannia;" the young men drawing every cart vied with each other in the vigour and picturesque character of their dances; the flags in every bower on the top of the rush-carts were waved triumphantly; the spangled and decorated banners carried before each band glittered in the bright noon; from every window hung flags or coloured draperies, handkerchiefs were waved, and loud huzzas broke to swell the exulting torrent of acclamation. The main thoroughfares were crowded by a multitude of folk in their gayest dresses; in side-streets were stalls with Eccles cakes, Everton toffy, and Ormskirk gingerbread; and booths with shows of every kind frequenting a country fair. Conjurors stood on their stages, watching for the passage of the procession to attract a crowd of gazers by their wonderful tricks. Mountebanks and clowns were ready to perform, when the streets were clear from the grand pageant of the day. There was a bear on the Butts, growling defiance at the dogs by which it was to be baited, and climbing at intervals to the top of the high stake to which he was chained. Then a pilot balloon of gay colours floated gracefully from a garden of the "Orchard," near the river, and the roar of guns boomed on the ear at short intervals as the pretty phantom rose in the still air to a great height, and then floated away in the tide of an upper current. When the twenty-first gun had been fired, the procession commenced its progress through the town, amidst the wildest shouts and gestures from the crowd. Yorkshire Street, especially at its steepest and most tortuous part, in the heart of the town, consisted five-and-thirty years ago either of quaint stone houses with mullioned windows, gothic doors, and peaked gables, or of white-and-black timber-houses projecting over first a low-browed shop, then with an overhanging story, containing often a wooden oriel, and higher a gabled story, whose bolder projection invaded the upper area of the street. Smithy Door, and Old Millgate, and other streets in the neighbourhood of the Collegiate Church of Manchester, half a century ago, consisted mainly of such structures, which have now to a great extent disappeared. Chester still abounds with them in a picturesque form. In this narrow and tortuous lane of ancient houses, the procession of rush-carts almost brushed the projecting gables. The men on the crown of each cart were covered with flowers flung by fair hands from the highest windows, just too far off to be reached by a friendly grasp. Overhead, webs of coloured flannel and calico stretched across from the peaks of opposite roofs, but little above the flagstaff of each crown. There was barely room for the great banners to pass. Every window was decorated and crowded. The bray of the bands resounded in the narrow steep street. There was a confusion of gay colours, an agitation of bright forms, a tumult of rude joy, the transient frenzy of a carnival, as each long train of white-shirted ribbon-covered men dragged its cart up the hill, pausing and dancing at intervals amidst the exultation of the crowd.

WARTON RUSH-BEARING.

THE inhabitants of the village of Warton, by Morecambe Bay, and their visitors, repair, on the Sunday nearest the 5th of August (St Oswald's Day), to the services of the church, and make good cheer within the rules of sobriety in their houses. The next day is spent in several kinds of diversions, the chief of which is usually a rush-bearing, in this manner :—They cut hard rushes from the marsh, and having made them up in bundles, they dress them in fine linen, silk, ribbons, flowers, &c. The young women then take these gay effigies in their arms and walk in procession, with music, drums, ringing of bells, and other demonstrations of joy, to the church, where they deposit the rushes over the cancelli. This ceremony performed, they return to the village, where scenes of festivity ensue, and the remainder of the day, and sometimes part of the night, is spent in dancing in the open air round the May-pole (adorned with evergreens and flowers), if the weather be fine; if not, in the houses. This is mentioned in Lucas's "History;" but the custom has fallen into disuse, as being no longer necessary.

WHALLEY RUSH-BEARING.

DR WHITAKER, in his history of the parish, says this was a high festival at Whalley. In the old churchwardens' accounts there are annual charges for dressing and cleaning the church, churchyard, &c., for this occasion. It is curious, however, to observe that even in 1617 the old festivals were beginning to decline. The

"Journal" says "much less solemnity than formerly." Canon Raines adds :—It was specially provided in the "Book of Sports" that women should have leave to carry rushes to the church for the decoration of the same according to their ancient custom. The old churchwardens' accounts have entirely perished from carelessness; but in those after 1700 laudable attention appears to have been paid to the cleansing of the church, and there are regular entries every year as follows :—" Paid for dressing the church against St James's Day, five shillings." The rushes were brought on the rush-cart by the north gate into the church free of expense. Garlands were suspended in the church and on the top of the steeple. It is about seventy years since the floor of Whalley Church was strewed with rushes; and after the occasion for its use ceased, the rush-cart door disappeared, though the festival itself was kept up, and the morris-dancers played their parts in it for more than seventy years afterwards. For fifty years, on the 5th August, the village was crowded like a fair, booths were erected, and horse-races and other rustic sports attracted numbers of people from the surrounding country. But the festival gradually declined, and within the last two years [before 1848] St James's Day, the rush-cart, and the festival, have altogether ceased in Whalley. St James's Day, old style, would be on the 6th August, and the rush-bearing day, the 5th August, would therefore be the Eve of St James'.

WAKES.

> "So blithe and bonny now the lads and lasses are,
>   That ever as anon the bagpipe up doth blow,
>   Cast in a gallant round about the hearth they go,
>   And at each pause they kiss. Was never seen such rule
> In any place but here at bonfire or at Yule;
> And every village smokes at wakes with lusty cheer.
> Then "Hey" (they cry) "for Lun and Lancasheere,"
> That one high hill was heard to tell it to his brother,
>   That instantly agreed to tell it to some other."
>
> —DRAYTON.

IT is necessary to distinguish between two ancient anniversaries. Every church at its consecration received the name of some patron saint, whose feast-day or festival became of course the festival of that church, which the people naturally celebrated with peculiar festivity. The day on which the edifice was actually dedicated was also kept as the established feast of the parish. These two feasts were clearly distinguished among the Saxons, and in the laws of Edward the Confessor the *Dies dedicationis* is discriminated from the *Propria festivitatis sancti*, that is, the dedication day was distinguished from the saint's festival. These feasts remained till the Reformation; when, in 1536, the dedication day was ordered to be kept, and the festival of the saint to be celebrated no longer. Anciently the dedication day could not have been observed with the same regularity as that of the patron saint, which was denominated "the church's holiday," and still remains in many parishes to the present time; while the dedication day is forgotten in most if not in all. The eve being of old considered a part of the day (Sunday commencing on Saturday at sunset), the services of the church commenced on the evening before the saint's day, and were called *vigils* or *eves*, and, from the late hour, *wæccan* or *wakes*. In a remarkable letter of Pope Gregory, written about the year 601, to the Abbot Melietus, he says—" When, therefore, Almighty God shall bring you to the most reverend man our brother bishop, St Augustine, tell him what I have, upon mature deliberation on the affair of the English, thought of; namely, that the temples of the idols in that nation ought not to be destroyed. Let holy water be made, and sprinkled in the said temples ; let altars be erected, and let relics be deposited in them. For since those temples are built, it is requisite that they be converted from the worship of the devils to the service of the true God ; that the nation, not seeing those temples destroyed, may remove error from their hearts, and knowing and adoring the true God, may the more familiarly resort to the same places to which they have been accustomed. And because they are wont to sacrifice many oxen in honour of the devils, let them celebrate a religious and solemn festival, not slaughtering the beasts for devils, but to be consumed by themselves, to the praise of God. Some solemnity must be exchanged for them, as that on the day of the dedication or the suffering days [*natalitia*] of holy martyrs whose relics are there deposited, they may build themselves booths of the boughs of the trees about those churches which have been turned to that use from temples, and celebrate the solemnity with religious feasting, and no more offer beasts to the devil." In compliance with these injunctions, in every parish, on the returning anniversary of the saint, little pavilions or booths were constructed of boughs, and the peopled indulged in them in hospitality and mirth. The feasts of the saint's day, however, were soon abused ; and even in the body of the church, when the people were assembled for devotion, they began to mind diversions and to introduce drinking. The growing intemperance gradually stained the service of the vigil, and so scandalised the Puritans of the seventeenth century, that numbers of the wakes were disused entirely, especially in the east and some of the western parts of England; but they are commonly observed in the North, and in some of the midland counties. The wakes gradually led to the establishment of the commercial or trade marts which are called *fairs*. The people resorted in crowds to the festival, and a considerable provision was needed for their entertainment. This induced the little country hucksters and traders to come and offer their wares; and thus arising many temporary erections for hospitality in the neighbourhood of the church, various booths were set up for the sale of different commodities. In larger towns, surrounded by populous districts, the resort of people to the wakes would be great, and the attendance of traders numerous; and this resort and attendance constitute a fair. The festival being a *feria* or holiday, it took itself, and connected to the mart, the appellation of *feria* or *fair*. These fairs were generally held in churchyards, and even in the churches, and also on Sundays, till the indecency and scandal were so great as to need reformation.—*For this and additional information see Whitaker's Manchester*, vol. ii. 440-448.

DIDSBURY WAKES.

THE *Stockport Advertiser* of August 5, 1825, contains the following paragraph :—" Didsbury wakes will be celebrated on the 8th, 9th, and 10th of August. A long bill of fare of the diversions to be enjoyed at this most delightful village has been published. The enjoyments consist chiefly of ass-races, for purses of gold ; prison-bar playing, and grinning through collars, for ale ; bag-racing, for hats ; foot-racing, for sums of money ; maiden plates, for ladies under twenty years of age, for gown-pieces, shawls, &c. ; treacled-loaf-eating, for various rewards ; smoking-matches ; apple-dumpling-eating ; wheelbarrow-racing, the best heats ; bell-racing, and balls each evening. 'Que nunc prescribere longum est.' The humours of Didsbury festival are always well regulated ; the display of youths of both sexes, vieing with each other in dress and fashion, as well as cheerful and blooming faces, is not exceeded by any similar event ; and the gaieties of each day are succeeded by the evening parties fantastically tripping through the innocent relaxation of country-dances, reels, &c., to as favourite tunes, at the 'Cock' and 'Ring o' Bells' inns."

ECCLES WAKES AND ECCLES CAKES.

An annual festival is held at Eccles, of great rustic celebrity and of high antiquity, as old probably as the first erection of the church, called " Eccles Wakes," celebrated on the first Sunday in September; and there is a wake at Swinton on the first Sunday after the 23d July, and another at Woodgate on Saturday in Whitsuntide. The Eccles wake commences on the Sunday, it is continued during the three succeeding days, and consists (amongst many other things) of feasting upon a kind of local confectionary called " Eccles cakes " and ale, with various ancient and modern sports. All the authorities agree in assigning the first institution of wakes to the annual assembly of the people to watch and pray on the festival of the saint to whom their church was dedicated, and this was doubtless originally the case in Eccles; the festival of St Mary the Virgin being on the 22d August, and the wake on the first Sunday after the 25th August, it has been asserted that the correspondence is tolerably well preserved. There is some error here; no festival of St Mary the Virgin falling on the 22d August. The Assumption (or death) was on August 15, and the 22d would be the octave of the Assumption. But the first Sunday after the 25th of August would be nearer to the feast of the Nativity of the Virgin (September 8) than to the Assumption. A Roman Catholic custom of making a kind of oatcakes, called "soul-mass cakes," on All Souls' Day (November 2), and giving them on that day amongst the poor, no longer exists in Eccles; and the couplet which the people were expected to repeat in return for this benevolence is almost forgotten—

"God save your saul,
Bairns and all."

The following is a copy of a bill which sets forth a programme of the sports of Eccles Wake :—

"ECCLES WAKE.—On Monday morning, at eleven o'clock, the sports will commence with that most ancient, loyal, rational, constitutional, and lawful diversion,

BULL-BAITING,

in all its primitive excellence; for which this place has long been noted. At one o'clock there will be a foot-race; at two o'clock a bull-baiting for a horse-collar; at four, donkey-races for a pair of panniers; at five, a race for a stuff-hat; the day's sport to conclude with baiting the bull 'Fury,' for a superior dog-chain.

"On Tuesday, the sports will be repeated; also on Wednesday, with the additional attraction of a smock-race by ladies. A main of cocks to be fought on Monday, Tuesday, and Wednesday, for twenty guineas, and five guineas the byes, between the gentlemen of Manchester and Eccles. The wake to conclude with a fiddling-match by all the fiddlers that attend, for a piece of silver." Wakes are probably as ancient as the introduction of Christianity into this county, and were at first purely religious festivals. But in course of time, as the festivities were prolonged into night, the Legend of St John the Baptist says that the attendants "fell to lecherie and songes, dances, harping, piping, and also to glotony and sinne, and so turned holynesse to cursydnesse." In the reign of Elizabeth, wakes were in part suppressed, but were again allowed by James I. in his "Book of Sports." Since then they have been carried on under varied programmes; but even now—

"Tarts and custards, creams and cakes,
Are the junkets still at wakes;
Unto which the tribes resort,
Where the business is the sport."

PART III.

SPORTS AND GAMES.

SPORTS AND GAMES.

INTRODUCTION.

MANY of the old open-air sports and games of Lancashire are now altogether lost, the names alone surviving. A few particulars as to the ancient customs in games and sports, as well as to those which still survive, shorn of their ancient garb, may interest the reader.

ANCIENT CUSTOMS IN GAMES USED BY BOYS AND GIRLS.

MERRILY SET OUT IN VERSE.

"Any they dare challenge for to throw the sledge,
To jump or leap over ditch or hedge ;
To wrestle, play at stool-ball, or to run,
To pitch the bar, or to shoot off a gun ;
To play at loggats, nine holes, or ten pins,
To try it out at football, by the shins ;
At tick-tacke, seize noddy, maw and ruff ;
At hot-cockles, leap-frog, or blindman's buff ;
To drink the halper-pots, or deal at the whole can ;
To play at chess, or pue, and inkhorn ;
T dance the morris, play at barley-brake ;
At all exploits a man can think or speak :
At shove-groat, venter-point, or crop and pile ;
At 'beshrew him that's last at any stile ;'
At leaping over a Christmas bonfire,
   at the drawing dame out of the mire ;
A shoot-cock, Gregory, stool-ball, and what-not ;
Pick-point, top and scourge, to make him hot."

These lines have been erroneously attributed by Baines, in his "History of Lancashire" (ii. 579), to the second Randle Holme, who merely quoted them as descriptive of Lancashire games and sports in the sixteenth and seventeenth centuries. They are from Samuel Rowland's "Letting of Humour's Blood in the Head-Vaine" (1600). Some of these names of games, and indeed the games themselves, having become obsolete, a few brief explanations may be necessary for the general reader :—*Stool-ball* is a pastime still practised in the North of England. It consists in simply setting a stool on the ground, and one of the players takes his place before it, while his antagonist, standing at a distance, tosses a ball with the intention of striking the stool; and this it is the business of the former to prevent, by beating it away with the hand, reckoning one to the game for every stroke of the ball; if, however, the ball should be missed by the hand, and touch the stool, the players change places; as they also do if the person who threw the ball can catch and hold it when driven back before it reaches the ground. The conqueror is he who strikes the ball most times before it touches the stool. Elsewhere, it is played with a number of stools and as many players. This seems to have been a game for women more than men, but occasionally it was played by young persons of both sexes indiscriminately, as the following lines show, from Tom D'Urfey's play of "Don Quixote" (1694) :—

"Down in a vale, on a summer's day,
All the lads and lasses met to be merry;
A match for kisses at stool-ball to play,
And for cakes and ale, and cider and perry.
Chorus—Come all, great, small, short, tall,—
Away to stool-ball."

Pitching or casting the bar was, in Tudor times, a favourite gymnastic exercise. A poet of the sixteenth century thinks it highly commendable for kings and princes, by way of exercise, to throw "the stone, the bar, or the plummet." Henry VIII. retained "the casting of the bar" among his favourite amusements. The sledge hammer was also used for the same purpose. *Loggats* (says Sir Thomas Hanmer) is the ancient name of a play or game, one of those made "unlawful" by the 33d Henry VIII. It is now called kittle-pins (*i.e.*, skittles), in which the boys often make use of bones instead of wooden pins, throwing at them with another bone, instead of bowling. Hamlet asks, "Did these bones cost no more the breeding, but to play at loggats with them?" *Nine-holes* was a boyish game played at the beginning of the seventeenth century. Nine holes are made in a square board, in three rows, three holes in each row, at equal distances, twelve to fourteen inches apart. The holes are numbered one to nine, so placed as to form fifteen as the total of each row. The board is fixed horizontally on the ground, and surrounded on three sides with a gentle acclivity. Every player being furnished with a certain number of small metal balls, stands in his turn by a mark on the ground, about five or six feet from the board; at which he bowls the balls. According to the value of the figures belonging to the holes into which the balls roll, his game is reckoned; and he who obtains the highest number is the winner. Another game, having the same name, was more recently played by schoolboys. A board was set upright resembling a bridge, with nine small arches, numbered one to nine; at this the boys bowled marbles. If the marble struck against the side or piers of the arches, it became the property of the boy owning the board; if it went through any arch, the bowler claimed a number of marbles equal to the number upon the arch it passed through. *Ten-pins* was in reality nine-pins. Moor, in his "Suffolk Words," says, "We have, like others, nine-pins, which we rather unaccountably call *ten-pins*, or rather *tempins*, although I never saw more than nine used in the game." Probably the game was once played with *ten* pins, as an evasion of the statute which made *nine* pins an unlawful game. The most ancient form of nine-pins was "cayles" or "kayles" (from the French *quilles*), which was played with pins, but all ranged in one row, and thrown at with a stick. These kayle-pins were afterwards called kettle or kittle-pins, and hence, by an easy corruption, skittle-pins. The game of *skittles*, however, differs materially from *nine-pins*, though requiring the same number of pins. At nine-pins, the player stands at a distance settled by mutual consent of the parties, and casts the bowl at the pins; the point is to beat them all down in the fewest throws. Skittles is played by bowling and tipping; the first at a given distance, the second standing close to the frame upon which the pins are placed, and throwing the bowl through in the midst of them. In both cases the number of pins beaten down before the return of the bowl (for it usually passes beyond the frame) are called fair, and reckoned to the account of the player; but those that fall by the coming back of the bowl are said to be foul, and of course not counted. One chalk or score is reckoned for every fair pin; and the game of skittles consists in obtaining thirty-one chalks precisely. Less loses, or at least gives the antagonist a chance of winning the game; and more requires the player to go again for nine, which must also be brought exactly to secure himself. *Football* needs no explanation. *Tick-tack* was a kind of backgammon, played both with men and pegs, and more complicated than the ordinary backgammon, or, as the French call it, *tric-trac*, whence our name of tick-tack. It is frequently referred to by English writers of the seventeenth century. *Seize noddy*, *maw* and *ruff*, were all games of cards. Sir John Harrington, after describing *primero*, perhaps the most ancient game of cards played in England, enumerates in rhyme the card games that succeeded it:—

"Then thirdly followed heaving of the *maw*,
A game without civility or law,
An odious play, and yet in court oft seen,
A saucy knave to trump both king and queen.
Then followed lodum, . .
Now *noddy* followed next."

In Thomas Heywood's play of "A Woman Killed with Kindness" (third edition, 1617), the game of *ruff* is mentioned, and is proposed to be played with honours. *Double ruff*, and *English ruff*, with honours, are mentioned in "The Complete Gamester" (1674), as distinguished from *French ruff*. *Noddy* is supposed to have been very similar to, if not the origin of, the game of *cribbage;* and *noddy-fifteen* is given in Carr's "Craven Glossary." Any number can play—the cards are all dealt out—the elder hand plays one (of which he hath a pair or a *pryal*, if a good player)—saying or singing, "There's a good card for thee," passing it to his right-hand neighbour. The person next in succession who holds its pair covers it, saying, "There's a still better than he," and passes both onward. The person holding the third of the sort (ace, six, queen, or what-not) puts it on, with "There's the best of all three." The holder of the fourth crowns all with the emphatic, "And there is niddy-noddee." He wins the tack, turns it down, and begins again. He who is first out receives from his adversaries a fish, or a bean, as the case may be, for each unplayed card. If *seize* have any particular signification, it may be the French *sixteen*, and in that case, if *fifteen-noddy* were made unlawful, they might play it with an additional point, just as ten pins may have been substituted for nine pins. *Maw* was played with a piquet pack of thirty-six cards, and any number of persons from two to six formed the party of players. At *ruff*, the greatest sort of the suit carried away the game; *ruff* became a term for a court-card, and to *ruff* meant to trump at cards. *Hot cockles* (said to be a corruption of the French *hautes coquilles*, but the French name for this game is *Main-chaude*, literally warm-hand) is a play in which one kneels, and, covering his eyes, lays his head in another's lap, and guesses who struck him. Gay describes this pastime in the following lines:—

> "As at hot cockles once I laid me down,
> And felt the weighty hand of many a clown,
> Buxoma gave a gentle tap, and I
> Quick rose, and read soft mischief in her eye."

Leap-frog and *blind-man's buff* are still favourite games. The line "To drink the halper pots, or deal at the whole can," is evidently an allusion to some competition in drinking, either in half or whole measures. Perhaps halper should be *halfer*. The pot of ale was once a measure; the pottle was two quarts; and the drinking off at once this measure of liquor was termed a "pottle draught." *Chess* is never likely to be obsolete. *Pue* is probably a misprint for *put*, a game at cards, still lingering in some districts. It was in vogue in the seventeenth century. *Inkhorn* is not known as a game. Inkhorn terms were fine words, savouring of the inkhorn. The *morris-dance* was a very ancient dance, in which the performers were dressed in grotesque costume, with bells, &c. It was sometimes performed by itself, but was much more frequently danced in processions and pageants, especially in those of the May-games. In the sixteenth century, it was frequently introduced on the stage. The bells on the dancers' dresses were to be sounded as they danced. They were of unequal sizes, and named the fore-bell, the second bell, the treble, the tenor or great bell; and mention is also made of double bells. In 1561, two dozen of morris-bells were valued at one shilling. There was no particular number of morris-dancers, usually five or more, besides two musicians (pipe and tabor), and the performer of the hobby-horse. The morris-dance is sometimes yet to be seen in Lancashire in connection with the rush-carts, the May-games, and the mummings about Christmas. *Barley-brake* was an ancient rural game, described by Gifford as played by six persons, three of each sex, who were coupled by lot. A piece of ground was then chosen, and divided into three compartments, of which the middle one was called *hell*. The couple condemned to this division tried to catch the others, who advanced from the two extremities; if they succeeded, hell was filled by the couple excluded by pre-occupation from the other places. In this "catching," however, there was some difficulty, as the middle couple, hand in hand, were not to separate before they had succeeded, whilst the others must break hands whenever they find themselves hard pressed. When all had been taken in turn, the last couple were said to be in hell, and the game ended. There is a description of the game in a little tract called "Barley-breake, or a Warning for Wantons" (4to, Lond. 1607). This game would seem to have left its traces in a boys' game still played in the North of England (especially in the East Riding of Yorkshire), in which a couple link hands, and sally forth from *home* (the modern substitute for *hell*), shouting something like "Aggery, ag, ag, ag's gi'en warning," and trying to tick or touch with the free hand any of a number of boys running about separately. These latter try, by slipping behind the linked couple, and throwing their individual weight on the joined hands, to separate them, without being first touched or ticked; and if they sunder the couple, each of the severed ones has to bear a boy "home" on his back. Whoever is touched is condemned to replace the toucher in the linked couple. *Shove-groat* is a variety of the old game of *shovel-board*. A shilling or other smooth coin was placed on the extreme edge of the shovel-board, and propelled towards a mark by a smart stroke with the palm of the hand. Sometimes a groat-piece was used, and in the present times a halfpenny; and the game of *shove-halfpenny* is mentioned in the *Times* of April 25, 1845, as then played by the lower orders. Taylor, the water-poet, states that in his time, the beginning of the seventeenth century, "Edward (VI.) shillings" were chiefly used at *shove-board*. *Venter-point* was a children's game of the sixteenth century, named but nowhere described. *Cross and pile* is the old name of what is now called "tossing," or "heads and tails," the coin now used being generally a halfpenny, of which the obverse or bust of the Queen is the "head," and the reverse, whether the figure of Britannia or the harp of the Irish halfpenny, or other device, is called the tail. The origin of the term "cross and pile" is not very clear. The cross, in form that of St George, its four arms of equal length, was the favourite form for the reverse of silver coins from the time of Henry III., and perhaps at one time facilitated the *fourthing* or *farthing* of the coin, *i.e.*, the dividing it into four equal quarters. But what was the *pile*? Not the pellets, for they were always inserted in the angles between the arms of the cross. Not the legend or reading on the coin, for that was found both on obverse and reverse. It does not appear to be from the Latin *pilus* (the beard), or *pilum* (an arrow or spear). Yet it was clearly the opposite side of the coin to the cross side. Grafton records, that in 1249 an order was made to coin a silver groat, which was to have on one side the picture of the King's face (Henry III.), and on the other a cross extended to the edge. In 1304, the controller of the King's Exchequer, by order of the King's treasurer, sent to the treasurer for Ireland twenty-four stamps for coining money there, viz., "three *piles* with six *crosses*, for pennies; the same for halfpennies; and two *piles*, with four *crosses*, for farthings." This at least shows that "cross and pile" were terms for the opposite sides of coins. The next sport is apparently a *foot-race* to the next stile. Leaping over a Christmas bonfire appears to be a relic of the leaping through or over the *bel-tain* fires in honour of Bel or Baal, at various festivals. The name of the next game contains a misprint. It should be *drawing dun out of the mire.* Dun was a favourite name for horse or mare of that colour, to which the saying "Dun is the mouse" doubtless refers. "*Dule upo' Dun*," a Lancashire tradition, is anglice the devil upon the dun horse or mare. The rural game is described as played with a log of wood representing *dun* (the cart-horse), and a cry is raised that he is stuck in the mire. Two of the company advance either with or without ropes, to draw him out. . They find themselves unable, call for help, and gradually the whole company take part, when *dun* is extricated of course; the fun consisting in the awkward and affected efforts of the rustics to lift the log, and sundry arch contrivances to let the ends of it fall on one another's toes. Chaucer and Ben Johnson have references to it. *Shoot-cock* is the same with our shuttlecock; was played by boys in the fourteenth century, and was a fashionable pastime among grown persons in the reign of James I. *Gregory* was a children's game of the sixteenth century. *Stool-ball* has been already noticed. Perhaps this second time it occurs in the verses it should be read *stow-ball*, which appears to have been a species of golf, and played with a golf-ball. *Pick-point* occurs in an enumeration of children's games in the sixteenth century. *Top and scourge* is simply the whipping-top, one of the most ancient of boys' pastimes, for it was in vogue amongst the ancient Greeks and Romans. *Peg-top* is a modern play.

BARLEY-BRAKE AND BUFF.

THIS game was formerly played in May. Randle Holme, the Chester antiquary, and heraldic deputy of Sir William Dugdale, mentions barley-brake as among the sports which prevailed in Lancashire, and which he thus records in doggerel from Rowland—

> "To play at chess, or pue and inkhorn,
> To dance the morrice, play at *barley-brake*,
> At all exploits a man can think and speak," &c.

Many of the games mentioned in his rude verses are now forgotten; but there is some reason to think that *barley-brake* still lingers in Lancashire and other counties under its more modern name of *prison bars*. It may be further observed that "Blindman's Buff" was formerly called "blende-bok," and has been supposed to be the same with the *jul* or *yule-bok*, the goat or stag of the Pagan Yule-tide. Rudbeck supposes this game to be a relic of the rites of Bacchus, who is pointed out by the name of *Bocke;* and he considers the hoodwinking, &c., of this game as a memorial of the bacchanalian orgies. From the Gothic celebration of these rites is perhaps to be deduced the Lancashire *boggart*, the name of an undefined sprite which has connected its name to Boggart Hole, in Pendle Forest (?), the scene of pseudo-witchcraft. The boggart is the terror of children; and when a horse takes fright at some object unobserved by its master, the vulgar opinion is that it has "seen th' boggart." Originally, the strange disguises worn by the principal mummer and representative of the *Bock* of Yule, have given rise to the superstition respecting a terrible sprite, the *Bocker*, which becomes in the provincialism of Lancashire the *boggart*. Mummers and maskers were finally suppressed by a statute of Henry VIII., which awarded against them an imprisonment of three months, and a fine at the discretion of the justices; so that in England the game of blindman's buff, and probably the modern entertainment of the masquerade, are the only relics of the *Bock* of Yule.

CLITHEROE SPORTS AND PASTIMES.

"VILLAGE wakes," says Mr Wright, "rush-bearings, and other rude customs of antiquity, continue to be observed in this locality; besides the practice of dressing up two figures as the king and queen, something in the Guy Fawkes costume, and carrying them round the borough boundaries. The very objectionable custom of *lifting* or *heaving* is not yet extinct at Clitheroe; and, reprehensible in all ages, it must be doubly so when simplicity characterises the religious observances of so many Christian sects." Another writer thus describes these practices in 1784 :—

"*Lifting* was originally designed to represent our Saviour's resurrection. The men lift the women on Easter Monday, and the women the men on Tuesday. One or more take hold of each leg, and one or more of each arm, near the body, and lift the person up into a horizontal position *three* times. It is a rude, indecent, and dangerous diversion, practised chiefly by the lower class of people. Our magistrates constantly prohibit it by the bellman, but it subsists at the end of the town; and the women have of late years converted it into a money job. I believe it is chiefly confined to these northern counties."

The *lifters*, however, have both ancient and high authority for the custom. They justify themselves by quoting the scriptural passage—" And I, if I be *lifted up*, will draw all men unto me;" and from the *Liber Contrarotularis Hospicii*, 17 Edward I., it appears that Edward Longshanks was lifted from his bed on Easter Tuesday by a party of ladies of the bedchamber. The writer has witnessed the process of *lifting* at Bowdon, near Manchester, within the last half dozen years, and he is informed that the ceremony is still continued. In 1774 fourpence was paid to the sexton at Eccles for " warning people against lifting at Easter."

COCK-FIGHTING AT MANCHESTER AND LIVERPOOL.

THE inhuman practice of fighting cocks appears to have been very prevalent amongst the upper classes in Lancashire during the last century. Almost every town had its cockpit; and not a few places and streets derive their names from this once so-called " national sport." In the "Manchester Racing Calendar," from 1760 to 1800, there are the following "RULES FOR MATCHING AND FIGHTING OF COCKS, which have been in practice ever since the reign of KING CHARLES II.

" 1. To begin the same by fighting the lighter pair of cocks which fall in match first, proceeding upwards towards the end, that every lighter pair may fight earlier than those that are heavier.

" 2. In matching, with relation to the battles, it is a rule always in London, that after the cocks of the main are weighed, the match-bills are compared.

" 3. That every pair of dead or equal weight are separated, and fight against others; provided it appears that the main can be enlarged by adding thereto, that ne battle or more thereby."

In accordance with these rules a "cock match" was fought "on the 15th of April 1761, and the three following days," which "consisted of twenty-eight battles," and was won by a Mr Diconson. The same gentleman was a competitor in the following year, when twenty-five battles were fought, and victory again declared in his favour. In 1772 "the ladies' stand" was first erected; and there was a "cock match" on the 13th of June, at the close of the races, "between the gentlemen of Yorkshire and the gentlemen of Lancashire," when the former were victorious in "twenty-two battles and nine byes." Subsequent matches are recorded in 1790, 1791, 1793, 1798, 1799, and 1800, at which the Earl of Mexborough, Sir Peter Warburton, William Hulton, Esq., Sitwell Sitwell, Esq., and Windsor Hunloke, Esq., appear as competitors. "The cockpit in Salford" is announced as the place where "the mains are to be fought."

In Liverpool similar sports were popular; for in 1790 "the great main of cocks between Thomas Townley Parker, Esq., of Ceurden, and John Clifton, Esq., of Lytham," is announced as "to be fought on Easter Monday, the 5th day of April, and the three following days, at the new cockpit in Cockspur Street—to show forty-one cocks each. Ten guineas each battle, and two hundred guineas the main." The doings of these four days are still matter for conversation amongst the old retainers of these two county families; and from what we have heard, it is well that the law has interfered to put a stop to such scenes of drunkenness, debauchery, and inhumanity.

ECCLES TITHES STAKED ON A COCKFIGHT.

A SINGULAR tradition prevails in Eccles, to the effect that in the reign of Henry VIII., or in that of Edward VI., the tithes of Eccles became the subject of a bet on a cockfight, and were won from Brandon, Duke of Suffolk, by Sir John Anderton, of Lydiate, in this county. According to this tradition, the tithes were granted to the Duke by his royal master, Henry VIII. Subsequent to this grant a cockfight took place in Westminster, when Sir John Anderton is said to have produced the first duck-wing cock that was ever fought at a main, with the vaunting challenge—

> "There's the jewel of England!
> For a hundred in hand,
> And a hundred in land,
> I'll fight him 'gainst any cock in England!"

The Duke of Suffolk, on finding that Anderton was able to make good his bet, produced another cock, and bet the tithes of Eccles parish as his share of the wager. Anderton won the battle, and became possessed of the tithes; and he afterwards, according to the story, sold them to Sir John Heathcote, of Longton, county of Stafford. So much currency has this story obtained, that duck-winged cocks are called "Anderton jewels" in Lancashire to this day. The whole story (adds Baines) appears to be a fabrication.

UP AND DOWN FIGHTING.

WRITING about 1832, Mr Baines, in his "Lancashire," says there is amongst the inhabitants of Bolton [and the neighbourhood] a mode of settling their quarrels by single combat that cannot be too strongly condemned. At almost every assize in Lancashire several individuals are tried for murder or manslaughter, arising out of battles, when, to the astonishment of strangers, evidence is given of parties mutually agreeing to fight "up and down," which includes the right of kicking—*punching*, or *purring*, as it is called in Lancashire—on every part of the body, in all possible situations, and of squeezing the throat, or "throttling," to the very verge of death. At races, fairs, and on other public occasions, contests of this nature are witnessed by crowds of persons who take part on each side with as much interest as is excited by the regular boxing-matches of the South. That death often occurs in such matches will not be thought extraordinary, especially when it is considered that clogs, or heavy wooden-soled shoes, covered with iron plates, and studded with large nails, are commonly worn in the districts where this barbarous custom prevails. To check these revolting contests, several of the judges, about seventy years ago, revived the almost obsolete punishment of burning in the hand, upon conviction of manslaughter arising from kicking. By an Act of the third year of George IV., cap. 38 [1822], that punishment is abolished; but the punishment of transportation for life, or for years, or imprisonment and hard labour not exceeding three years, is extended to this crime; and it is understood that the highest infliction will be resorted to, if necessary, for the purpose of putting an end to a practice which is a disgrace to a civilised country. Persons best acquainted with the habits and pastimes of the inhabitants say that the custom of up and down fighting, with purring, was less frequent amongst the forty thousand inhabitants of 1831 than it was amongst the fifteen thousand inhabitants of 1773; and they augur that, from the combined operation of the terrors of the law, the dissemination of religious instruction, and that spirit of civilisation which is slowly but perceptibly spreading through the district, it will shortly only be known as a matter of history.

HUNTING AT EXTWISTLE HALL.

MOST of our Lancashire gentry appear to have been fond of field-sports; and their prowess has frequently been made the subject of local songs and ballads. The late Mr Harland included one of these—"The Stonyhurst Buck Hunt"—in his "Early Lancashire Ballads;" and the following composition relates to the same "noble sport," by one of the Parkers of Extwistle, near Burnley. From some memoranda, in a copy of "Merlinus Liberatus," for 1699, the present owner of Extwistle and Cuerden considers "the Owd Squire" to have been Robert Parker, of Extwistle, who married a co-heiress of Christopher Banastre, of Banke, and by her obtained Cuerden. He kept a "Journal of Events," which includes the days he went hunting and killed "haires."

OWD SQUIRE PARKER O' EXTWISTLE HALL.

"Come all ye jolly sportsmen, give ear to me all,
An' I'll sing you of a huntin at Extwistle Hall.
Sich huntin, sich huntin, you never did see;
So come, jolly sportsmen, and listen unto me.
    Sich huntin, sich huntin, you never did see;
    So come, jolly sportsmen, and listen unto me.

"There were Squire Parker, and Holden o' th' Clough,
T' one mounted on Nudger, and t'other on Rough;
An' tantivy, tantivy, the bugles did call,
To join in that huntin fra Extwistle Hall.
    Sich huntin, sich huntin, you never did see;
    So come, jolly sportsmen, and listen unto me.

"They hunted fra Roggerham to Wyecoller Moor,
But t' buck kept ahead and made th' horses to snore;

There were th' Owd Dog and Pincher, but Rover bet all
That started that morning fra Extwistle Hall.
    Sich huntin, sich huntin, you never did see ;
    So come, jolly sportsmen, and listen unto me.

"They hunted to Langridge, and then back again,
Till by Pendle Water the buck it were ta'en ;
Some horses they stumbled, some riders did fall,
For they'd hunted *beawt* restin fra Extwistle Hall.
    Sich huntin, such huntin, you never did see ;
    So come, jolly sportsmen, and listen unto me.

"Owd Nudger kept leadin, and let nought come near,
An' it neighed an' it *marlocked* when th' hunters did cheer ;
So come, jolly sportsmen, an' join wi' me all
In a health to Squire Parker o' Extwistle Hall.
    Sich huntin, sich huntin, you never did see ;
    So drink to Squire Parker, Rover, Nudger, an' me."

The above song was taken down from the singing of "Blacking Tommy," *alias* "Tommy o' Raddles," *alias* Thomas Walker, who can *sing* the song, but not *recite* it. The word *beawt* signifies *without;* and *marlock* is an expressive dialectical word signifying *pranks*, or *playful tricks*.

MISCELLANEOUS GAMES.

ARCHERY BUTTS.

THE butts, or the archery ground for Burnley, was situated in that portion of Keighley Green on which the cotton-mills belonging to Messrs Spencer & Moore now stand. In those "good old days" the *ley* was a narrow strip of flat land, on the banks of the river Brun, bounded by a "scar" on the one hand, and by a nicely wooded steep on the other. Some old cottages still bear the name of "The Butts." "Scar Foot," and "Scar Top" are mentioned in title-deeds to property, but these have recently been modernised into Church Street.

BULL-BAITING.

THIS inhuman practice has been followed within the last fifty years, both at Chatburn and Waddington, near Clitheroe. This sport, however, is now quite extinct; but a lady still resides in Burnley who ran up into the attic when the last baited bull broke loose from its tormentors at Chatburn.

HAND-BALL.

THIS is still a favourite play in East Lancashire, especially with schoolboys and girls. Four stones are placed in the form of a lozenge. One of the party is then selected to give the ball. On its being thrown, the boy or girl on the outside of the row hits it with the hand. The thrower then runs for the ball, and if she can hit the striker before he or she reaches the next stone, the one who is hit becomes the thrower, and the other takes a place at the head of the line. By increasing the number of stones, more players can be accommodated; and each stone is called "home."

BANDY-BALL.

THIS game is played with a ball of wood and stout cudgels. The ball is struck in the same manner as "golf," and that side which drives it first across a given line wins the game.

SPELL AND NUR.

SPELL and nur is played somewhat differently in the neighbourhood of Burnley, from what is said of it by

Strutt in his "Sports and Pastimes." The game has also been discussed in *Notes and Queries*. If the ball is struck so as to diverge too much either to the right or to the left of fixed marks, the player loses the number of his *wide* balls. These limits are agreed upon by the players before the game is commenced.

TIP.

"Tip," or "tipcat," is still played at Burnley; but the game is locally known as "playing at t' *bad*." "Bad" is a North-country word descriptive of the short thick piece of wood driven by the players. He who can drive the *bad* the greatest distance in so many strokes wins the game.

BLACKTHORN.

Any number of boys and girls can play at "blackthorn." Two or three, or it may be only one, stand at a line or mark, placed at some distance from another line, along which all the rest of the players stand in a row. The following dialogue then takes place:—

"Blackthorn, blackthorn, blue milk and barleycorn;
How many geese have you to-day?"
Ans.—"More than you can catch and carry away."

They players then run towards each other's marks, and if any one be caught before he gets *home* to the opposite mark, he has to carry the one who catches him to the mark, where he takes his place as an additional catcher. In this way the game goes on till all are caught.

FIVES.

This game is frequently played by boys at both public

and private schools. The pupils at the Burnley Grammar-School do not confine themselves to *five* players on one side. That party which succeeds in keeping up the ball for the longest space of time wins the game. The factory operatives are also very fond of the game, the cotton-mills affording sufficient blank wall space for the purpose.

PRISON BARS.

THIS game is much practised in East Lancashire. It is quite a favourite play with schoolboys; and they perform it exactly as laid down by Strutt in his "Sports and Pastimes," p. 79, Tegg's edition.

QUOITS AND BOWLS.

THESE are still favourites with most classes, and ample scope is afforded for both plays at most of our watering-places on the western coast. "Bowling-greens" are very common. A quoiting-ground forms an appendage to almost every cricket-field in East Lancashire.

SKATES.

A PECULIAR form of skates is used in some parts of Lancashire. A long piece of iron is made smooth at the bottom edge; the back and front are then made sharp, and are turned up at right angles to the flat edge. When these points are driven into the soles of the skater's shoes or clogs, he is fully equipped.

SLINGING.

SLINGING is much practised as an amusement by boys and young men. There are three kinds of slings in use—

First, A piece of leather forms the centre; two equal strings are then attached to it. The stone is then placed in the leather portion, and both strings are held in the hand. On a whirling motion being given to the whole, one string is let loose, and the stone is thrown forward with great velocity.

In the second form, a flexible stick takes the place of one of the strings, and the other string is wrapped once or twice round the stick. Motion is then communicated to the stone by a quick vertical stroke from behind to the front of the person slinging.

The third method is by fastening the stone into a cloven stick and then projecting it forward. When throwing *clay bullets*, the stick is pointed at the top in the form of a cone, and the bullet is firmly pressed upon it. These missiles are then thrown either by a vertical or a horizontal motion, at the pleasure of the slinger.

TRIPPET.

THIS game is played in the fields, and was very popular in East Lancashire some forty years ago. It is still practised by the colliers in this district. The players choose a smooth water-worn boulder of sandstone or limestone, with a gently sloping side. The trippet is about two inches long, and is made of holly. It is about one inch in diameter in the middle, and slopes off towards each end in a somewhat conical form. A portion of the under-side is then made flat, and this is called "the belly." The trippet is then placed upon the sloping side of the boulder, with the point overhanging; and the player, having provided himself with a long, flexible, heavy-headed club, gently taps the trippet so as to make it rise from the stone. As it falls, he strikes the trippet with all his might, and the player who drives it the greatest number of yards in a certain number of strokes wins the game.

IGNAGNING AND IGNAGNUS.

SOME years ago a morris or sword-dance known by this name was common in the Fylde. Some fifty years ago there were seven actors in it. A "merryman" first entered the house for permission to act. This being granted, there advanced a "Toss-pot" in rags, the Grand Turk and his son, St George, a Doctor, and a Bessy. St George and the Turk fight; the latter falls; but the Doctor, after boasting of his qualifications and travels, brings him again to life, saying—

"I've a bottle in my pocket called alicumpane:
Rise, brave Turk, and fight the battle again."

The whole concludes with a song. A horse-head was carried [the "hobby"], and this was formerly a sport of Whitsuntide; but now its successor, named "Jolly Lads," is performed at Easter. I believe it to be a remnant of the Danish sword-dance; but what is the derivation of ignagning? I have been told it was in honour of the sun—a kind of *agnalia*; whilst others say that it derives its cognomen from *Ignis Agnæ.*—*Notes and Queries*, v. 315.

OTTER-HUNTING IN THE FYLDE.

THOMAS TYLDESLEY, of Myerscough Lodge and Foxhall (Blackpool), in his diary, under the date of Friday, August 28, 1713, records that he "went an otter-hunting, and killed an otter near New Mill, which Cuddy Threlfall and I dressed. We were a great many, good company—Cuddy Threlfall and Barton, Thomas Barton, and all the neighbourhood—and we ate the whole otter. I paid for Wilding, Cuddy Threlfall, and self, 3s.; so to bed. We drank the house dry." James Lomax, Esq., of Clayton Hall, was long noted for his love of otter-hunting, and his pack of hounds were notorious throughout the whole of Ribblesdale.

KERSAL MOOR RACES.

THE yearly Manchester Whitsuntide races were established on Kersal Moor in the year 1730. Afterwards a long controversy arose on the propriety of continuing or discontinuing the races in a large manufacturing town. Ashton Lever, Esq., and William Hulton, Esq., advocated the races, which were opposed by Edmund Chetham, Esq., Mr John Byrom, M.A., and Mrs Ann Chetham, through whose exertions they were discontinued from 1745, the year of the second Jacobite rising, to about 1760, when they were resumed. For many years these local races formed one of the chief attractions to Manchester, and the population of the large manufacturing district of which it is the centre, during the Lancashire annual holiday at Whitsuntide. A few years ago the site of the races was removed from Kersal Moor to some flat ground forming a delta of the river Irwell, between Broughton Suspension Bridge and Pendleton, near Castle Irwell, the house of Mr Fitzgerald, the owner of the ground. Here the races were held for many years in the Whitsuntide week; but of late railway and other excursions and pleasure-trips have largely competed with the races in the popular favour of some half million of holiday Lancashire lads and lasses.

KERSAL MOOR RACES IN THE EIGHTEENTH CENTURY.

KERSAL MOOR, or, as provincially pronounced, "Karsy Moour," was one of the oldest race-courses in the kingdom, and was unrivalled for the crowds of merry gazers who annually witnessed its sports. "Nimrod," in an article in the *Sporting Magazine* for 1822, thus incidentally writes: "No course I was ever on is so well kept as Manchester. I have ridden over it amongst a hundred thousand spectators, and nothing can be better than the clear way for the race-horses, and the good-humour of the people." So far back as 1730, races were first established on the Moor. In that year John Byrom issued a pamphlet against them, condemning all such sports on the score of their immoral tendencies. Nevertheless, the meetings were continued until 1745, in which year Prince Charles Edward Stuart marched into the town at the head of his Highland clans. Kersal Moor races were discontinued during fifteen years, the influence of Byrom and his friends being sufficient to prevent their renewal, until Wednesday, the 1st October, 1760. Manchester races consisted then, as now, of three days' sport; but, uninfluenced by Whitsuntide, they took place on the 7th, 8th, and 9th September.

The prizes of the meeting were restricted to one for each day, and were made to yield plenty of running, being thoroughly earned by multiplied heats of three or four miles each. The first official printer of our race-lists was Mr Joseph Harrop, appointed in 1765. In 1766 there was no race on the middle day "for want of horses," and blank days occurred on several other occasions. The sports were extended over four days in 1767, when a silver cup was added for hunters. After a trial of three years, the number of racing days was reduced to the former standard. Previously the races had been held in August, September, or October; but in 1772 Whitsuntide became the recognised race-week. In that year a ladies' stand was erected, and the lack of diversion was compensated by the presence of the fair sex, who are stated to have "shone forth a pleasing sight to many thousands of spectators, in all the beauty of their sex, in all the gaiety of fashion, and with that delicacy of behaviour which inspires the heart," and so on. The ten years next ensuing yielded nothing of interest, though programmes of the races were regularly advertised, and the stakes were frequently interspersed with matches. Although John Byrom died in 1763, the opposition which he had commenced to the sports died not with him, but was renewed at intervals by other persons until 1782, when the ensuing manifesto, signed by the borough-reve, constables, and forty others, was issued to the public:—"We, the undersigned gentlemen, being of opinion that it would be for the interest of the town that the races should be discontinued, are determined to subscribe to them no longer." Despite the borough-reve and all the constables, &c., the Whitsuntide diversions were enjoyed that year as usual. Another ten years of mediocre racing must be passed over, and then (1792) came a step in advance, in the shape of four days' sport, and a stake increased to £100. In 1793 and 1794 there were five days' races, commencing on the Monday, there yet being only one stake a day contested, all of which were in heats. From 1795 to 1804 there were usually two prizes daily, and in the latter year Mr Houldsworth's name first appears on the list.—" *Our Turf, our Stage, and our Ring*," *by R. W. Procter.*

MANCHESTER RACES ON THE NEW COURSE, NEAR CASTLE IRWELL.

WITH the extinction of races on Kersal Moor, it seemed probable that the Manchester meetings would suddenly end, and their name be lost by amalgamation with some friendly rival. In this strait it was suggested that Radcliffe Bridge races might be accepted as a substitute; next the good folks of Horwich invited us to their bleak moor; then Newton did its best to please us, by fixing its races to our time—the Wednesday, Thursday, and Friday of Whitweek. At the eleventh hour, however, when all these claims had been mooted, and when White Moss had been rejected, a site was secured near Castle Irwell. Apart from association, I have never had much fancy for the new course at the foot of the old moor. Being on a dead level, there is no convenient hill within its circle of ropes and chains whence the heads of the crowd may be overlooked. One of the pleasantest features of our new course is the river Irwell, winding round three sides of the arena. The river is also the source of occasional merriment. As the approaches to the race-ground are jealously guarded by toll-men, it follows that many urchins, penniless tramps, and artizans out of employ, are usually excluded. Of these unfortunates, some turn listlessly homewards, while others, more persevering, gather in groups along the bank of the stream, and select a place for fording. The youngsters then strip, and fasten their bundled apparel upon their heads; the men turn up their trousers, slinging their shoes and stockings over their shoulders; thus prepared, they enter the water, some crossing with comparative ease, but others, on dropping a cap or swimming a stocking, or sinking deeper than they expected, lose heart and return, to the infinite amusement of those on the winning side. After the river, the suspension bridge that spans it is the chief point of interest. Several times have I curiously examined the mechanism of this structure, since 1831, in which year it betrayed forty or fifty marching soldiers, treating them to a plunge-bath in the stream beneath when they least expected or desired such a visitation. Though several of these involuntary bathers were severely injured, no one was drowned or killed. The first race on the new course [in May 1847], for the Wilton Stakes, ended in a dead heat; which tie was considered a favourable omen. On account of the Art Treasures Exhibition there were four days' races in 1857. During the race for the "Exhibition Stakes" a serious accident occurred. Josephine, one of the competing horses, fell at the back of the course, through catching her leg against the rails, and her boy-rider, Johnson, fell under her. Upon the filly rising from the ground, the jockey was conveyed to the grand stand, where it was seen that his collar-bone was broken. In the races of 1861, a wild, unmanageable horse, named North Lancashire, ran on the rails, and threw over his rider, Motley, who received a fracture of the right leg. While galloping riderless along the course, the horse knocked down a boy, inflicting a severe concussion of the brain.—*Procter's* "*Our Turf, Stage, and Ring.*"

Several years ago the races were transferred to the present ground at Old Trafford.

FOOT-RACES BY NUDE MEN.

A CORRESPONDENT in *Notes and Queries* says:—" During the summer of 1824 I remember seeing at Whitworth in Lancashire [a hamlet in the parish, and three miles north of the town of Rochdale], two races, at different periods, of this description. On one occasion two men ran on Whitworth Moor, with only a small cloth or belt round the loins. On the other occasion the runners were six in number, stark naked, the distance being seven miles, or seven times round the moor. There were hundreds, perhaps thousands, of spectators, men and women, and it did not appear to shock them, as being anything out of the ordinary course of things. It is with reference to this usage, no doubt, that the Lancashire riddle says—

> 'As I was going over Rooley Moor, Rooley Moor shaked,
> I saw four-and-twenty men running stark nak'd ;
> The first was the last and the last was the first.'

The answer is—The twenty-four spokes of a wheel."

Races by nude men are not yet extinct in many parts of Lancashire, notwithstanding the vigilance of the county police.

SCHOOL HOLIDAYS IN THE EIGHTEENTH CENTURY.

WE frequently hear that, in the eighteenth century, old customs, festivals, and holidays were much more—much better, as some would say—observed than at present. In some articles of agreement, made in December 1790, between the trustees of the Liverpool Blue Coat Hospital and Mr James Meredith of Manchester, for the labour of two hundred children in "pin-making," for a term of eleven years, it was stipulated that the following holidays should be allowed the boys:—

Christmas, fourteen days, (for amusement).
Good Friday.
Easter, two afternoons, and from three o'clock the third day.
Whitsuntide, the same.
Shrove Tuesday.
Ash Wednesday.
Conversion of St Paul, 25th January.
King Charles' martyrdom, 30th January.
Purification, 2d February.
St Mathias, 24th February.
Annunciation (Ladyday), 25th March.
St Mark, 25th April.
St Philip and St James, 1st May.
Ascension-day (Holy Thursday).
Restoration of King Charles (Royal Oak-day), 29th May.
St Barnabas, 11th June.
St John the Baptist (Midsummer-day), 24th June.
St James (July 25), Liverpool summer fair.
St Bartholomew, 24th August.
St Matthew, 21st September.
St Michael (Michaelmas quarter-day), 29th September.
Liberty-day.
St Luke, 18th October.
King's inauguration.
St Simon and St Jude, 28th October.
All-Saints, 1st November.
Gunpowder Plot, 5th November.
Martinmas (Liverpool winter fair), November 11.

St Andrew's-day, 30th November.
St Thomas (shortest day), 21st December.

In all, these vacancies make about six weeks holidays in the year—less than is now given in boarding and private schools, but very much more than working boys, apprenticed or otherwise, now enjoy. The most remarkable feature of the above list is, that, with the exception of the fortnight at Christmas, and three afternoons in the Easter week, and the like at Whitsuntide, all the holidays of the year are of single days (twenty-seven in all), averaging more than two in every month of the year. There were three in October and four in November. Now, for apprentices, there are, in addition to Sundays, only two days' holiday legally demandable, viz., Christmas Day and Good Friday. But the custom in Lancashire is to give, in large manufacturing establishments, the whole of the Whitsuntide week as a yearly holiday; and in shops and small establishments, the whole, or the afternoons, of three days; in many cases in the country, Monday, Tuesday, and Wednesday; but in Manchester and the neighbouring district, the three or four race-days, Wednesday, Thursday, and Friday—Saturday being usually set apart for wives, sisters, and daughters from the country to go into Manchester and stare about them, whence it is derisively called "Gaping Saturday." In Blackburn, the annual holidays are Easter Week; in Burnley, the three days of the July fair.

TREACLE-DIPPING.

THE late Mr Gregson, in his "Gimcrackiana," describes amongst the sports of the visitors at Southport, treacle-dipping, sack-running, and steering soap-tailed pigs to their styes. In a note to his verses on Southport, he observes that some of these pastimes are not to be found in Strutt, such as the elegant amusement termed "treacle-dipping," which he believes found its way to Southport from some place in the neighbourhood of Bolton. For those to whom it may not be familiar, he adds a short description :—"A large dish is placed on an exalted station, and into it is poured a quantity of treacle, till about three or four inches in depth; a few shillings or sixpences are then thrown in. *Needy adventurers* then essay to dive into this silver mine, and bring up the metal with their teeth, upon which their faces are wiped with feathers—thus forming altogether a *delicious* spectacle!" Dipping for apples, or money, in mugs full of water is not uncommon throughout Lancashire, and sometimes forms the subject of heavy wagers. The apples chosen for the sport are tolerably large, and the performers have to dip for them into the water with their hands tied behind their backs. He who catches most apples in his mouth within a given time, wins the wager. In the case of money, it must be brought up in the mouth from the bottom of the mug.

PART IV.

PUNISHMENTS.

PUNISHMENTS—LEGAL AND POPULAR.

INTRODUCTION.

AMONG the old legal punishments, descending, many of them, from Saxon times, the chief, or at least the most remarkable in Lancashire, were the stocks, the whipping-post, the cucking or ducking stool, the tumbrel, the scold's brank or bridle, the pillory, and the gallows. Of those popular punishments, which were inflicted in the spirit of Lynch-law for offences which the ordinary processes of law and modes of legal punishment would not reach, the most striking were riding the stang and ringing the pan. The following are a few brief notices of these.

STOCKS, WHIPPING-POSTS, &c.

THERE is, or was, at Walton-on-the-Hill, about three miles from the Liverpool Exchange, on the Preston road, an iron stocks. It stood close to the churchyard wall; and within at least two years (before January 1859) a person was confined there by order of the local magistrates of the district. I don't remember for what offence. —*Notes and Queries*, 2d series, vii. 39.

STOCKS, &c., AT BURNLEY.

THE remains of the stocks and whipping-post are still standing close to the pedestal of the old Market-cross, in Burnley. The punishment of sitting in the stocks has frequently been inflicted on notorious drunkards within the last twenty years; but the writer has never known the whipping-post used. Both Padiham and Colne still retain the framework of these instruments of torture.

THE SCOLD'S BRANK OR BRIDLE.

HANGING up in the Warrington Museum may be seen a representation of a withered female face wearing the brank or scold's bridle; one of which instruments, as inflexible as iron and ingenuity can make it, for keeping an unruly tongue quiet by mechanical means, hangs up beside it. Almost within the time of living memory, Cicily Pewsill, an inmate of the workhouse, and a notorious scold, was seen wearing this disagreeable head-gear in the streets of Warrington, for half an hour or more.

One can hardly conceive a punishment more degrading to the offender, or less calculated to refine the spectators, and yet it seems to have been common in every part of England, and there are few places where a brank or scold's bridle is not shown as the effective mode in which our fathers curbed an unruly tongue. Cicily Pewsill's case still lingers in tradition, as the last occasion of its application in Warrington, and it will soon pass into history.—*Beamont's* "*Warrington in the Thirteenth Century.*"

SCOLD'S BRIDLE AT HOLME.

DR WHITAKER, the historian of Whalley, formerly possessed a scold's brank, which had evidently done much duty. Dr Plott says:—" This artifice is much to be preferred to the ducking-stool, which not only endangers the health of the party, but gives liberty of tongue betwixt every dip. . . . The offender, by order of the magistrate, when the brank is fastened with a padlock behind, is led round the town by an officer, to her shame." The present occupier of Holme is not aware what has become of his grandfather's brank.

THE CUCK-STOOL OR DUCKING-STOOL.

As recently as the beginning of the eighteenth century this machine for the punishment of scolds was in use in the parish and town of Liverpool. It was a chair suspended by a long pole over some pool of water; and the scolding woman being tied fast in the chair, could be ducked more or less deeply in the pond, as those on its bank raised their end of the pole. It is, says Baines,

impossible now to fix the date when the chair of correction was first introduced into Liverpool, or to say when, by the improvement in female manners, it was no longer found to be necessary; but that it was in request as late as the year 1695 may be inferred from an item in the parochial expenditure of that year, which runs thus :—
" Paid Edward Accres for mending the cuck-stool, fifteen shillings." For many ages the ducking-stool stood at the south end of the town of Ormskirk; but from the improvement in female manners, or the refinement in modern taste, it was removed in 1780. According to Blount, this cooling apparatus was in use in the Saxon era, when it was named the *scealfing-stole*, and described to be a chair in which quarrelsome women were placed, and plunged under water. The poet Gay celebrates this correctional chair, which was evidently in use in his time, in the following terms (Pastorals, iii. v. 105) :—

> " I'll speed me to the pond where the high stool
> On the long plank hangs o'er the muddy pool—
> That stool the dread of every scolding quean."

DUCKING-PITS, &c., AT BURNLEY.

THIS mode of punishing female offenders has long been disused in Burnley and the neighbourhood. The places, however, can still be identified. The pit for Burnley was formed on what is now termed Brown Hill. When the present genteel residences were erected there, the pond was filled up. The ducking-pits for the Pendle district were formed by the side of the northern branch of the river Calder, here locally termed "Pendle Water." The ford across the river at that point is well known as the " Duck-Pit Hippings."

CUCKING OR DUCKING-STOOL, LIVERPOOL.

IN the "Moore Rental" (1667-8), its editor, Thomas Heywood, Esq., F.S.A., observes that "the ducking (properly cucking) stool, at this period, with the pillory and stocks, ornamented every English market-town. Misson gives an elaborate account of the machinery for ducking scolding women, the trebuchet and the stool; and the punishment he describes as "pleasant enough." Bakers and brewers "who offended the statute" were subject to immersion, as also cuck-queans, which Lord Coke (3d inst. 219) and Mr William Gifford held to mean scolds, though other etymologists will have the word to signify the female of cuckold; and on reading this last critic's two notes upon the subject (Johnson's Works, ii. 482, iv. 424), we were almost led to believe that a woman was sometimes ducked because her husband was unfaithful. In the last edition of Burns (v. 246), Hawkins is quoted to show that after conviction for scolding, on indictment, the ducking must be inflicted. The last trace of the cucking-stool in Liverpool is the order for its repair, 1695, still remaining on the parish books. In Manchester, Barritt saw one standing in the pit—since the Infirmary Pool—now the Flags—half a century later.

The ducking-stool, according to Mr Richard Brookes' "Liverpool from 1775 to 1800," was in use in 1779, by the authority of the magistrates, in the House of Correction, which formerly stood upon Mount Pleasant, in that town. Its use there is noticed in Howard's "Appendix to the State of Prisons in England and Wales" (p. 258), and it is also alluded to by Mr James Nield, the philanthropist, in the *Gentleman's Magazine* for 1803.

THE DUCKING-STOOL IN THE FYLDE.

DIFFERENT persons now living, says Rev. W. Thomber in 1837, well remember that formidable machine the cuck-stool, once the dread of scolds, standing in Great Carlton. The stool or chair was placed at the end of a long pole, balanced on a pivot, and suspended over a pond of water, in which the offender was ducked. At Poulton, he adds, a few are still living who remember the remains of the chair fixed over the cuck-stool at the Breck, for the punishment of scolds. Poulton must surely have been infested with these scourges of domestic happiness, for no less than three ponds there all bear the name of cuck-stool. It was in use even to a late period; for the last female doomed to undergo this punishment, escaped by the interference of Madame Hornby, who became surety for her future good behaviour.

PENANCE STOOL.

IN the belfry of Bispham [Bishop Ham] parish church was formerly deposited a simple-looking wooden frame, formed of four pieces of wood with cross-bars, &c. This was described by old people as having been formerly used as a penance-stool. The offending parties were fastened to the stool by means of cross pieces of wood. The frame has recently been removed; but to what place is not known.

KIRKHAM DUCKING-STOOL.

THE ancient borough of Kirkham, in Amounderness, formerly possessed a bridle, or brank, for scolds, as well as a ducking-stool. A pool near the old workhouse long bore the name of the Cuckstool Pit, but it is now filled up.

MANCHESTER GALLOWS AND TUMBREL.

AN inquisition at Preston in 1359, found that Manchester had been held by its lords time out of mind, not as a borough, but as a market-town, with the privileges to market-towns belonging, including the right to punish all breakers of the assise of bread and ale, as well as butchers, tanners, regulators, &c., with right also of gallows and tumbrel. Where the *gallows* stood in Manchester is not known. Those for the Hundred of Salford were fixed at a little distance from the town of Salford, in a field still called the Gallows Field, on the banks of the Irwell, leading from Boat-house Lane to the lock, and opposite the great Hulme Meadow. The *pillory*, or neck-stocks, stood in the market-place till 1812, when it was removed with the common stocks, which stood beneath it. The *tumbrel* (says Baines) was the same instrument of correction as the *cuck-stool*, which is described by our Saxon ancestors as "a chair in which scolding women were plunged into water." In Domesday it is called *Cathedra Stercoris*, and was anciently used for the punishment of brewers and bakers who transgressed the laws. "Some (says Blount) think it is a corruption from *ducking-stool*, others from choking-stool, because women plunged in water by this means were commonly suffocated." In

Saxon times the fosse, over which the correctional stool was suspended, was used for the ordeal of plunging. In the ancient collection of laws entitled "*Regia Majestas Scotiarum*," it is stated that criminal pleas belonged to those barons who held their courts with "*Sac et soc furca et fossa* [gallows and pit], *toll et theam, infangtheof et utfangtheof.*" On the words "furca et fossa," Sir Henry Spelman remarks, that they express the right of hanging male and drowning female criminals; and adduces an instance in which the latter punishment was used in the reign of Richard II. "The Manchester stool (says Rev. John Whitaker) remained within these few years (1775) an open-bottomed chair of wood, placed on the end of a long pole (balanced upon a pivot), and suspended over the large collection of water called Poolhouse, or Pool Fold, which continued open until about the middle of the seventeenth century. It was afterwards suspended over the water of Daub Holes (afterwards the Infirmary Pond), and was used to punish scolds and common prostitutes."

BEHEADING A THIEF.

DR Whitaker remarks that from an old perambulation record of the township of Wiswall, near Whalley, it appears that one of the meres, or landmarks, was called "Jeppe knave grave," for one Jeppe, says the record, "ki fust decolle come laron" (who was beheaded as a thief). Jeppe (pronounced Yep) is a monosyllabic Saxon name; but this punishment could not have been prior to the Conquest, for the Saxon laws imposed either a money fine or banishment for theft, which they did not punish capitally. It is said that Earl Waltheof was the first person upon whom the sentence of decapitation was executed, in the year 1075. The beheading of thieves appears to have been a Norman punishment, and seems to have been specially applied to cases of *furtum manifestum,* or thieves caught in the act. In such cases the right of beheading the offenders belonged to the Earls of Chester, and was probably imported into Lancashire by the Halton branch of the Lacies, on their succeeding to the fee of Clitheroe.

THE OLD APPEAL OF MURDER.

AN incident in local history, says Mr Beamont, will illustrate the ancient custom in law of appeal. On the occurrence of the murder of Sir Botiler, usually named "the Bewsey Tragedy," as described in one of the Harleian MSS., we learn that Lady Butler pursued the murderers of her husband, and indicted them; but that, being married to the Lord Grey, he made her suit void. The substitution of the word appealed,' for indicted, is requisite to make the passage intelligible; for a wife's second marriage, while it had no effect upon an indictment, would certainly make void her appeal against her husband's murderers. In the sense then used, an appeal did not mean a resort to a higher tribunal from the decision of a lower, in order to obtain the reversal of the judgment,—which is the ordinary acceptation of the term; but it signified a criminal prosecution by one private person against another, on account of some particular injury he has suffered, rather than for the offence against the public. In England appeals of this kind were formerly permitted in treason, murder, rape, mayhem, and arson. In robbery, mayhem, and arson, the parties injured must be the appellants. In rape, the appeal must be made either by the husband or the next of kin. In murder, the appeal is given to the wife, on account of the loss her husband; and therefore, if she marries again before or pending her appeal, the appeal is gone. But if there should be no wife, or she herself be implicated or suspected, the appeal devolves upon the next heir-male of the murdered ancestor.

DOING PENANCE IN THE FYLDE.

ABOUT half a century ago, says Mr Thornber, in 1837, the frail member, the victim of the seducer, did public penance within Poulton Church; and, barefoot, clothed in white, with a lighted candle in each hand, she had to pass along the aisles, a spectacle of mirth and jeering to an unfeeling crowd. Jane Breckul was the last to undergo this painful exhibition at Poulton; for the cries of this unfortunate girl, melting the hearts of the well-disposed, raised a clamour against it, which led to its discontinuance. A woman who died only last year (1836) was the last offender who performed this penance in the church of Bispham, and stood upon a stool, the remains of which, till lately, might be seen in the belfry of the ancient tower.

STANG RIDING.

THE practice of what is locally termed "stang riding" was practised in Lancashire some forty years ago. When a man or woman is detected in an act of unfaithfulness, a framework of two long poles is procured, across which is placed a flat board, to serve as a seat. The person who has offended is then caught by the crowd, and tied fast to the seat with cords. A procession is then formed, and the culprit is carried aloft on the shoulders of four men, attended by a crowd, who make all the discordant noises they can, on pots, pans, tea-trays, &c., as they pass along the road. On arriving at the front of any house, the procession halts, and the leader of the gang proclaims the names of the parties, with the time and place where the fault has been committed. When the real parties cannot be captured, a substitute is found, and the procession passes along as if the offenders were really present. The writer accompanied one of these processions, in the neighbourhood of Blackburn, when quite a youth; and the feud thus created was not allayed for many years.

"Buck-thanging" is a Lancashire punishment still practised by school boys. The offender is taken and placed on his back; four boys then seize each an arm, or a leg, and the person is then swung as high as possible, and then allowed to fall with a heavy bump on the ground. "Stretching" is a variation of this, for there is then no throwing up, but each leg and arm are pulled different ways, in the manner of a rack, so as to produce excruciating pain.

"Tossing in the Blanket," or "pack-sheeting," is still practised in the neighbourhood of Burnley. This is done when a sweetheart jilts her lover, and weds another. The forsaken one is then placed on a blanket, or sheet, and is then tossed by four persons, who hold the corners. A fine is then inflicted, which is immediately spent at the next public-house.

"Back-slamming" is another of these punishments. In this case, the offender is swung against a door, or wall, by two or more persons, who hold him, face upwards, by the arms and legs, and thus turn him into a sort of battering ram.

"Mischief Night" is well known, and much amusement, and occasionally anger, is caused by the practice of fastening doors, smearing the handle, stopping up chimneys, laying emblematical plants, or shrubs, at the doors, or in the windows, so as to please, or irritate, the occupants. The eve of All Fools' Day is not yet forgotten.

RINGING THE PAN.

IF a couple be found courting on a Friday night, they are frequently treated to an impromptu concert. The musical instruments usually employed are the frying-pans, shovels, tongs, pokers, and, indeed, any implements which can be made to produce a sufficiently discordant noise. A pretended bellman usually precedes the procession, and at stated intervals calls out—

"Oh ! dear a me !
A. B. and C. D. (mentioning names),
Court six neets aot o' seven,
Un corn'd let Friday neet olooan."

The writer saw this ceremony performed in the neighbourhood of Burnley twice during the year 1868. The actors term the ceremony " ringing the pan."

NOTCHEL CRYING.

ON Wednesday (in March 1859), there was, at Accrington, an extraordinary instance of the disgraceful practice of "notchel crying." The public bellman went round the town announcing that a certain man (an inhabitant of the town) would not, from that day forward, be answerable or accountable for any debt which his wife might contract. On the afternoon of the same day the same important functionary was employed by the wife to inform the inhabitants of Accrington that, as she was up to that day straight with her husband, she would not be answerable for any debts which he might contract;

and stated, by way of additional information, that she had been allowed by him five shillings a week to find herself and him in meat and lodging; and that he was also not a very constant husband; and that if he had brought home the money which he had given to other women, he might have maintained them in very comfortable circumstances. Great crowds followed the bellman up and down during his oration. This ceremony is occasionally performed at the present time; but it is gradually giving way to the posting of small placards on the walls of the town or village where the unthrifty one resides. Not long ago a fair one retorted on her lord by a counter announcement, to the effect that as he had long been supported by her earnings, she would decline to keep him any longer, and tradesmen might beware accordingly.

WIFE SELLING.

IT is not uncommon for wives to be sold by their husbands. There is a wide-spread popular error that this is a legal transaction, when the wife is brought into the place of sale with a halter round her neck, and when the buyer obtains a written receipt for the money he has ventured upon her. Some years ago, a case of this kind occurred near Haslingden; and, on one occasion, it was urged in a county court that the real husband was not liable for his wife's debts, since he had sold her some time before for half-a-crown.

PART V.

POPULAR RHYMES, PROVERBS, SAYINGS.
AND SIMILES.

POPULAR RHYMES, PROVERBS, SAYINGS, AND SIMILES.

INTRODUCTION.

THE popular rhymes, proverbs, similes, &c., of Lancashire are very numerous. Many of them date from prehistoric times, and have been handed down by tradition from generation to generation with little or no variation. Some of the more common of these have found resting-places in the works of Tim Bobbin, Waugh, Brierley, Staton, Wilson, Martindale, and others, and have thus become a portion of our Lancashire literature; the rest are still current in the undisturbed nooks and corners of our county. It would require a volume to include all the folk-rhymes and wise-sayings of the peasantry of Lancashire; and hence a few only of the more curious or important are here included.

POPULAR LOVE-RHYME.

THE following lines very forcibly express the condition of many a country milkmaid, when motherly influences, or other considerations, render her incapable of giving a final decision upon the claims of two rival suitors. The rhymes may be changed so as to suit other Christian names at pleasure :—

> Heigh ho! my heart is low,
> My mind runs all on one;
> W stands for William true,
> But J for my love John.

WIGAN NURSERY SONG.

> LITTLE John Jiggy Jag,
> He rode a penny nag,
> And went to Wigan to woo-oo-oo.
> When he came to a beck [brook],
> He fell and broke his neck;
> Johnny, now how dost thou do-oo-oo?
> I made him a hat
> Out of my coat-lap,
> With stockings of pearly blue-ue-ue,
> A hat and a feather,
> To keep out the cold weather;
> So Johnny, dear, how dost thou do-oo-oo?

WINWICK CHURCH RHYME.

> THE church at little Winwick,
> It stands upon a sod;
> And when a maid is married there,
> The steeple gives a nod.

> Alas! how many ages
>   Their rapid flight have flown,
> Since on that high and lofty spire
>   There's moved a single stone!

PRESCOT, HUYTON, AND CHILDWALL.

> PRESCOT, Huyton, and merry Childow,
> Three parish churches all in a row:
> Prescot for mugs; Huyton for ploydes;
> Childow for ringing and singing besides.

[Ploydes—ploys—merry meetings; although some think "ploughs" are meant.]

POPULAR RHYMES.

> Them that buys beef buys bones;
> Them that buys land buys stones;
> Them that buys eggs buys shells;
> Them that buys ale buys nought else.

> Many men has many minds,
>   But women has but two;
> Everything is what they'd have,
>   And nothing would they do.

> New moon! new moon! I pray to thee:
> Tell me who my true love shall be;
> Whether he's dark, or whether fair;
> And what the colour of his hair.

> In "ford" and "ham," in "ley" and "ton,"
> Most old English surnames run.

PROUD PRESTON.

PROUD Preston, as the town has long been termed, was probably so called from its being the residence of genteel families in days of yore, before the introduction of the cotton trade; having been, as Dr Whitaker says, "the resort of well-born but ill-portioned and ill-endowed old maids and widows." The paschal lamb couchant, with the letters P.P. (for *Princeps Pacis*, Prince of Peace), form the armorial bearings of the town. Hence, perhaps, the old lines—

> "Proud Preston,
> Poor people;
> High church,
> Low steeple."

The name in the first line yet adheres to the place. The prefix in the second is no longer strictly applicable. Nor is the last line now true; for in 1815, the tower of the church, which was then only about the height of the nave, was pulled down, and a new one of proportionate size erected. In 1853, the old church also disappeared, and the present beautiful structure was built on the same site.

CHRIST'S CROFT.

ROGER DE POICTOU, for the services of his family to Duke William, in the Norman conquest of England, received all the lands between the Ribble and the Mersey, as a gift from the Conqueror. Lancashire does not appear in the Domesday survey as such, but these lands are described as "inter Ripa et Mersham." Subsequently the appellation "Christis Crofte" was given to this extensive portion of South Lancashire, and it is celebrated as a place of security in troublesome times, probably from its being comparatively wild and uninhabited—

> "When all England is alofte,
> Safe are they that are in Christis Crofte;—
> And where should Christis Crofte be,
> But between the Ribble and Mersey"

THE THREE RIVERS AT MYTTON.

THE Hodder, which divides Lancashire from Yorkshire for a considerable portion of its course, joins the Ribble at Winkley, in Aighton, and winds along a beautiful vale, forming the southern boundary of the parish of Mytton. The Calder, issuing from the deep hollows of Whalley and Read, meets the Ribble at Hacking, a short distance below Mytton Church. The confluence of these three rivers gives additional breadth and depth to the main stream, and at times disastrous floods are the consequence. This has given rise to a distich which has in it something of a depreciatory character:—

> "The Hodder, the Calder, Ribble, and Rain,
> All joined together, can't carry a bean."

Another version is—

> "Hodder and Calder, and Ribble and Rain,
> All meet together in Mytton demesne."

It has been conjectured that Mytton = Myd-town = Mytton, from its being situated, as it were, in the midst of the three rivers.

THE THREE HILLS.

An old rhyme says that—

"Ingleborough, Pendle Hill, and Penygent,
Are the highest hills between Scotland and Trent."

The recent ordnance survey has proved this to be a fallacy; for Pendle Hill, being 1831 feet above the level of the sea, is nearly 800 feet lower than Grey Friar, in the north of Lancashire, and considerably lower than Whernside in Yorkshire. However, the following version may be true :—

"Pendle Hill, Penygent, and little Ingleborough,
Are three such hills as you'll not find by seeking England thorough."

LANCASHIRE RIDDLES.

Red within, and red without;
Four corners round about.
Ans.—A brick.

All hair except the head ;—
Guess me right and go to bed.
Ans.—A cow-tie.

Four stiff standers,
Four dillydanders,
Two hookers, two snookers,
And a flip-flap.
Ans.—A cow.

Clink, clank, under the bank;
Ten against four; try once more.
Ans.—A girl in pattens, milking.

Little Nanny Netticoat
  Has a white petticoat;
The longer she stands
  The shorter she grows;
Now cross both your hands,
  And tell me who knows.
        Ans.—A candle.

We have a horse
  Without any head;
He is never alive,
  And will never be dead.
        Ans.—A clothes-horse.

As round as an apple,
  As deep as a cup;
All the Queen's horses
  Can't draw it up.
        Ans.—A well.

A riddle, a riddle,
  As I suppose;
Full of eyes,
  But never a nose.
        Ans.—A sieve.

Long legs, crooked thighs,
Little head, and no eyes.
        Ans.—Tongs.

Humpty-dumpty sat on a wall,
Humpty-dumpty got a great fall;
Threescore men, and threescore more,
Can't make Humpty as before.
        Ans.—A broken egg.

Old Mother Twitchett has but one eye,
And a long tail which she makes fly;
And every time she goes over a gap,
She leaves a piece of her tail in a trap.
        Ans.—Needle and thread.

Meal-porridge hot,
Meal-porridge cold,
Meal-porridge in a pot,
Nine days old,
Beef and bacon boiled in a hat;
In four letters spell me *that*.
Ans.—T-h-a-t.

Higgledy-piggledy,
Here we lie;
Picked and plucked,
And put in a pie.
Ans.—Pigeons.

LANCASHIRE RHYMES.

Lancashire law—
No stakes, no draw.

This is often quoted by those who, having lost a wager, do not wish to pay, on the ground that no stakes had been deposited.

As foolish as monkeys
Till twenty or more;
As bold as lions
Till forty and four;
As cunning as foxes
Till threescore and ten,
They then become asses,
Or something—not men.

WEATHER RHYMES.

If red the sun begins his race,
Expect that rain will fall apace.

The evening red, the morning gray,
Are certain signs of one fair day.

If woolly fleeces spread the heavenly way,
No rain, be sure, disturbs that summer's day.

In the waning of the moon,
A cloudy morn—fair afternoon.

When clouds appear like rocks and towers,
The earth's refreshed by frequent showers.

When Pendle wears its woolly cap,
The farmers all may take a nap.

Owd Know [*i.e.*, knoll, a hill between Rochdale and Rossendale] hes bin awsin [offering] to put hur durty cap on a time or two to-day; an as soon us hoo can shap to see it, ther'll be waytur amang us, yo'll see.

Of the Duddon and other streams in the north of Lancashire, a local expression states that, "Up with a shower, down in an hour."

PROVERBS.

It is of no use laying sorrow to your heart when others only lay it to their heels.

Mouse-coloured dun is the foulest colour under the sun.

A Friday's flit will not long sit.

My butter-cake always leets [falls] th' butter-side down.

Two are company, three are none.

Too much of ought is good for nought.

All this for nothing, and more for a penny.

Long and lazy, little and loud,
Fair and foolish, dark and proud.

One year's seeding makes seven years' weeding.
If you see a pin and let it lie,
You'll need a pin before you die.

You're a long time out of your money if you take me for a flat [foolish person].

I'm nod gooin to a fair to buy thee for a foo [fool]; if ah doo, ah shall wear [spend] my brass [money] badly.

SIMILES.

Just tak' th' chill off it [ale].

Aw're us't that aw could ha' swallut it iv it had bin as cowd as snowbo's; bo' mi clock-wark's gettin like owd Gimp's cart-shaft—rayther temporary.

As hee's th' Teawer o' Babel, an' a breek or two o' th' top on 't.

Aw'm thawin' neaw, like a snowbo' on a top-bar.

Aw've no moor use for a penknife nor Queen Victorey has for a yeld-hook [heald-hook].

A foowt-bo' 'ut 'll beawnce like a yung widow at a club-dinner.

He doanc't abeawt th' floor like a scopperill.

As toof as Jone o' Buckler's barn-beef.

As still as a mile-stone.

"Every mon to his likin, but no moor o' yor stew for me," as Holloper said when he fund th' ratton-bwones in his lobscouse.

"Neaw for summat fresh," as Adam o' Rappers said when he roll't off th' kitchen slate into th' midden-hole.

Similes.

He danc't up an' deawn war nor a drunken pace-egger.

As stiff [dead] as a maggot.

As cramm'd [ill-tempered] as a wisket, an' as 'cute as Dick's hat-band.

That winter 'ut things wurn so bad bent him deawn like a windle.

His hant wur as thin as a comm [comb].

He 're as quiet as a stopt clock; he 're stark deead.

Aw 'd no brass [money] o' mi awn; nobbut what had as monny legs as an earwig.

We 're o' oo a litter, like Kitter pigs [*i.e.*, the pigs of the sand-knockers of Smallbridge].

It 's war [worse] nor muckin wi' sond an' drainin wi' cinders.

His e'e-seet cuts across somewheer abeawt th' end ov his nose as sharp as a pair o' sithors.

"Every one to ther likins," as owd George o' Jammy's sed when he swallut th' suvverin.

Off aw seet deawn th' fowt, like a thrail dog.

It 'ud melt th' heart o' a whet-stone, or, what's harder, a putter-eawt.

That 's same as owd Nanny Roger's blynt hoss; it 's a ripper.

He sprawlt like a stricken tooad upo' the greawnd.

As quiet as a chapel.

He 're straight as ony picken-rod,
And limber as a snig.

Goo trailin' abeawt
Like a hen at 's i' th' meawt [moult].

Rascots i' th' ward ar' as thick as wasps in a hummobee neest.

As thrunk as Throp's wife, when she hang'd hersel' in th' dish-cloot.

As cross as an ex [the letter x]

Hoo keck'd as stiff as if hoo'd swallud a poker.

As droy as soot.

As fat as a snig, as smoot as a mowdywarp, an as plain as a pike-staff.

As gaunt as a grewant [greyhound].

As mute and modest as mowdywarps.

As stiff as a gablock [crowbar].

As gawmless as a goose.

As hongry as a rotton.

Me throttle's as dry as a kex [gex = gewse = *Long saxifrage*].

It 'd weeary a grooin tree.

He skens [squints] ill enough to crack a lookin'-glass welly.

He's as feaw [ugly] as an empty pot ole o'er beside bein as dirty as Thump o' Dolly's 'at deed wi bein wesht.

He stares like a tarrier-dog uts watchin a ratton.

Aw 've no moor use for a book nor a duck has for a umbrell.

Aw 'st keep comin ogeean, yo may depend;—like Clegg Ho' boggart.

As rich as Cheetham o' Castleton.

They swore like hoss-swappers.

Tim Bobbin cud write a clear print hond, as smo as smithy smudge.

As consated as a wisket [basket].

He used to be as limber [lively] as a treawt when he 're young; bud neaw he's us wambley [shaky] and slamp [tottering] as a barrow full o' warp sizin.

As hard as a cobbler's lapstone.

A face as long as Solomon Sampson's sow; which could never learn to talk, but was a devil to think.

Poor and peart, like the parson's pig,

Puffing like a porpoise-pig.

Squilting like a duck in thunder.

Grinning like my granny at a hot puff-cake.

Like a mule at a nettle early in spring.

Grinning like a clown through a horse-collar at Eccles wakes for a pound o' 'bacco.

As patient as Willy Wood's horse, ut died one day in a fit o' patience, waitin for fodder.

LANCASHIRE SAYINGS.

Kent and Keer
Have parted many a good man and his mere [mare].

[The river Kent, at low water, flows in several channels over the sands, to the middle of Morecambe Bay. The Keer enters upon the sands in a broad and rapid current, rendering the passage over it at times more dangerous than fording the Kent. Many have perished in fording both rivers when swollen, and in crossing the adjacent sands, without due regard to the state of the tide].

"All we, like sheep, have gone astray."

[In a letter of Henry Tilson, Bishop of Elphin, dated April 2, 1651, the prelate writes—" I trist to do God service in the exercise of my ministry amongst that moorish and late rebellious plundering people [at Cumberworth]. When I went first to Rochdale, you may remember what the old ostler at the baiting willed me to do. "Take with you (said he) a great box full o' tar, for you shall find a great company of scabbed sheep."]

As fierce as a dig. [A dig is a duck.]

As drunk as David's old sow.

Grinning like a Cheshire cat chewing gravel.

Never done like Pilling Moss.

As common as ploughs.

His e'en twinkled like a farthing rushlight.

Quite young and all alive,
Like an old maid of forty-five.

What everybody has to do, nobody does it.

Hoo howds up hur yed like a new bowt tit.

A steady person is said to be "like Colne clock—always at one;" *i.e*, always the same.

Birtle [or Bircle] folk are a deeal on 'em sib an' sib, rib an' rib,—o' oo a litter,—Fittons and Diggles, and Fittons and Diggles o'er again.

He 'll sit a fire eawt ony time, tellin' his bits o' country tales.

Newyer's days keep'n comin reawn, like old Ratcher's cream-jug, 'ut never stopt till someb'dy wur laid under th' table.

Yo 're puttin yo'r yed in a dog-kennel neaw.

He's ta'en his reed and geirs in, lang sin' [*i.e.*, he's dead].

On a bed a mon lee, that favvert he're wavin his last draw-deawn o' life.

A plum-pudding.—At eawr club-dinner it coom on th' table i' thunner an' leetnin [blazing brandy], an' had welly ha sweel't a chap's ee-brees off wi' lookin at it. That were th' sort for shiftin' ther ribs, an' makkin 'em tak' ther wynt thick.

Good ale.—Noan o' yor brew'd besoms this; bo' gradely stingo. A quart o' this o' th' top ov a beef-stake 'ud mak' a chap's ribs feel do'some [healthy], would nor it? Well, here's luck! That's what aw co' milk o' paradise, or natyer's pap. Yo' may seawk at it till yo're blynt, an' ne'er be satisfied.

Wur eawr Sally crause? Bo' aw no 'casion t 'ax that if hur tung wur no' fast. Her temper 'll ne'er be meawlt [mouldy] wi' keepin'.

Two gradely red-hot Jacobins o' th' Gallythumpian breed, 'ut could smell a pa'son a field off, an' 'ud rayther see a quart o' ale upo' th' table any time nor goo an' harken him prache.

It favourit him to a wrinkle.

Owder and th' maddher.

Don' yo know what we ha' opo' th' throne o' Englan' just meet neaw? A mother an' her childer, mon! And a gradely dacent little woman, too, as ever bote off th' edge o' a moufin.

Iv that's aw th' arran yo hav', aw deawt yo 've made a lost gate.

Aw ail mich o' naut yet, whan aw'm meyt whot [able to eat meals] an' sich like.

Folk connut expect to ha' youth at bwoth ends o' life, aw guess; an' we mun o' un us owd be, or young dee, as th' sayin' is.

It 's cowd enough theer to starve an otter to deeath i' winter-time.

Folk at 's a dur to keep oppen connut do 't wi' th' wynt. [Folk that have a house to maintain cannot do it with the wind.]

Owdham rough yeds. Bowton trotters. Smo'bridge cossacks. Heywood " monkey-teawn."

Anti-vegetarian diet.—I loike summat at 's deed ov a knife.

Country people say that town's folk have nothing wholesome about them. They 're o' offal and boilin' pieces.

He 'll seawk lamp-oil through a 'bacco-pipe, iv onybody 'll give him a droight o' ale to wesh it deawn wi'.

Iv yo'rn up at th' Smo'bridge, yo'dd'n be fit to heyt yerth bobs and scaplins welly [small fragments]. Th' wynt 's cleean up theer, an' ther 's plenty on't, and we con help ersels to 't when we liken.

Aw 's ne'er get eawt o' this hoyl, till aw'm carried eawt feet foremost.

Keep yor heart eawt o' yor clogs.

It's a fine thing is larning; it ta'es no reawm up, mon; an' then th' baillies connut fot it, thea sees.

Aw'm noan one o' th' best, yo know; naw, nor th' warst nothur, Jone. Happen not; but thee'rt too good to burn, as hea't be [too good to burn, howsoever it be].

That clock begins o' givin short 'lowance, as soon as ever aw get agate o' talkin.

Aw'd sooner see thee nor two fiddlers, ony time.

They [cheap-trippers] felt fain at they 'rn wick.

Tormentil grows oftenest abeawt th' edge o' th' singing layrock neest.

Solomon's seal—to cure black e'en wi'.

We're o' somebory's childer.

The sign of the Roebuck and Grapes—"Sitho, sitho', Mary, at yon brass dog, heytin' brass marrables!"

Enoof is us good us o feeost.

Sit thee deawn, and thee 'll be less bi th' legs.

A quart ov ale wouldn' come amiss; and he wouldn't wynd aboon wonst afore he'd see'd th' bottom o' th' pot.

Lord John, th' Wheyver.—Aw think they'n ha' to fot Lord Jone back to wheyve his cut deawn. To my thinkin, he'd no business t' ha laft his looms. But aw dare say he knows his job better nor aw do. He'll be as fause as a boggart, or elze he'd never ha' bin i' that shop as lang as he has—not he

Th' best o' folk need'n bidin' wi' a bit, sometimes.

See yo, tae this cheer; it's as chep sittin' as stonnin', for ought aw know.

Aw'll find you some gradely good stuff [oat cake]; an' it's a deael howsomer [wholesomer] nor loaf, too, mind yo.

It's some o' a cowd neet. Meh nose fair sweats again.

Thee 'rt noan one o' th' warst mak' o' folk, as rough as t' art.

"That's just reet," as Ab' o' Pinders said when his woife bote her tung i' two.

Owd woman, yo desarv'n a cumfutabble sattle'ment i' th' top shop [heaven] when yo de'en.

By th' mass, iv aw're heer a bit moor, aw'd mae some rickin i' this cawve-cote [some noise like springing a watchman's rattle in this calf-house] too.

Whay, mon yo'dd'n fair sink into a deead sleep, an fair dee i' th' spell, iv one didn't wakkin yo up a bit neaw and then.

Aw'd goo as far as owther graiss grew, or waytur run, afore aw'd live amoon sich doins.

By Guy, he's hardly wit enof to keep fro' runnin' again waytur.

Thi' dd'n just getten a yure o' th' owd dog into 'em; an' they sit afore th' fire, as quiet, to look at, as two pot dolls.

Up [chimbley] wi' tho; soot's good for th' ballywurch; an' it'll be a bit ov an' eawt for tho.

Yo're a rook o' th' biggest nowmuns at ever trode ov a floor.

Aw never sprad my e'en upo' th' marrow trick to this i' my loife.

Are yo noan flayed o' throwing yor choles [jaws] off th' hinges?

Ther's moor in his yed nor a smo'-tooth comb con fot eawt.

It's enough to ma'e onybody cry their shoon full.

A bad trade'll spoil a good mon sometimes, iv he'll stick weel to 't.

Keep yor peckurs up.

Tho' we live'n o' th' floor, same as layrocks,
We'n goo up, like layrocks, to sing.

Theaw geawses within two tumbles ov a leawse.

I oather anger't some he-witch, or the Dule threw his club o'er me 't mornin when I geet op; for misfortins coom on me as thick as leet.

Fworse is medsn for a mad dhog.

Gexin's [guessing] akin to lyin.

Proof o' th' puddin's i' th' eatin.

Sich wark as this ma'es me t' scrat where aw dunno itch.

Thoose 'ut couno' tell a bitter-bump fro' a gillhooter [a bittern from an owl].

As sure as a tup's a sheep.

They'n th' bigg'st meawths i' yon country at ever aw seed clapt under a lip! Aw hove one on 'em his yure up, to see iv his meauth went o' reawnd; but he knockt me into the dhitch.

He's one o' thoose at 'll lend onybody a shillin', iv they'n give him fourteenpence to stick to.

On receiving a present of game from a son.—It isn't so oft 'at th' kittlin brings th' owd cat a meawse, but it hes done this time.

Thae 'rt to white abeawt th' ear-roots to carry a gray toppin whoam, aw deawt.

Aw wouldn't lend te a dog to catch a ratton wi'.

[Some statesmen might do] to sceawr warps, or to wesh barrils eawt at th' back o' th' Bull's Yed; but are no moor fit to govern a nation nor Breawn at the Shore, or Owd Batterlash, at beat waytur far runnin!

Boarding 's t' best laving (*i.e.*, putting the feast on the board is the best invitation).

Love 's a philter, they sayn, to mak' th' dead wick [quick].

As uneasy as a keeper wi' varmint.

Better so than run off fleyed [affrighted] loike a heawnd cotched poaching.

A mow o' hay's as soft i' moi arms as moi owd wench.

Colliers v. Farm Labourers.—What t' farreps, mon, dost gaum [suppose] us chaps as tears t' guts eawt o' th' eairth arn nobbut a set o' gaumrils [dullards] an' neatrils [idiots], loike fellies as scrat holes for praties loike rattons, an' niver crooks their backs but t' mow gress, or t' ma'e a doike? Thae be far.

To the question,—"What have you got there?" a

common reply is—"Lay-o'ers [lay-overs, *i.e.*, thumps] for meddlers."

To the query, "Where did you get it?" the answer is, "Where Kester [Christopher] bought his coat." To the further inquiry—"Where wur that?" the ready reply is, "Where 't wur to be hed."

PROVERBS.

He that would have his fold full
Must keep an old tup and a young bull.
He who will have a full flock
Must have an old stagge [gander] and a young cock.

A cod's head is a cod's head still,
Whether in a pewter or a silver dish.

Good-will, when getten, is as good as gowd [gold].

A creaking door hangs long o' th' hinges.

There's a hill again a slack, all Craven through. (About equivalent to "every bean hath its black.")

"No, thank you," has lost many a good butter-cake.

He'll go through th' wood, and ta' th' crummock [crooked stick] at last.

Candlemas-day coom and goan,
Th' snow lies on a whot stoan.

If you willn't when you may,
When you will, I'll say you nay.

The third time throws best; or, pays for all.

Stroke with one hand and strike with the other.

When ability faileth friendship decayeth.

He shall find my frowns lie buried with his follies, and my favours to be revived with his good fortunes.

'Bout's bare, but it's yeasy. *Bout*, Lancashire for *without*, *i.e.*, he that is without money is bare, but it is easy [safe] travelling—he has no fear of robbery. John Byrom quotes this proverb in a letter after noticing an alarm about highwaymen, and adding—"This is a terror that poor folks know nothing on."

POPULAR RHYMES AND PROVERBS.

WE take the following, which relate to the north-eastern and north-western borders of Lancashire, from a paper, by Mr A. C. Gibson, Esq., F.S.A., on "Popular Rhymes and Proverbs." As to the prosperous and beautiful village of Bowness, on Windermere—

"New church, old steeple,
Poor town, and proud people."

The Vale of Troutbeck opens upon Windermere about midway between Bowness and Ambleside, and is divided into three Hundreds, each of which maintains a bridge over the stream, a bull for breeding purposes, and a constable for the preservation of order,—severally known as "the Hundred Bridge," &c. Hence the men of Troutbeck are given to astonish strangers by boasting that their little chapelry possessed "three hundred bridges, three hundred bulls, and three hundred constables." It is probable that some revengeful victim of this quibble perpetrated the following :—

"There's three hundred brigs i' Troutbeck,
Three hundred bulls,
Three hundred constables,
And many hundred *feuls* !"

There is an old school rhyme—

> "God made man, man made money;
> God made bees, bees made honey;
> God made the devil, the devil made sin;
> God made a hole to put the devil in."

An old farmer in Furness, whose worldly goods had been subjected to the tender mercies of the law, is said to have added to this the following couplet:—

> "But the devil hissel made lawyers and 'turnies,
> And placed 'em at U'ston and Dawton in Furness;"

that is, at Ulverston and Dalton, pronounced as in the rhyme. In High Furness it is said that "the towns are finished and the country unfinished." The first part of this paradoxical adage has arisen from the custom of distinguishing Hawkshead, the only town the district boasts, as "a finished town," because it has shown no increase, either in extent or population, probably for centuries. The second part refers chiefly to the western border of High Furness, where the chapelry of Seathwaite extends along the Lancashire side of the river Duddon, in the upper part of its course, and the scenery is remarkably wild; so that the arrangement, or rather the non-arrangement, of—

> "Crags, knolls, and mounds confusedly hurled,
> The fragments of an earlier world,"

has given to the minds of certain imaginative observers the impression that the fair work of creation has been left somewhat incomplete there. Wordsworth tells of a traveller who, having arrived at Seathwaite over-night, walked out before breakfast; and being asked, on his return to the little public-house, how far he had been, replied, "As far as it is *finished!*" The soil and climate of Seathwaite are not favourable to the production of the finer varieties of grain. The high grounds are all sheep pastures, and the "few small crofts of stone-encumbered ground," divided by dry-walls, and attached to each tenement, are devoted to the growth of summer grass and winter fodder for the hardy cattle, and of oats and potatoes for the equally hardy families. This limited range of agricultural produce is remarked upon in two jingling verses, wherein nearly all the farms in Seathwaite are mentioned—

"Newfield and Nettleslack,
　Hollinhouse and Longhouse,
Turner Hall and Under-Crag,
　Beckhouse, Thrang, and Tongue-house,
Browside, Troutwell, Hinging-house,
　Dalehead, and Cockley Beck,
Yan may gedder o' t' wheat they grow,
　And nivver fill a peck !"

In the fall of the year, a caller at any Seathwaite farm-house will notice upon a hanging-shelf, or some such repository, a bundle of what looks rather like dirty straw, but which, on examination, turns out to be half peeled rushes saturated with fat ; and are the principal, if not the sole provision made for the supply of light to the household in the evenings of winter. In the dales around Seathwaite a proverbial saying may be heard to the effect that "a Seathwaite candle's a greased seeve ;" *seeve* being Cumbrian for rush. Another domestic custom in Seathwaithe has given rise to another proverb. The week's meat (generally mutton) is all boiled on the Sunday for broth, and the cold meat is eaten on the other six days of the week. This dried mutton is not very nice when eaten hot, but when cold is excellent ; while the broth is simply detestable, so much so, that people in the neighbouring dales, when they find their soup watery, their tea washy, their porridge thin, or their toddy weak, will say—"It's hot and wet, like Seathwaite broth;" implying, of course, that this is all that can be said in its praise. Another saying, "We've no back-doors in Seathwaite," indicates the primitive character of their domestic arrangements, as well as their intolerance of modern household conventionalities. It is quoted by their neighbours to illustrate these wants, and is used also when any person, of homely manners and habits, is expected to observe some unaccustomed requirement of a more advanced state of civilisation. It is said to have had its birth in a Seathwaite youth taking a basket of provision to the front door of a gentleman at Coniston; and on being desired by a servant to go to the back, replying, in a tone of remonstrance, "We've neah back-dooars i' Seeathet!" The road from Cumberland to Furness winds sharply round the foot of the mountain called Black Combe. The people of Broughton-in-Furness hold that nothing good ever came round that nook.

Mr W. Dobson, of Preston, says—"It is a very common expression to say of a person having two houses, even if temporarily, that he has 'Lathom and Knowsley. These were formerly the Lancashire seats of the Earls of Derby. Lathom, on the death of the ninth Earl in 1702, passed by descent to his daughter Lady Ashburnham, and ultimately by sale to the Booth family, the representative of which now owns it. Knowsley passed with the earldom to the heir-male, and is now the seat of the head of the Stanley family. Though separate possessions for above a hundred and fifty years, the expression 'Lathom and Knowsley' still survives. Another proverb relates to one of these houses—'There's been worse stirs than that at Lathom,' alluding, no doubt, to the havoc made there when the Parliamentary forces took it in 1645. This saying comes in when a flitting, a whitewashing, or any other domestic 'stir' of an unpleasant nature, makes an apology needful on the score of untidiness and confusion."

Fuller, in his "Worthies," notices only two Lancashire proverbs. The first he gives — " Lancashire fair women," which is doubtless the origin of our more modern phrase of " Lancashire Witches." " I believe " (adds the quaint old worthy) " that the God of nature, having given fair complexions to the women of this county, Art may save her pains (not to say her sins) in endeavouring to better them. But let the females of this county know, that though in the Old Testament express notice be taken of the beauty of many women — Sarah, Rebecca, Rachel, Abigail, Tamar, Abishag, Esther,—yet in the New Testament no mention is made at all of the fairness of any woman; not because they wanted, but because grace is chief gospel beauty. Elizabeth's unblamableness, the Virgin Mary's pondering God's Word, the Canaanitish woman's faith, Mary Magdalen's charity, Lydia's attention to Paul's preaching, —these soul-piercing perfections are far better than skin-deep fairness." The other proverb cited by Fuller is—

"It is written upon a wall in Rome,
'Ribchester was as rich as any town in Christendome!'"

He adds: "We suppose some monumental wall in Rome, as a register whereon the names of principal places were inscribed, then subject to the Roman empire; and probably this Ribchester anciently was some eminent colony (as by pieces of coins and columns, there daily digged out, doth appear). However, at this day, it is not so much as a market-town; but whether decayed by age or destroyed by accident, is uncertain." Antiquarians were formerly much divided in opinion as to whether this was the site of the ancient Roman station Rerigonium, or that of Coccium. This question may now be considered to be set at rest by the discovery of the site of Coccium at Walton-le-dale, by Mr Hardwick, who has fully described it in his " History of Preston."

"As old as Pendle Hill."—"This," says Captain Grose, "is generally understood to mean coeval with the creation; although, if it be, as some have supposed, the effect of a volcano, its first existence may be of a later date."

> "If Rivington Pike do wear a hood,
> Be sure the day will ne'er be good."

A mist upon Rivington Hill is considered to be a sure sign of foul weather.

"Stop-ford law—no stake, no draw."—Stockport is the place meant, nearly one-half of which borough is in Lancashire. "This proverb," says Grose, "is commonly used to signify that only such as contribute are entitled to drink of the liquor."

"The constable of Openshaw sets beggars in stocks at Manchester."—Grose erroneously puts this among Cheshire proverbs, and adds: "Ray has not given the meaning of this proverb, nor can I guess at it." This, however, may mean that when the constable of Openshaw found Manchester sparks enjoying themselves too freely in his district, he could follow them home, and then have them placed in the stocks for drunkenness and disorderly conduct.

The Lancashire proverbial saying, "As drunk as blazes," is probably corrupted from "as drunk as Blaizers." The day of Bishop Blaize, February 3, the patron saint of the wool-combers, is celebrated every seventh year by a procession of the masters and workmen in the woollen manufacture. The procession is accompanied by music, maskers, morris-dancers, &c., and the festivities of the latter part of the day become, for the most part, drunken orgies. Hence, probably, the origin of the saying.

When a person is much addicted to talking unnecessarily, he is often said to be able to "Talk a horse's leg off;" and there is a variation of this saying which asserts that such a one will "Talk th' leg off a brass pan."

God bless hur! Aw could eyt hur to a thum-buttercake, that aw cud.

Dun yo think yon chap's o his weft in? He's summat like Owd Calamity wur, when they tee'd him deawn i bed and then shavet his toppin.

He beeats Wrynot; an Wrynot beats the Dule, he does.

It is not the hen that cackles most that lays most eggs.

Jackasses never can sing well, because they pitch their notes too high.

A mouse that has only one hole is easily taken.

A woman's tongue wags like a lamb's tail.

A small house has a wide throat.

Attorneys' houses are built upon the heads of fools.

Those who are doing nothing are doing ill.

Brawling curs never want sore ears.

Truth and sweet oil always come to the top.

It is all in the day's work.

Robin Hood could bear any wind but a thaw wind.

The devil's children always have the devil's luck.

Like a pig's tail—going all day, and nothing done at night.

A wise head makes a still tongue.

Every dog considers himself a lion at home.

One half of the devil's meal runs to bran.

There's no getting white meal out of a coal-sack.

He has none of his chairs at home (*i.e.*, he is wrong in his head).

Don't stretch thy arm further than thy sleeve will reach.

Every herring should hang by its own gills.

They are not all thieves that dogs bark at.

There's more flies caught with honey than alegar.

That man is safest who always serves a good conscience.

A man might as well eat the devil as the broth he's boiled in.

"As thick (friendly) as inkle weavers." Inkle, or beggar's inkle, is a kind of coarse tape used by cooks to secure meat previously to being spitted; and by farriers to tie round horses' feet, &c. The introduction of this kind of tape was from the Low Countries during the persecutions of the sixteenth century. The traffic was carried on by a few foreign weavers, who kept the secret among themselves; and being of one trade, country, and religion, of course became staunch and familiar friends. Hence the expression.

The proverb, "It is the still (quiet) sow that eats up the draff," is prevalent in Scotland as well as in Lancashire. "As the sow fills the draff sours," also occurs in the North. The dialects of the North counties are very similar to the Lowland Scotch.

If he had as much brass (money) as he has in his face he would be a rich man.

Heart healing reacheth to the bottom of the sore.

The more common the good the better it is.

Envy may have its wish, but will miss its end.

Who more bold than blind Bayard?

One scabbed sheep may infect the whole.

Better late than never.

Enough you've got—then ask for noa more.

It is good to cut our coats according to our cloth.

The burnt child dreads the fire.

Great hopes are quickly dashed.

Hopes come oft in heaps.

Much would have more.

Excessive shows of sorrow spend themselves quickly.

A plain rule—the briefer the better.

Malice seldom underdoes its work.

Home is home, though never so homely.

What men do weakly, God overrules wisely.

'Tis an old proverb, that those that fare well and flit have St Patrick's curse.

They say, self-sore is no sore, but certainly 'tis the worst of sores.

It has become a proverb—Better workmen the worse husbands.

It is an old saying—The soft drop wears the hard stone by frequent falling.

Affliction seldom comes alone.

As a dog or storm drives sheep together, so do afflictions God's people.

Truth seeks not corners, but some causes need shifts.

As dogs set men a-fighting, so wicked people use to stir up strife.

Some may better steal a horse than others look o'er the hedge.

Crosses come with comforts.

Experience is the mother of wisdom.

Prudence saves handsomely what indiscretion spends vainly.

He bites as keen as an otter; he can dinge [indent] iron.

You'll sooner get blood out of a stone, than get him to give you anything.

He's a keen un; he'll flay two cats for one skin.

He'll never get on; his back's too stiff; there's a booan in it at willont bend.

They're as like as two peys [peas]; their wives wouldn't know toan fro' t' other.

He's a good un, is Jack; he never says dee [die].

There's noa good in him, I can see, by t' cast of his een.

As queer as Dick's hat-band, that went nine times round, and wouldn't tie.

He's as deeof as a dur nail; but offer him owt, and he'll hear you a mile off.

Like a cat; always leets on his feet.

It's noa yuse tynin t' yate [shutting the gate] when t' hoss is stown.

When poverty enters the door, love flies out at the window.

Many years ago, during a violent thunderstorm, Jem O' Bradeley's wife asked him to pray. The answer was, "Pray thysel;" and she began, "Thou shalt have no other gods but me." Bradeley, hearing this, declared that he would "be beawt then." This incident gave rise to the now common expression—"If that's all, I'll be Jem O' Bradeley on 't, I'll be beawt."

CHAPTER OF PROVERBS.

By the Rev. THOMAS WILSON, B.D., Head-Master of Clitheroe Grammar School, 1775-1813.

BUONAPARTE, the bully, resolves to come over,
With flat-bottomed wherries from Calais to Dover;
No perils to him in the billows are found,
For "if born to be hanged, he can never be drowned."

From a Corsican dunghill this fungus did spring,
He was soon made a captain, and would be a king;
But the higher he rises, his conduct's more evil,
For "a beggar on horseback will ride to the devil."

To seize all we have, and then clap us in gaol,
To devour all our victuals and drink up our ale,
And to grind us to dust, is the Corsican's will,
For they say "all is grist that e'er comes to his mill."

To stay quiet at home that great hero can't bear,
Or perhaps "he would have other fish to fry" there;
So as fish of that sort do not suit his desire,
He "leaps out of the frying-pan into the fire."

He builds barges and cock-boats and crafts without end,
And numbers the host which to England he'll send;
But in spite of his craft, and in spite of his boast,
"He reckons, 'tis true, but 'tis not with his host."

He rides upon France, and he tramples on Spain,
And Holland and Italy holds in a chain;
He says Britain he'll conquer, and still understands,
"That one bird in the bush is worth four in his hands."

He trusts that his luck will all dangers expel,
"But the pitcher is broke which goes oft to the well;"
And when our brave soldiers this bully surround,
"Though he's thought penny-wise, he'll pound-foolish be found."

France cannot forget that our fathers of yore,
Used to pepper and butcher, at sea and on shore ;
And we'll speedily prove to this mock Alexander,
"What was sauce for the goose will be sauce for the gander."

I've heard, and I've read in a great many books,
Half the Frenchmen are tailors and "t'other half cooks ;"
We've trimmings in store for the knights of the cloth,
"And the cooks that come here will but spoil their own broth."

It is said that the French are a numerous race,
And perhaps it is true, for "ill weeds grow apace ;"
But come when they will, and as many as dare,
I suspect they'll "arrive the day after the fair."

To invade us more safely these warriors boast,
They will wait till a storm drives our fleet from the coast,
That 'twill be "an ill wind" will be soon understood,
For a wind that blows Frenchmen "blows nobody good."

They would treat Britain worse than they've treated Mynheer,
But they'll find that "they've got the wrong sow by the ear ;"
Let them come, then, in swarms, by this Corsican led,
And I'll warrant we'll "hit the right nail on the head."

PART VI.

MISCELLANEOUS SUPERSTITIONS AND OBSERVANCES.

MISCELLANEOUS SUPERSTITIONS AND OBSERVANCES.

INTRODUCTION.

THERE are many superstitions and observances still current in Lancashire which do not readily admit of classification. Some of these are, no doubt, due to the earliest settlers in the county; others have been introduced by those who have successively conquered and colonised the district; and the rest have probably had their origin in the local circumstances by which the peasantry have been surrounded. Natural phenomena never fail to arrest the attention of an ignorant population; and their effects are always attributed to causes, which, so far as they can judge, appear sufficient for their production. Unaccustomed to reason, it is enough for them, when one circumstance frequently follows another, to suggest that some occult relation exists between them; and hence the omens and auguries, the spells and incantations, the weather-wisdom and the medical lore, which prevail in the undisturbed nooks and corners of our county.

It would not be difficult to assign many of the following items to their respective sources, and to explain their probable import in accordance with commonly received theories; but we have contented ourselves with merely noting their existence, leaving for others the task of forming a comparative folk-lore from the abundant materials which are in course of being collected. Every one of the following instances is current in some portion of the county; not a few have been familiar to the writer from childhood; and the rest have been written down as they occurred, almost from the mouths of the narrators. So far as is known, the majority of these examples have never before found their way into any printed collection of the folk-wisdom of this or any other county. Under this limitation, the folk-lore of

BIRDS

FURNISHES several curious superstitions. Popular opinion states that if we turn over any money which we may happen to have in our pockets, when we first hear the cuckoo in the spring, we shall thereby secure a prosperous year. Lovers are told that if they will take off their left shoe when the cuckoo is first heard, they will find a hair in it of the same colour as that of their respective future husbands or wives. Children greet them, on their first appearance, with

"Cuckoo! Cuckoo! cherry tree,
Lay an egg and give it me."

They are popularly said to indicate length of life according to the number of times they shout out their only notes. Hence, they are addressed in the following terms, and their answers are considered ominous by those who put the questions :—

"Cuckoo! cuckoo! cherry tree,
Pretty bird, come tell to me,
How many years! Before you fly,
How many years before I die?"

The story of the "Babes in the Wood" appears to have

done good service for the robin. Farmers and their servants are frequently told that if they kill a robin their cows will give blood instead of milk; and they are also said to cover dead bodies with leaves whenever they are suffered to lie out of doors unburied. Crows are said to bespatter persons with dung who have neglected to provide some new article of dress for Easter Sunday; and boys who are sent to scare them away from the crops imagine that they do it most effectually by screaming out—

> "Crow! crow! fly away;
> Come again o' Setterday,
> Crow! crow! get out o' my seet,
> Or I'll eat thy liver to morn at neet."

The magpie augury assumes different forms in different counties. The following is prevalent in East Lancashire:—

> "One for sorrow; two for mirth;
> Three for a wedding; four for birth;
> Five for the rich; six for the poor;
> Seven for a bitch; eight for a ———;
> Nine for a burying; ten for a dance;
> Eleven for England; twelve for France."

CATS.

THE hairs from cats are considered to be very detrimental to health; and these animals are not unfrequently sent away from a house, or destroyed, when any child, or young person, begins to show symptoms of bad health. When cats' hairs get into the stomach, they are supposed to be almost indigestible, but that they admit of being dissolved by eating a portion of an eggshell every morning fasting. This medicine is frequently prescribed. If a cat sleeps in a child's cradle, or on its bed, it is supposed to inhale the child's life, and disease soon follows. When we desire a cat to stay at home, we must grease its feet with new butter and it will not wander away. Again:—a witch and a cat are always good company. Their natures are much alike; and hence, they help to form a portion of every "load of mischief."

Superstitious observances respecting the health and preservation of

CHILDREN

ARE very numerous, and are constantly practised in our nurseries and cottages. Young children are often reminded that they ought not to walk backwards in a room, or on a road ;—if they do, death will soon deprive them of their mothers. Many persons consider it sinful to give a child the same Christian name as another who is dead: one female remarked to the writer that "id wor gooin ageean God Omeety as hed ta'en t'other away." A child with two crowns, or two circular tufts of hair, will live in two kings' reigns. Very few nurses will convey a child *down*-stairs the first time it is removed from the room; they always carry it *up* a few steps, if possible, towards the attic, in order that it may hereafter *rise* in the world. For want of other means the nurse sometimes mounts a chair with the child in her arms. The belief in changelings is not yet extinct; especially amongst the lower Irish population.

A person now living in Burnley firmly believed that her withered, consumptive child was a changeling. She told the writer that it would not live long; and when it died, she said "the fairies had got their own." Our peasantry also hold that unbaptized children neither go to heaven nor to hell; but wander in an intermediate state, and become either fairies or pixies. Baptism is said to drive the devil out of children; and negligent mothers are frequently reminded that they become better tempered and have better health after they have been christened.

When an infant smiles in its sleep our nurses say that the angels are whispering to it; but when it starts up in terror, then some demon is tormenting it. Precocious children are seldom long-lived;—they are often reminded that they "are too fause [wise] to live." If children are weighed before they are a year old; or if their finger nails are *cut*, instead of being *bitten* off, during the same period, bad health and misfortune will follow. When children cut their teeth early, their mothers are supposed to be prolific; the old adage being—

"Soon ith goom [gum]; quick ith woom [womb]."

The good or ill fortune of children is the subject of several predictions. Female infants with small white hands are considered to be "born ladies." Their future success in life is frequently tested by means of tickling their knees, while the following words are being repeated:—

"If you're to be a lady,
As I expect to see;
You will neither laugh nor smile,
While I tickle on your knee."

Occasionally nurses may be detected tying three pieces of straw to the top of a stick. This is done in order to test the the disposition of a strange child; for it is said that—

"Three straws stuck on a staff
Will make a baby cry or laugh."

COURTSHIP

Is always an engrossing subject, and has appropriated its full share of omens and superstitious ceremonies. The dictum that "Long courtships make bad marriages," is never questioned by any; for it is well known that—

> "Happy is the wooing
> That's not long a-doing."

In cases of extreme haste, we are told that, "Cold pudding cures hot love;" and are at the same time reminded that, "It is best to be slow to make haste." Rubbing against a newly-married couple is said to be infectious; and if an unmarried person stumbles on going up-stairs, it is taken as a sign of early marriage. When a bramble, or briar, or a thorn branch, adheres to a lady's dress when she is walking with her lover, it is a sure omen that he will be faithful. The same encouraging information is obtained by placing sprigs of the tea plant on the back of one hand and striking them with the other. If they stick firmly to the hand which strikes them, so will the lover whose intentions are being tested. Should a young female attend church when her own banns are published, her children will be born deaf and dumb as a punishment for her want of decency. No one ought to try on her wedding-dress before the day of the marriage; for popular opinion affirms that if she does, she will never live happily with her husband. Fortune in marriage is still tried in Lancashire as it was in the days of Gay; his "Spell" has lost nothing of its force by lapse of time:—

> "Two hazel nuts I threw into the flame,
> And to each nut I gave a sweetheart's name;

> *This* with the loudest bounce me sore amazed,
> *That* in a flame of brightest colour blazed;
> As blazed the nut, so may thy passion glow,
> For 'twas *thy* nut that did so brightly glow."

Priority of time as to marriage is frequently determined by means of the "merrythought" bone of a fowl. Two persons take hold of it with their smallest fingers, holding the bone the forked side downwards; and the one who breaks the largest piece from the bone will be the first to be married. It is considered to be highly improper for lovers to see each other on a Friday evening. When a couple are found transgressing this rule, they are followed home by a crowd beating frying-pans, shovels, tongs, or any implements that will make a discordant noise when struck, whilst the leader of the gang loudly proclaims the crime they have been committing. Great care ought to be taken when the day of the marriage is selected. The popular dictum is—" As the day of the wedding so will be the married life of the couple." The sun ought to shine on every wedding party, for, "Happy is the bride that the sun shines on." On no account refuse to relieve a beggar on that day, lest you be subjected to crosses, denials, and disappointments through life. Sunday is considered to be a very improper day for marriages, and hence they are seldom celebrated on that day, especially in country churches. In East Lancashire Thursday appears to be the favoured day; and this is in accordance with the practice of our Scandinavian ancestors, although it is somewhat at variance with the following metrical regulations:—

> "Monday for health—Tuesday for wealth—
> Wednesday best day of all;
> Thursday for losses—Friday for crosses—
> Saturday no luck at all.

FISH AND BACON

ARE included in the same category of superstitions, and various rules have been laid down for the guidance of family purveyors. Shell-fish are not considered to be wholesome in any month whose name does not contain the letter R. There is, however, one exception :—

> "Cockles and ray
> Come in in May."

Pigs are popularly said to be able "to *see* the wind," in consequence of their restlessness before and during stormy weather. We are advised never to kill domestic pigs during the waning of the moon; for then their flesh is unwholesome, and will not absorb the salt. The following caution is also current throughout the county :—

> "Unless your bacon you would mar,
> Kill not your pig without the R."

HAIR.

THE folk-lore of hair contains several curious items. We are told that if a horse-hair be placed in a stream of running water, it will soon become alive; but those who are only very slightly acquainted with natural history will be able to correct and also to explain the origin of this mistake. If a hair be placed on a schoolboy's hand, it is expected to split the cane with which the schoolmaster is punishing him. When the splitting does not take place, the hair will so deaden the pain as to make it scarcely felt. Youths generally pluck hairs from the heads of their playmates on each return of their birthdays. They also pull the hair upwards at the back of the head, in order to ensure them a lucky and prosperous year. This is locally termed "randling." When a child is bitten by a dog, the bite is said to be effectually cured by binding a few hairs from the dog over the wound. As "like cures like," no hydrophobia can possibly result. During 1872 an assault case was heard before two of our county magistrates, which arose from the owner of a dog refusing to give some of its hairs to the mother of a child that had been bitten. Red-haired persons, we are told, do not soon turn grey; their passions are more intense than those whose hair is of a different colour; and they are not unfrequently reproached with having descended from the Scots and Danes. Red-haired children are supposed to indicate infidelity on the part of the mother; they are consequently looked upon as unlucky, and are not wanted in a neighbour's house on the morning of New Year's Day. Hair on the arms is considered to betoken coming riches; for "When hairy mich, you'll soon be rich;" and when the hair of the eyebrows meets over the bridge of the nose, it is taken as an indication that the person who possesses this peculiarity will certainly be hanged.

MEDICINE.

MEDICAL properties enter largely into the common notions of our peasantry. Most heads of families possess a knowledge of herbs and roots sufficient to enable them to treat ordinary diseases with considerable success; and at the proper seasons they never fail to lay in an ample stock of these simples for future use. Herbals are in much request; and herb doctors are met with in every town and village, who profess not only to know what herbs to prescribe for any given disease, but also to gather them "when their proper planets are ruling." There is, however, much to be added to this medical folk-wisdom which is purely superstitious. Thus, in order to cure warts, we are instructed to put the same number of small pebbles into a bag as there are warts; then to drop the bag where *three* or *four* roads meet, and the person who picks it up will obtain the warts in addition. Warts will also disappear soon after they are rubbed with a black snail; but it must afterwards be impaled on a spike of the hawthorn, or no effect will be produced. A farmer, lately resident in Cliviger, found one of his visitors suffering from toothache, and after exhorting him to have more faith in Jesus, gave him the following charm, written on paper, which he was to wear suspended from his neck, and over his heart, in full assurance that he would never again suffer from pain in his teeth. "As St John sat on a stone weeping, Jesus passed by, and saw him, and said, 'Why weepest thou?' And John answered and said, 'Because my tooth doth ache.' Jesus answered and said, 'Whosoever keepeth this charm for the sake of me, his teeth shall never ache again.' The same is good and for ever." Placing a cold iron key on the nape of the neck is frequently practised in order to stop bleeding at the nose. When persons are afflicted with tumours of any kind, they are advised to rub them with a dead man's hand. Smoke from a lime-kiln, the fumes from ammonia, or liquor from a gas-manufactory, are remedies for whooping-cough. This disease is also supposed to be cured by passing the patient *nine* times round the body of an ass. Those who suffer from rheumatic pains are advised to carry small potatoes in their pockets, which are held not only to cure, but to prevent a return of the disease. Consumption is believed to be produced, in many cases, by drinking water which has been boiled too long; and it is frequently sought to be cured by digging a hole into the earth and causing the patient to lie down and breathe into it. This remedy is supposed to be effectual in cases of ordinary coughs, asthmas, whooping-cough, low spirits, and hysteria. Twin children are said to be sympathetic; when one is suffering the other is more or less affected. The same medicines cure both. When one dies the other is expected to increase in strength, and to enjoy more vigorous health. In the vegetable kingdom, the bane and the antidote always grow near each other. The common dock is the antidote to the nettle; and hence we are told from childhood that when we are stung by a nettle we must rub the leaf of the dock over the part, repeating the words—" Nettle come out, dock go in;" and the smarting will gradually cease.

MONEY.

THERE are several curious aphorisms current in the county respecting money. When we obtain possession of a piece of gold, we are sometimes advised to rub it over both eyelids, and we shall, in consequence, soon see more. When a rainbow appears we must mark the spot where it touches the earth, and we shall there find a pot of gold by digging. Bad luck soon follows the finding of a sixpence, unless it happens to be crooked. This notion has passed into a proverb, since—

"A coin that's crook
Brings more to t' rook [heap]."

Many persons will not part with money that has moulded. The pieces are not only considered to be lucky, but have the property of attracting others to them. Young persons may occasionally be detected in the act of stirring a cup of tea, or other liquid, so as to cause it to rotate rapidly, and produce a circle of foam in the centre. The quantity of foam indicates the amount of money which will ultimately be bequeathed to the persons who thus try their fortunes.

OMENS

ARE drawn from a variety of circumstances. Some of them are trivial enough, whilst others are both curious and interesting. Occasionally they contain words which have passed from our lexicons; but on examination they will be found to have been derived from the speech of our ancestors a thousand years ago. Thus, when a corpse is soft and pliant, it is said to be *lennock*, and is a sure sign that there will soon be another death in that family. The same misfortune is predicted when horses are restive at a funeral. If a dove fly into a house where any one is dead, or on the point of dying, the person at whose feet the bird falls will die next. Deaths, or accidents, always happen in *threes;* the coroner will have to hold three inquests in the town, or village, where one is rendered necessary. When the relatives of a person in ill health are troubled with "*broken* dreams," out of which they start in terror, it is considered that they are a sure indication that the patient will die. The same event is frequently predicted when bees forsake a hive, or crickets the hearth. Most of our peasantry retain a firm belief in the appearance of ghosts and apparitions. They even consider it possible for some persons, born at particular hours, to see their own spirits. When this is the case, it is considered certain that those persons will soon die. There are, however, certain evenings in the year, and particular hours of those evenings, when spirits are more frequently abroad. Twilight and midnight are favourable times, and so is daybreak during the winter season. Hence we are told that if a person sits in the church porch from eleven o'clock to one, on St Mark's Eve, he will see the spirits of those who are doomed to die during the next year pass by and enter the church. If his own spirit be amongst them, it will turn round and look him in the face; and should he fall asleep in the porch he may assure himself that he will be one of the first victims.

The caution that we must avoid passing under a ladder, lest we should come to be hanged, has probably descended to us from early practice at Lancaster; but no conjecture can be hazarded as to the origin of the superstition which asserts that when an ass brays it betokens the death of a weaver or an Irishman. Undue levity is frequently checked by the remark, that "if you *sing* before breakfast, you will *cry* before supper." A flat hand, or a dimpled chin, is supposed to indicate an open, liberal disposition; whilst crooked fingers and hooked nails betoken avarice and covetousness in the persons who are so unfortunate as to possess such peculiarities.

Should the sun shine through the fruit trees on Christmas-day, it is an indication that there will be a plentiful supply of fruit during the next season; the same is inferred as to grain, if, after dull weather, the sun bursts out upon the farmer as he is sowing his seed. In the rite of confirmation, those upon whom the bishop lays his *right* hand consider themselves most fortunate, since they are thereby insured of a prosperous-career through life. The person who takes the last piece of bread from a plate during any meal is favoured with a double omen; for he or she will either be blessed with a handsome partner, or die unmarried. Good fortune is supposed to be indicated by specks on the nails; and they have different significations, according to the fingers on which they may make their appearance. The common adage says—

> "Specks on the fingers,
> Fortune oft lingers.
> Specks on the thumbs,
> Fortune surely comes."

Our marriageable females are not devoid of that curiosity which attaches to their sex. They are sometimes anxious to ascertain the intentions of their admirers, and various modes of prying into the future are resorted to in order to acquire the desired information. On such occasions popular opinion directs that if a lady desires to infer the name of her future husband she must peel an apple without breaking the rind, and hang the shred on a nail behind the door—the initials of the name of the first gentleman who enters the house after this has been done will be the same as those of the person she will marry. If she desires more special information she must stitch two nuts in the sleeve of her chemise, and give them the names of the two persons respecting whom she may entertain expectations; then the one of these who is the first to give her a kiss will be her future husband.

Burning apple pippins is a very common test, and is practised in almost every cottage. In this case we are directed to place two pippins on the mouth of a pair of tongs, so as to touch each other. The lady who is performing the experiment now gives her own name to the left-hand pippin, and that on the right must bear the name of the person whose intentions are being tested. The tongs must now be placed in a hollow portion of the fire, where the heat is most intense, and if both pippins fly off on the *same* side, the parties will be married; if on *opposite* sides, there will be no union; and if both burn together without flying off, the gentleman will never propose to the lady who is placed beside him.

WEATHER WISDOM

Is generally to be sought among the farming population. Their out-door avocations lead them to observe the states of the atmosphere, and they have treasured up many items of weather-lore, which embody much close and continued observation. Some of these scraps have been thrown into rude rhymes, easily remembered, and are handed down, without much alteration, from generation to generation. Frost on the shortest day is said to indicate a long winter:—

> "A hoar frost;
> Third day crost;
> The fourth lost."

Eclipses are popularly believed to have great influence on the weather for many months after the events. During the late wet season (1872), it was frequently remarked that the eclipse on June 6th had "shaken the weather all to pieces." When the Aurora Borealis is visible, rough winds and heavy rain are expected to follow in a few days; this appearance is also said to indicate war, especially when the displays are of a dark red colour. We are often told that whatever kind of weather we have on a Friday, we shall have similar weather on a Sunday,—"sic a Friday sic a Sunday," is known as an item of weather-wisdom both in the north of England and in Scotland. When rooks return to their roosting places in groups, they are said to be "coming home," and rain is expected soon to follow. Horses, cows, and sheep always make for the hedges, and stand with their tails to the wind when rain is about to fall. If bats are seen during the day, warm weather is predicted; and invalids are assured of improvement by the adage—

"When the wind is west,
Health is always best."

Certain days and months have their distinctive characteristics expressed in appropriate rhymes, thus—

"If Candlemas day be fair and clear,
There will be two winters in one year."

And further—

"February fill dyke,
With either black or white."

"Whenever April blows its horn,
It fills the barns with hay and corn."

"March wind and May sun,
Make clothes white and maids dun."

"Sunshine and rain
Bring cuckoos from Spain;
But the first cock of hay,
Flays the cuckoo away."

To those who are not acquainted with Lancashire provincialisms, it may be necessary to add that a "cock of hay" means a small heap, and represents that stage in hay-making which immediately precedes the larger heaps locally termed "rickles." "Flays" is obviously equivalent to "frightens." Predictions as to coming winter are derived from several sources. Those who are apprehensive of much sickness from warm open weather in December, are consoled by the assurance that—

"As the day lengthens,
So the cold strengthens."

At an earlier date we are assured that—

"If on the trees the leaves still hold,
The winter coming will be cold."

The poultry in our farm-yards also furnish their quota to our weather-maxims, for—

"When the cock moults before the hen,
We shall have weather thick and thin;
When the hen moults before the cock,
The ground will be as hard as block."

In seedtime and harvest there is need for much judgment and circumspection; and hence several items are still current on these subjects. Our farmers are advised that—

"When the sloe tree is white as a sheet,
Sow your barley whether it be dry or weet."

Again—

"If the moon shows a silver shield,
Be not afraid to reap your field."

And lastly, since the ass is considered to be extremely sensitive to changes in the weather—

"When the donkey sounds his horn,
It is quite time to house your corn."

WITCHCRAFT

STILL keeps its hold on the minds of many of our peasants. They never doubt its reality, although their conceptions of its effects, and the powers of those who are supposed to practise the art, have undergone much modification since the time when witchcraft was made a capital crime. At present, reputed witches are supposed to employ themselves much more in doing mischief than in "raising storms and causing great devastations both by sea and land." Witch feasts are now unknown; nor do "the old crones" now fly through the air on broomsticks; but they are supposed to be able to cause bad luck to those who offend them; to produce fatal diseases in those they desire to punish more severely; and to plague the farmers by afflicting their cattle, and rendering their produce almost unprofitable. Sickles, triple pieces of iron, and horse shoes, may still be found on the beams and behind the doors of stables and shippons; which are supposed to possess the power of destroying, or preventing, the effects of witchcraft; and self-holed stones, termed "lucky-stones," are still suspended over the backs of cows, in order that they may be protected from every diabolical influence.

When cream is "bynged," and will produce no butter by any amount of churning, it is said to be bewitched, and a piece of red-hot iron is frequently put into the churn, in order that "the witch may be burnt out," and that butter may be produced. To prevent cream from being bynged, dairy-maids are taught to sing when churning—

"Come, butter, come;
Peter stands at t' yate,
Waiting for a butter cake;
Come, butter, come."

When we see a fire on the top of a hill, we are sometimes assured that the flame is a witch-fire, and that the witches may be seen, from a distance, dancing round it at midnight. It is firmly believed that no witch, nor even any very ill-disposed person, can step over anything in the shape of a cross. Hence persons are advised to lay a broom across the doorway when any suspected person is coming in. If their suspicions are well-grounded, the witch will make some excuse and pass along the road. The power of a witch is supposed to be destroyed by sprinkling salt into the fire *nine* mornings in succession. The person who sprinkles the salt must be the one affected by the supposed witchcraft, and as the salt drops down must repeat, "Salt! salt! I put thee into the fire, and may the person who has bewitched me neither eat, drink, nor sleep, until the spell is broken." During 1871 a young man, resident near Manchester, suspected his own mother of having bewitched him, and the above spell was repeated in the presence of the magistrates before whom he was summoned, in consequence of his inhuman conduct to his mother. There is also a female resident near Burnley, who refuses to live with her husband, because she suspects him of having bewitched her on many occasions.

MISCELLANEOUS SUPERSTITIONS

And observances are abundant throughout the county. They relate to a variety of subjects connected with the daily life of the peasantry; some are used as safeguards from evil; and others for the purpose of securing prosperity to their ordinary undertakings. Very few persons will cut their nails on a Sunday, for—

> "Better that man had never been born,
> Who cuts his nails on a Sunday morn."

Those who are removing into another house are advised to place a Bible, some oatmeal, and some salt in the cupboard of the new house, in order that they may have prosperity during their stay. Some persons are said to be *born* unlucky; nothing they attempt prospers; and this notion has passed into the oft-repeated remark that "They are always in the lane when luck is in the field." It is considered to be very unlucky to break any glass vessel, more especially a mirror; for that reflects both ourselves and our fortunes. The "lucky-bone of a fowl is frequently worn in the pocket in order to insure prosperity; and crooked pins possess the same property when they are cast into a well of clear water. These pins are popularly supposed to bring whatever good luck the persons may *wish* for who thus deposits them. When a new suit of clothes is put on for the first time, the wearer is expected to pay "bebbrage," or a forfeit, so that his clothes may wear well. If a person has a run of bad luck at cards, he is advised to change his chair, or turn it round, in order that fortune may turn to him. Foxglove flowers are popularly termed fairy caps; for these imaginary beings are supposed to wear them. Tea is considered to be a cooling drink for summer, and a heating one for winter. If we crush a beetle on the road, we are told that we shall cause it to rain on the morrow; and when blisters rise on our tongues, they are a sure sign that we have been telling lies.

On the first day of April, boys are frequently sent for "pigeons' milk," or "strap oil," and sometimes get thrashed for their ignorance. Pale-faced persons are said to have *white* livers; thin-lipped women are considered to be very ill-tempered; and if we ask advice from a woman, we are advised always to take her first suggestions, since her *instinct* is an unerring guide. When we are in doubt respecting the propriety of commencing any new undertaking, or with respect to taking any step in life which involves risk, it is usual to open the Bible for direction. The first verse that meets the eye is supposed to contain a hint as to the course we ought to adopt. The aristocracy sometimes complain that their estates are rapidly being absorbed by the money-making, trading population. If the Lancashire adage be true, their misfortunes will only be temporary. We frequently hear it affirmed that "It only takes *three* generations from clogs to clogs." This evidently means that a father will get riches during the time he wears clogs; that his sons will squander his money and estates; and that their children will come to wearing clogs again. This is no doubt correct in numerous instances; but there are many marked exceptions.

It is customary for tailors or friends to give a boy a penny when he puts on his first suit. This is done that he may have good luck during the time he wears it. Children are also advised to wrap up a tooth, after it has been extracted, in a piece of brown paper with salt, and then burn it in the fire. If this is not done, they are informed that they will have to seek their teeth in hell. When we see a "Will o' the Wisp," we ought to thrust the blade of a clasp-knife into the ground, and lie down upon it. The Wisp is supposed to be a demon, which leads persons into quagmires, but is afraid of sharp implements, and hence will soon disappear. On the fifth day of November, and on St John's Eve, two fires are occasionally lighted out of doors, not very far from each other. Young persons, of both sexes, then chase each other between them; in utter ignorance, however, that this "passing between two fires" is of early eastern origin, and was formerly of much significance.

The virtues of the symbol of the cross are acknowledged by our peasantry on many widely different occasions. If the fire will not burn readily, almost every housewife will place the poker against the bars, and amongst the coals, so as to form a cross, in full confidence that the fire will soon burn briskly. Blackberries are considered to be unwholesome, and ought not to be eaten, after the spiders have covered them with their silken webs; for then "the Devil has thrown his club over them." Very few mothers will suffer the full moon to shine in at the bedroom windows when their children have retired to rest; for the popular opinion is, that her rays will cause the sleepers to lose their senses. Should children observe the moon looking into their rooms, they are taught to endeavour to avert her influence by repeating the words—

"I see the moon;
The moon sees me.
God bless the priest
That christened me."

Common salt is considered to have many purifying qualities; and a plateful is frequently placed on the chest of a corpse, under the impression that it will prevent the body from swelling. Miners are in general very ignorant, and consequently very superstitious. Very few of them go to work without some charm being hung round the neck, or worn in the pocket. Gambling is one of their besetting sins, and they possess quite a code of observances in order that every one may leave off a winner. No one will whistle when he is working in the mine, under the idea that the roof may fall upon and smother him.

The near approach of visitors is indicated by various omens; and rules are laid down by which even their sex may be distinguished. Thus:—a flake of soot on the *first* bar of the fire-grate betokens a boy visitor; on the *second* a man; on the *third* a woman; and on the *fourth* a girl. If the hands are clapped before the flake, it will fly off at the end of as many strokes as there will be days before the visitor arrives. The number of flakes also indicates the number of persons who will visit the house within the limited time. Our modern Lancashire witches are celebrated for their beauty; and many of them are not a little proud of their fair complexions. Maid-servants possess this weakness in common with their mistresses; some of them employ *natural* cosmetics in order to preserve their beauty, and may be detected washing themselves in cold spring water for this purpose, or in May dew during that month of the year. This is said, and with much truth, to have the property of removing freckles from the skin. The old adage is still in full force—

> "Those who wish to be fair and stout,
> Must wipe their faces with the dish-clout;
> Those who wish to be wrinkled and grey,
> Must keep the dish-clout far away."

Thin oatmeal bread is much used by the operatives in Lancashire; and may be found on the rack in almost every house. From this our youths have obtained the name of "Oat Cake Lads," and under this designation have rendered themselves notorious during several popular commotions. At certain seasons of the year, groups of children parade the villages, and demand a piece of oat-cake at every house; while some rattle at the door the rest sing—

> "One for Peter; two for Paul;
> Three for Christ, who made us all.
> Up with your kettle—down with your pon;
> Give us some oat cake, and we will begone."

At Christmas they are more jealous of one another, and are desirous of securing all the presents individually. Hence, each boy or girl visits the houses alone; and both early in the morning and late at night we may hear a feeble voice at our doors plaintively calling—

> "I wish you a merry Christmas,
> And a happy New Year;
> Your pocket full of money,
> Your cellar full of beer.
> The road is very dirty,
> But my shoes [or clogs] are very clean;
> I've got a little pocket,
> To put a penny in.
> I knock at the knocker,
> I ring the little bell;—
> Please give me then a penny,
> For singing this so well."

As will have been seen in the early portions of this work, several of our local legends turn upon the stratagems by which the devil has been outwitted. This is a portion of our folk-lore which we hold in common with many different races of people; and has probably been imported into our country by some of our earlier colonists. At Hothersall Hall, near Ribchester, a demon is supposed to be "laid" under a laurel tree until he can spin a rope from the sands of the River Ribble, which runs near the house. The same stratagem occurred to a schoolmaster resident at Cockerham, near Lancaster, on the shores of Morecambe Bay, when he was at his wits' end how he might avoid being carried bodily off to hell. Some local rhymester has woven the story into rude verse; but the transcriber has mislaid his reference to the old magazine in which the composition first appeared:—

"THE DEVIL AT COCKERHAM."

"A story strange I'll tell to you,
Of something very old and new.
New—because of it you've never heard;
Strange—even now, upon my word.

"The devil his presence hath maintained;
He came unfettered and unchained;
In the churchyard his form was seen,
His habit mixed of blue and green;
Such ne'er before, or since, was seen.

"What time his reverence had escaped,
When the wide gates of hell wide gaped;
He with his horrid crew in plight,
From thence on lowly earth alight.

"As smoke uprolleth from some mighty fire,
These spirits blue and green rise from the mire;
All shapes and sizes they at will assume—
Of grovelling snakes, or warriors decked with plume.

"Wandering up and down the earth,
Midst scenes of sorrow, scenes of mirth;
Till at last the devil tired hard,
Alights in Cockerham Churchyard;
Invisible, but still he prowled
About, and oft at midnight howled,
Scaring the natives of the vale,
Dwelling in neighbourhood of my tale.
All things went wrong, and nought was right,
None could do aught, try as they might;
By night, by day, his presence was felt,
When they ate or fasted, stood or knelt.

" The people at length in assembly met,
And appointed the schoolmaster the devil to get ;
To try his skill if he could not master,
And with his power the devil bind faster ;
So proud of his station, and confidence placed in him,
He determined to seek and try to chasten him.

" One day in the school, in the corner of churchyard,
The windows all fastened, the doors all barred,
With the gypsies' blarney, and the witches' cant,
He drew him forth with his horrible rant.

" Amazed stood the pedagogue, frightened to see,
A spirit in harness from head to the knee ;
With eyes large as saucers, and horns on his head,
His tail out behind, a dread shadow he shed.

" All silent he stood, the master quaked more,
And tried to move, as if for the door ;
The spirit his tail gave a wag from behind,
Now for his doom ! the master made up his mind.
' Ay,' thought he, ' I 'm now in a pickle,
But wouldn't I mangle him, if now I'd my sickle !'
So to put on a bold face, he straightway began—
' Who art thou ? answer, fiend or man ? '
' Know I 'm the devil, hear and tremble,
And unless thou attendest me, thou 'lt soon me resemble ;
And unless by thy lore thou anon entanglest me,
By the shivers and brimstone, mangled thou 'lt be.'

" 'Twas said in a voice deep as thunder outpoured,
'Twas a terrible sound, as a lion had roared.
Aghast stood the master, his limbs oscillating,
Too frightened to speak, or to think, contemplating !
' Quick,' said the devil, ' three questions thou must put,
Or otherwise off with me thou must to my hut.'

" This put the chap more in a terrible flutter,
His voice now had gone, he could only mutter ;
At length, after thrice essaying, he thus began—
' Tell me, kind sir,' (O Moses ! how wan
Was the fellow's countenance as he began)—
' How many drops of dew on yon hedges are hinging ? '
The devil and imps flew past it swinging ;

He numbered them all. And the man in his walks,
Said—'In this field how many wheat stalks?'
At one swoop of his scythe, the stalks he all trundles,
And bound them up quick in manifold bundles,
And gave him the number, as he held them in hand.

" Now the poor fellow's was a pitiful case,
As plain might be seen from his long length of face.
'Now make me, dear sir, a rope of your sand,
Which will bear washing in Cocker, and not lose a strand.'

" The devil and mate then went down to the strand,
In a jiffy they twisted a fine rope of sand,
And dragged it along with them over the land ;
But when they brought the rope to be washed,
To atoms it went—the rope was all smashed.

" The devil was foiled, wroth, and gave him a shaking ;
Up he flew to the steeple—his frame all a-quaking.
With one horrid frig—his mind very unwilling,
He strode to the brig o'er Broadfleet at Pilling."

Pilling is a small town and chapelry in the parish of Garstang, and has long been noted for its moss. In the year 1745, there was an irruption of this moss, similar to that of Solway Moss in 1771. Part of it, near Heskam House, gradually rose to a great height, and then moved slowly towards the south, covering more than one hundred acres of land under cultivation. The vast supplies of turf for fuel obtained from this dreary waste has given rise to the saying—" As inexhaustible as Pilling Moss." The " Devil's Stride," from Cockerham to Pilling, must have been, at least, the orthodox *seven* miles in length.

APPENDIX.

LANCASHIRE WITCHES TRACT.

APPENDIX.

THE LANCASHIRE WITCHES.

INTRODUCTION.

FROM internal evidence, it may be inferred that the author of the following rare tract probably lived in the early days of James I.; for although the Pendle Forest Witches form the burden of the story, they are nowhere alluded to as having suffered capital punishment at Lancaster, which many of them did in 1612. Another batch very narrowly escaped the same fate in 1633.—*See Whitaker's Whalley; Potts's Discoverie, by Crossley; or Croston's Samlesbury Hall.*

THE FAMOUS HISTORY OF THE LANCASHIRE WITCHES,

CONTAINING the manner of their becoming such; their enchantments, spells, revels, merry pranks, raising of storms and tempests, riding on winds, &c. The entertainments and frolics which have happened among them; with the loves and humours of Roger and Dorothy. Also, a Treatise of witches in general, conducive to mirth and recreation. The like never before published.

CHAPTER I.

The Lancashire Witch's Tentation, and of the Devil's appearing to her in sundry shapes and giving her money.

LANCASHIRE is a famous and noted place, abounding with rivers, hills, woods, pastures, and pleasant towns, many of which are of great antiquity. It has also been famous for witches, and the strange pranks they played. Therefore, since the name of Lancashire witches has been so frequent in the mouths of old and young, and many imperfect stories have been rumoured abroad, it would doubtless tend to the satisfaction of the reader to give some account of them in their merry sports and pastimes.

Some time since lived one Mother Cuthbert, in a little hovel at the bottom of a hill, called Wood and Mountain Hill [Pendle], in Lancashire. This woman had two lusty daughters, who both carded and spun for their living, yet were very poor, which made them often repine at and lament their want. One day as Mother Cuthbert was sauntering about the hill-side, picking the wool off the bushes, out started a thing like a rabbit, which ran about two or three times and then changed into a hound, and afterwards into a man, which made the old beldame to tremble, yet she had no power to run away. So putting a purse of money in her hand, and charging her to be there the next day, he immediately vanished away, and old Mother Cuthbert returned home, being somewhat disturbed between jealousy and fear.

Chapter II.

Strange and wonderful apparitions; how one witch had power to make another; and other strange things.

THE old woman opened not her purse until she came home, and then found in it ten angels; so, calling to her daughters, she told them what had happened. The wenches rejoiced that the treasure of the house had increased, that they might stuff themselves with beef and pudding which they had long been strangers to; and advised their mother to go again as he had ordered, and so she did. The first thing she saw was a tree rising out of the ground which moved towards her, and, to her surprise, multiplied into a very thick wood round her, so that she was afraid of losing herself, when on a sudden she saw a house, and heard the sound of musick. This appeared most strange; however, she took courage and went towards it, when she found a great many women all dancing and revelling; and the house appeared like a stately palace, and the tables were furnished with a great variety of delicacies. The dance being ended, she was desired to sit at the table with the rest, but she scrupled it at first, till at length, being hungry, she fell roundly to. After dinner the matron which received her, by striking the floor with her wand, caused divers of the familiars, in the shape of cats, bears, apes, &c., to enter and dance antic dances, whilst she played on the gridiron and tongs. This done, taking Mother Cuthbert aside, she demanded how she liked the cheer and sport? She answered, very well; but desired to know where she was and her company? Mother Crady then told her that she was Witch of Penmure [Penmaenmawr], a great mountain in Wales, and the rest were her countrywomen of the same faculty; and being desirous to have her of the fraternity [sisterhood?] she had contrived this way to entertain her, to show that she might always live jocund and merry. Mother Cuthbert, overcome with persuasions, consented, when immediately they anointed her breast with a certain ointment, then, speaking a charm or two, they gave her the rest to use upon occasion, and also in another box a little thing like a mole, that was to be her imp. So, all mounting upon a coal-staff, away they flew and she with them; but they left her at the door of her own house, and kept still on their way with the wind.

CHAPTER III.

A Lancashire witch enchants the Mayor of the town, who had caused her to be whipped; with the circumstances attending.

MOTHER CUTHEBRT being thus entered into the society of witches, by the force of her ointment, and counsel of her imp, who could speak when he pleased, and turn himself into divers shapes, finding the power she had, began to play many pranks.

Sometime before this, the Mayor of Lancaster had caused Mother Cuthbert to be whipped, for breaking his pales to make her a fire in the cold winter, which she resented much; and now, knowing her power to revenge it, she trudges thither, where she found him carousing with many friends. She took an opportunity to slip a letter into his hands, and retired unknown, which he had no sooner perused, but telling his company he must run a race, he immediately went into the next room, and stripped himself stark naked, then taking a hand whip, he ran into the street, lashing his sides and back, crying "There he goes! I win! I win!" Whilst the people followed, calling him to stay, thinking he was distracted, yet he ran on to the further end of the town, lashing himself till he was bloody. At which time, coming to his wits, he was in the greatest consternation, swearing the devil had put this trick upon him; for all the time he imagined he had been on horseback, and was riding a race, not feeling the lashes he gave himself till he had completed his number, and filled the measure of the witch's resentment.

Chapter IV.

The old woman's two daughters become witches, and one of them, in the shape of a mare, is revenged upon her false sweetheart and rival.

Mother Cuthbert, growing more and more perfect in her art, resolved to bring in her daughters for a snack and thereupon communicates to them all that had befallen her. They were content to be ruled by the mother, and she anointed them, and used the best means she was able to make them perfect in their new trade.

Their names were Margery and Cicely. The first was courted by Roger Clodpate, a plain, downright country fellow; but he was wheedled from her by Dorothy, a gentleman's dairymaid not far distant. This vexed Margery, and made her resolved to be revenged for it; so one day as they went abroad in the fields about courtship, she, by casting up dust in the air and other enchantments, raised up a mighty storm of rain, which so swelled the ditches that they overflowed in their way and stopped them; but as they began to think of going back, Margery immediately transformed herself into the shape of a black mare, and came gently towards them; when Roger, glad of the opportunity, first mounted his sweetheart, and then got up himself. But they were no sooner in the middle of the water than she threw them heels overhead, and ran away laughing, soon recovering her shape; while Roger and Dorothy were in a piteous case, and forced to trudge home, like drowned rats, with the story of their unfortunate disaster.

CHAPTER V.

A witch rescues a man, who was going to gaol, and plagues the bailiffs, by leading them a dance over hedge and ditch.

A POOR man, being arrested by a cruel creditor for debt, and he not being able to pay it, they were carrying him to Lancaster Gaol, when Mother Cuthbert met them, and desired to know the matter. The officers answered her very surlily, pushing her aside, which, raising her choler, she said, "But you shall let him go before we do part." And they said he should not. Whereupon she bade the poor man stop his ears close; and then she drew out a pipe which had been given her by the Witch of Penmure, and then set piping, and led them through hedges and thorns, over ditches, banks, and poles, sometimes tumbling, and other times tearing and bruising their flesh, while the poor fellow got time enough to make his escape ; but the catchpoles cried out for mercy, thinking the devil had led them a dance. At length she left them in the middle of a stinking pond, to shift for themselves.

CHAPTER VI.

Of a Lancashire witch being in love with a gentleman ; of her haunting him in the shape of a hare, and obtaining her ends.

CICELY, the youngest daughter of the Lancashire witch, being in love with a gentleman's son about a mile from their home, was resolved to have him in her arms at any rate ; wherefore, knowing he admired hunting, she often turned herself into a hare to make him sport, and still drew him towards her mother's house ; for when he went that way he was used to call to chat with them, the which caused in Cicely the first fatal passion. But once this had liked to have proved fatal ; for the charm wanting somewhat of its force, one of the foremost hounds catched her by the haunches, just as she was entering her creep-hole, and gave her a terrible pinch ; and happy was it for her that she was so near, or her loving had been for ever spoiled. The young man, commonly losing the hare about this house, began to wonder, and supposing it to have run in at the sink, he entered the house, where he found Cicely rubbing of her back ; but not meeting what he sought, nor looking for such a transformation, he departed, and she for the future grew cautious of showing him any more sport of that kind. But when he was going to be married to a beautiful young gentlewoman, she by enchantment caused the lady to lose herself in a wood, and there cast her in a deep sleep for a day and a night. In the meantime she personated the bride; but knowing it could not long continue, she cast him likewise into a deep sleep, and then fetched the young lady to his arms, that when they both awaked, they thought they had been all the time together.

CHAPTER VII.

Mother Cuthbert enchants several thieves, and takes away the money; with the manner of setting spells.

OLD Mother Cuthbert going along the road, she overheard some thieves bragging of a mighty purchase they had made, whereupon she resolved to herself that she would come in for a share; and accordingly she muttered some words, on which the horses began for to stumble, which made them [not the horses, but the thieves] curse and swear. At length they supposed they heard the rattling of clubs and staves, as if the whole city had been up in arms to seize them; and finding they could not spur their horses on, nor make them stir a foot, they got off, leaving the portmanteaus behind them, and ran away on foot. The prize she conveyed home, and hearing some poor people had been robbed, she gave them back what they had lost. The fright the rogues were put into was caused by enchantment, in which she was so good a proficient, that she would often set spells on the highway, so that any being robbed, the rogues had no power to get away.

The description of a spell.—A spell is a piece of paper written with magical characters, fixed in a critical season of the moon and conjunction of the planets; or, sometimes, by repeating mystical words. But of these there are many sorts.

Chapter VIII.

The manner of a witch-feast; or, a general meeting.

THERE being a general meeting of the witches, to consult for merry pranks, and to be even with any who had injured them, one of them must needs bring her husband with her; but charged him and made him promise that, whatever he saw or heard, he should not speak a word of it. To this he promised to be obedient. He was carried thither in the night, but he knew not what way; and there he found a stately palace (to his thinking), furnished with goods of exceeding value; and it shined in the night with artificial lights as at noonday. Here they had all manner of good cheer, and he was as frolicsome as the merriest. The man observed his covenant till he came to eat, when, looking about and seeing no salt (for it seems witches never use any), he, before he was aware, cried out, "What, in God's name, have we no salt here?" Upon this, all the lights immediately went out, and the company flew away; so dreadful is the name of God to those servants of Satan. Storms of rain and hail, attended with lightning and terrible claps of thunder, ensued. The rain poured on him, the wind blew, and instead of a palace, when daylight appeared, he found himself in an old uncovered barn, about twenty miles from home. And from that time he never desired to go with his wife to see curiosities.

Chapter IX.

The Humours of Roger and Doll, with the manner how they were served by a Lancashire Witch.

ROGER and Dorothy being got in a merry humour, one day meeting with Margery, began to swear at her, and called her "Leaden Heels," but she passed by as if she minded it not. They had not far to go before there was a stile to go over;—but when they was on the top, they could not get down on either side, fancying there was ponds of water round about them, till some travellers came by, who, finding them thus mounted on the wooden horse in a strange posture, made them dismount. However, not satisfied, she watched their motions, and found them in a barn that stood by the road, where the cows used to be driven in to be milked. There, being seated upon the straw, toying together, and wondering at what had happened, . . . Margery, who stood there invisible, sprinkled Roger with a certain dust, which changed his very countenance, making it appear to his mistress like an ass's head; which so frighted her, that she gave a lusty spring, and throwing him quite down, she got up, running, and crying out, "The devil! the devil!" This so terrified Roger, that he followed, crying out, "What ails you, my dear?—what ails you?" In this manner, to the laughter of a great number of people, they ran until they were so tired, they were forced to lie down, being no longer able to hold out. Thus, at this time, her revenge was satisfied.

Chapter X.

How some Witches, revelling in a gentleman's house, served the servants who surprised them.

It happened one time that a great number of Lancashire witches were revelling in a gentleman's house in his absence, and making merry with what they found, the dogs not daring to stir—they having, it seems, the power to strike them mute. However, during the frolic, some of the servants came home, and, thinking they had been ordinary thieves, went to seize them. But they happened to catch a Tartar; for, each taking one, they flew away with them, who in vain called for help, till they had lodged them on the top of very high trees; and then raised prodigious storms of thunder and lightning, with hard showers of rain, they left them there to do penance for their intrusion.

Chapter XI.

A brief Treatise on Witches in general, with several things worthy of notice.

About this time great search was made after witches, and many were apprehended, but most of them gave the hangman and the gaoler the slip; though some hold that when a witch is taken she hath no power to avoid justice. It happened as some of them were going in a cart to be tried, a coach passed by in which appeared a person like a judge, who, calling to one, bid her to be of good cheer and take comfort, for neither she nor any of her company should be harmed; and on that night all the prison locks flew open, and they made their escape; and many, when they had been cast into the water for a trial, have swam like a cork. One of them boasted she could go over the sea in an egg shell. It is held on all hands that they adore the devil, and become his bondslaves, to have for a term of years their pleasure and revenge. And indeed many of them are more mischievous than others in laming and destroying of cattle, and in drowning ships at sea, by raising storms. But the Lancashire Witches we see, chiefly divert themselves in merriment, and are therefore found to be more sociable than the rest.

CHAPTER XII.

A short description of the famous Lapland Witches.

THE Lapland witches, they tell us, can send wind to sailors, and take delight in nothing more than raising of storms and tempests, which they effect by repeating certain charms, and throwing up sand into the air. The best way to avoid their power is to BELIEVE IN GOD, who will not suffer them to hurt us; for here they are held to be restrained. As many mistake their children and relations to be bewitched when they die of distempers somewhat strange to the unskilful, so one poor woman or other is falsely accused of things which they are entirely ignorant of. So it has often happened.

This may suffice as to what comically or really happened, or related to witches; or such as are imagined to be possessed with evil and familiar spirits.

THE EAGLE AND CHILD.

(*See page* 19.)

Probably the most curious version of this legend is that contained in Hare's MSS., vol. ii.; which has been printed by the Lancaster Herald in the seventh volume of the *Journal* of the British Archæological Association. As the orthography is almost unintelligible to most readers the spelling is here modernised.

"THE FAUSE FABLE OF THE LORD LATHOM. A FAYNED TALE."—When the war was 'twixt the Englishmen and the Irishmen, the power of the English so sore assaulted the Irishmen, that the king of them, being of Ireland, was constrained to take succour, by flight, into other parts for his safeguard; and the queen, being pregnant and great with child, right near her time of deliverance, for dread of the rudeness of the commonalty, took her flight into the wilderness, where her chance was to suffer travail of child; bringing forth two children, the one a son, the other a daughter; when after by natural compulsion, she and such gentlewomen as were with her was constrained to sleep, insomuch that the two children were ravished from the mother; and the daughter, as it is said, is kept in Ireland with the fairies. Insomuch that against the time of death of any of that blood of Stanleys, she maketh a certain noise in one quarter of Ireland, where she useth [to stay].

The son was taken and borne away with an eagle, and brought into Lancashire, into a park called Lathom Park, whereas did dwell a certain Lord named the Lord Lathom; the which Lord Lathom walking in his park heard a child lament and cry, and perceived the skirts of the mantle lying over the nest side, and made his servants to bring down the child unto him.

And whereas both he and his wife being in far age, and she past conceiving of child; considering they never could have issue; reckoning that God had sent this child by miracle, they condescended to make this child their heir, and so did. At length this Lord Lathom and his wife deceased, and this young man, which was named Oskell of Lathom, reigned and ruled this land as right heir, and he had to issue a daughter which was his heir and child by the Lady Lathom.

It chanced so that one Stanley, being a younger brother of the House of Wolton in Cheshire, was servant to the Abbot of West Chester; this young man Stanley was carver to the Abbot, and he would not break his fast on the Sunday till he had heard the High Mass. Insomuch that it chanced one Sunday when the meat was served on the table, he had so great hunger he carved the pig's head, and conveyed one of the ears of the pig and did eat it.

When the Abbot sat down, and perchance missed this pig's ear, he was miscontent and in a great fume, and reviled so extremely and so heinously this young Stanley, that he threw the napkin at his head, and said he would do him no more service and departed. And he came to the king's court and obtained his service, and proved so active a fellow that the renown sprang and inflamed upon him, insomuch that the fame and bruit descended from him around this realm.

And when, as the use then was, that noble adventurers would seek their fortune and chance into divers and strange nations, one renowned gallant came into England, and he called as challenger for death and life, come who list. Insomuch that the king commanded this Stanley to cope with him ; and, to make short protestation, his chance was to overthrow the challenger and obtain the victory.

Then the king made him knight, and gave him certain lands to live on.

After this foresaid Stanley came for marriage to the daughter of Oskell of Lathom, which was found in the eagle's nest, and obtained her favour, and espoused her. And then after the death of Oskell he was Lord Lathom, and enjoyed it many years. And for such service as he did afterwards the king made him Lord Stanley ; and he was the first lord of the name; and so by that reason the Stanleys descended of Lathom give the eagle and child in their arms.

SAMLESBURY HALL AND THE LADY IN WHITE.

MIDWAY between Blackburn and Preston, on a broad and rich plain of glacial drift, stands the famous old Hall of Samlesbury. The view towards the south comprehends the wooded heights of Hoghton ;—on the east the background is filled in by the elevated ridges which run through Mellor, Ramsgreave, and Billington to Pendle ; —the west is occupied by Preston and the broad estuary of the Ribble, the ancient Belisama ;— and on the north the correctly-named Longridge leads on to the heights of Bowland ;—thus enclosing a landscape which, for picturesque beauty, and historic interest, has few equals in the country.

It was here, in the early part of the reign of Henry II., that Gospatric de Samlesbury was seated in his ancestral home; surrounded by rich pastures and shut in by primeval forests of oak, from which the massive timbers were selected which formed the framework of the magnificent structure erected during the reign of Edward III. The family pedigrees tell us that Cicely de Samlesbury married John de Ewyas about the middle of the thirteenth century; but, dying without male heir, his daughter was united to Sir Gilbert de Southworth, and the property thus acquired remained in the possession of his family for upwards of three hundred and fifty years. It was then sold to the Braddylls, and ultimately passed into the hands of Joseph Harrison, Esq., of Galligreaves, Blackburn; whose eldest son, William Harrison, Esq., now resides at the Hall.

After the disposal of the property by John Southworth, Esq., in 1677, the house was suffered to fall into decay. For many years it was occupied by a number of cottagers; it was afterwards converted into a farmhouse, and passed through various stages of degradation from neglect. Mr Harrison, however, determined that this fine old structure should be no longer thus desecrated. With a wise and just appreciation he restored both the exterior and the interior of the house in accordance with their original design; and under his hands the Old Hall at Samlesbury has become one of the most interesting and instructive mansions in the county.

Sir John Southworth was the most distinguished personage of his race. He was high in military command during the early years of the reign of Elizabeth — he mustered three hundred men at Berwick; and served the office of Sheriff of Lancashire in 1562. His possessions included Southworth, Samlesbury, Mellor, besides lands in eighteen other townships; but he was illiterate, bigoted, and self-willed. His rigid devotion to the faith of his ancestors led him to speak rashly of the changes introduced into the national religion; he also acted unwisely in contravening the laws, for which he was ultimately cast into prison, and otherwise treated with much severity until his death in 1595.

Tradition states that during his later years one of his daughters had formed an intimate acquaintance with the heir of a neighbouring knightly house. The attachment was mutual, and nothing was wanting to complete their happiness except the consent of the lady's father. Sir John was thereupon consulted; but the tale of their devoted attachment only served to increase his rage, and he dismissed the supplicants with the most bitter denunciations. "No daughter of his should ever be united to the son of a family which had deserted its ancestral faith," and he forbade the youth his presence for ever. Difficulty, however, only served to increase the ardour of the devoted lovers; and after many secret interviews among the wooded slopes of the Ribble, an elopement was agreed upon, in the hope that time would bring her father's pardon. The day and place were unfortunately overheard by one of the lady's brothers, who was hiding in a thicket close by, and he determined to prevent what he considered to be his sister's disgrace.

On the evening agreed upon both parties met at the hour appointed; and as the young knight moved away with his betrothed, her brother rushed from his hiding place, and slew both him and two friends by whom he was accompanied. The bodies were secretly buried within the precincts of the domestic chapel at the Hall; and Lady Dorothy was sent abroad to a convent where she was kept under strict surveillance. Her mind at last gave way—the name of her murdered lover was ever on her lips, and she died a raving maniac. Some years ago three human skeletons were found near the walls of the Hall, and popular opinion has connected them with the tradition. The legend also states that on certain clear, still evenings a lady in white can be seen passing along the gallery and the corridors, and then from the Hall into the grounds: that she there meets a handsome knight who receives her on his bended knees, and he then accompanies her along the walks. On arriving at a certain spot, most probably the lover's grave, both the phantoms stand still, and, as they seem to utter soft wailings of despair, they embrace each other, and then their forms rise slowly from the earth and melt away into the clear blue of the surrounding sky.

THE DRAGON OF WANTLEY.

THE story of the Dragon of Wantley has been claimed for several districts. Hunter, in his "Hallamshire," 1820, claims that locality for the scene of the conflict; but Mr Gregson, in his "Fragments," pp. 151-2, shows pretty conclusively that the tradition must be assigned to More Hall, in the Hundred of West Derby. Sir William de la More, who flourished about 1326, was a noted warrior. He distinguished himself at the battle of Poictiers, and was knighted by Edward I. His prowess gained him great fame, and he is supposed to have been the hero of the legend; although a similar story is told of Sir Thomas Venables, of Golborne David, in the county of Chester. It is not improbable that the issue of some family feud or Border fray is there allegorised by the author of the ballad, which is reprinted in the "Fragments" from a broadside issued for Randal Taylor, near Stationers' Hall, London, 1685.

A TRUE RELATION OF THE DREADFUL COMBATE BETWEEN
MORE OF MORE HALL AND THE DRAGON OF WANTLEY.

OLD stories tell how Hercules
A dragon slew at Lerna,
With seven heads and fourteen eyes,
To see and well discerna;
But he had a club
This dragon to drub,
Or he had ne'er don't, I warrant ye,
But More of More Hall,
With nothing at all,
He slew the Dragon of Wantley.

This dragon had two furious wings,
Each one upon each shoulder,
With a sting in his Tayl,
As long as a Flayl,
Which made him bolder and bolder.
He had long claws,
And in his jaws,
Four and forty teeth of iron,
With a hide as tough as any buff,
Which did him round inviron.

Have you not heard that the Trojan horse
Held seventy men in his belly?
This Dragon was not quite so big,
But very near I'll tell ye,
Devour did he,
Poor children three,
That could not with him grapple;
And at one sup
He eat them up,
As one should eat an apple.

All sorts of cattle this Dragon did eat,
Some say he'd eat up trees,
And that the forest sure he would
Devour up by degrees.

For houses and churches
Were to him gorse and burches,
He eat all and left none behind,
But some stones, dear Jack,
Which he could not crack,
Which on the hills you will find.

In Yorkshire fair, near Rotherham,
The place I know it well ;
Some two or three miles or thereabout,
I vow I cannot tell ;
But there is a ledge
Just on the hill edge,
And Matthew's house hard by it ;
Oh ! there and then
Was this Dragon's den,
You could not choose but spy it.

Some say this Dragon was a Witch;
Some say he was the Devil ;
For from his nose a smoke arose,
And with it burning snivil ;
Which he cast off,
When he did cough ;
In a well which he did stand by,
Which made it look
Just like a brook
Running with burning brandy.

Hard by a furious Knight there dwelt,
Of whom all towns did ring,
For he could wrestle, play at staff,
Kick, cuff, box, huff,
Call son of a witch,
Do any kind of thing ;
By the tail and the main,
With his hands twain,
He swung a horse till he was dead,
And that which was stranger,
He, for very anger,
Eat him all up but his head !

Three children, as I told, being eat;
Men, women, girls, and boys;
Sighing and sobbing, came to his lodging,
And made a hideous noyse,
Oh! save us all, More of More Hall,
Thou peerles Knight of these woods;
Do but slay this Dragon,
We won't leave us a rag on,
We'll give thee all our goods.

Tut, tut, quoth he, no goods I want,
But I want, I want in sooth,
A fair maid of sixteen, that's brisk,
And smiles about the mouth;
Hair as black as a sloe,
Both above and below,
With a blush her cheeks adorning;
To 'noynt me o'er night,
Ere I go to fight,
And to dress me in the morning.

This being done, he did engage
To hew this dragon down;
But first he went new armour to
Bespeak, at Sheffield town.
With spikes all about,
Not within, but without,
Of steel, so sharp and strong,
Both behind and before,
Arms, legs, all o'er,
Some five or six inches long.

Had you but seen him in this dress,
How fierce he look't and big,
You would have thought him for to be
An Egyptian Porcu-pig;
He frighted all,
Cats, dogs, and all,
Each cow, each horse, each hog.

For fear did flee
For they took him to be
Some strange, outlandish hedgehog.

To see this fight, all people there
Got upon trees and houses;
On churches some, and chimneys some,
But they put on their trowses;
Not to spoil their hose.
As soon as he rose,
To make him strong and mighty,
He drank by the tale,
Six pots of ale,
And a quart of aqua-vitæ.

It is not strength that always wins,
For wit doth strength excel;
Which made our cunning champion
Creep down into a well;
Where he did think,
This dragon would drink,
And so he did in truth;
And as he stoop't low
He rose up and cryed, bo!
And hit him in the mouth.

Oh! quoth the Dragon; pox take you! come out
Thou that disturb'st me at my drink;
And then he turned and spit at him—
Good lack! how he did stink,
Beshrew thy soul,
Thy body is foul,
Thy dung smells not like balsame;
Thou son of a witch,
Thou stink'st so sore,
Sure thy dyet is unwholesome.

Our politick knight, on the other side,
Crept out upon the brink,
And gave the Dragon such a doust,
He knew not what to think;
By cock, quoth he,

Say you so, do you see,
And then at him he let flie:
With hand and with foot,
And so they went to 't,
And the word it was—Hey, boyes, hey!

Your word, quoth the Dragon, I don't understand,
Then to 't they fell at all;
Like two wild bears, so fierce, I may
Compare great things with small.
Two dayes and a night
With this Dragon did fight
Our champion on the ground;
Tho' their strength it was great,
Yet their skill it was neat,
They never had one wound.

At length the hard ground began for to quake,
The Dragon gave him such a knock;
Which made him to reel,
And straightway he thought
To lift him high as a rock,
And thence let him fall;
But More of More Hall,
Like a valiant son of Mars,
As he came like a lout,
So he turned him about,
And hit him a kick on the back.

Oh! quoth the Dragon with a sigh,
And turn'd six times together;
Sobbing and tearing, cursing and swearing,
Out of his throat of leather.
Oh! thou rascall,
More of More Hall,
Would I had seen you never;
With the thing at thy foot,
Thou has prick't my gut,
Oh! I am quite undone for ever!

Murder! murder! the Dragon cryed,
Alack! alack! for grief;

Had you but miss't that place you would
Have done me no mischief.
Then his head he shak't,
Trembled and quaik't,
And down he layed, and cried;
First on one knee,
Then on back tumbled he,
So groaned, kick't, burst, and dyed.

OSBALDESTON HALL.

THE origin of this ancient structure dates from Saxon times. It was evidently the home of Oswald; for this is merely another form of the name, and *ton* designates the homestead on his estate. This family does not appear to have been dispossessed by the Normans, the county was then perhaps too wild and uncultivated to be attractive to the conquerors; and hence we find Eilfi of Osbaldeston, a Saxon, living in the twelfth century, who had a son whose name appears in documents about 1245. The property continued in the family without interruption until 1701, when it passed into collateral lines on the death of Thomas, son of Edward Osbaldeston, the last male heir of his race. During the Tudor and early Stuart sovereigns the Osbaldestons formed one of the most distinguished families in the county; several of its members received the honour of knighthood, and one of them was connected by marriage with the Earls of Derby. They founded a Chantry in the parish church of Blackburn, and until recently a brass plate in the family chapel contained the figure of a man in armour, underneath which was the following inscription—" Here lyeth the bodye of Sir Edward Osbaldeston; a charitable, courteous, and valiant knight, qui obiit A.D. 1636, æt. 63."

The Hall at Osbaldeston is now in a dilapidated condition. From what remains it is evident that the house formerly consisted of two wings, and a large central portion set further back. On three sides it was protected by a moat, while the fourth side was swept by the river Ribble. Several ranges of transomed and mullioned windows attest the grandeur and magnificence of the place when finished by Sir Edward during the reign of the first Stuart. The large drawing-room is nearly entire, and over the fireplace are some elaborate carvings, containing the family arms with their numerous quarterings, and the initials of John, Edward, Margaret, and Maud Osbaldeston. Excessive subdivisions of the estates, consequent upon large families, led to the decline of the house, until at last the remnant was disposed of for a trifling consideration. There is one room in the old Hall whose walls are smeared with several red marks, which tradition states can never be obliterated. They have some resemblance to blood, and are considered to have been caused when one of the family was brutally murdered. It is said that there was once a great family gathering at Osbaldeston Hall, at which every member of the family was present. The feast was ended, and the liquor was flowing freely round when family differences began to be discussed. These ended in anger and 'recriminations, until at length two of the company challenged each other to mortal combat. Friends interfered and the quarrel seemed to be allayed, but soon after the two accidentally met in this room, and Thomas Osbaldeston drew his sword and murdered his brother-in-law without resistance. For this crime he was deemed a felon, and forfeited his lands. Ever since that time the room has been haunted. Tradition says that the ghost of the murdered man continues to visit the scene of the conflict, and during the silent hours of night it may be seen passing from the room with uplifted hands, and with the appearance of blood streaming from a wound in the breast.

MELLOR HALL, OR ABBOT HOUSE.

MELLOR Hall, or Abbot House, is an ancient structure of the early Tudor period. It formerly possessed an antique porch and pointed gables, but these have long since disappeared. The internal walls and partitions were formed of "raddle and daub," held together by upright and cross beams which reached from wall to wall. The upper rooms were reached by a spiral stone staircase, and the floor of that over the hall was formed of yellow clay spread on "raddles" at least a foot thick. A portion of the south-west angle of this room had been partitioned off, and was known by the name of the "Priest's room." This was probably the hiding-place for one of the missionary priests when the Hall was occupied by a junior branch of the Southworths of Samlesbury. Tradition states that the last owner of that name wasted all his property, and was ultimately compelled to beg for bread. A large flat stone was formerly pointed out upon which the old man used to sit while he chanted in tremulous tones—

"When I was young and in my prime,
All these fields down here were mine;
But now I'm old, and grown so poor,
I'm forced to beg from door to door."

THE LEGEND OF SIR TARQUIN.

MANCUNIUM, Mamecestre, the modern Manchester, was probably founded by Agricola, in the year A.D. 79. It continued in the hands of the Romans, until their final departure from Britain, during the reign of Honorious, about A.D. 425. After the Romans left the country, their camp on the Irwell was occupied by the native Britons, who had again to give place to the victorious Saxons. These hardy warriors appear to have become masters of Lancashire about A.D. 618, when they seized the old Roman station at Mamecestre, which more than a century before is fabled to have been occupied by a semi-mythic personage named Sir Tarquin. Tradition states that he was "a giant in size and a monster in brutality." Be this as it may, the Britons made two desperate attempts under King Artnur and his knights, to retake this stronghold; and Sir Tarquin is said to have fallen a victim to the prowess of Sir Lancelot du Lake in single combat, during the second attack.

After the death of King Arthur, the Saxons and Danes regained their ascendancy; but the tradition has outlived the success of the Britons. The combat between the two knights not only forms an interesting incident in the "Morte d'Arthur;" but has been alluded to by Shakspeare in the second part of his Henry IV.; and preserved to us in Bishop Percy's valuable "Reliques." There is also an extended version of the metrical legend included in the privately printed "Memoirs of the Mosley Family;" but we prefer to give the original ballad, merely localising it by the words included within brackets.

"When Arthur first in court began,
And was approved King,

By force of arms great victories wanne,
   And conquest home did bring.

Then into England straight he came,
   With fifty good and able
Knights, that resorted unto him,
   And were of his Round Table.

And he had jousts and tournaments,
   Whereto were many prest;
Wherein some knights did far excell,
   And eke surmount the rest.

But one Sir Lancelot du Lake,
   Who was approved well,
He for his deedes and feats of armes,
   All others did excell.

When he had rested him awhile,
   In play, and game, and sport,
He said he would go prove himselfe,
   In some adventurous sorte.

He armed rode in [Lancashire]
   And met a damsel faire,
Who told him of adventures great,
   Whereto he gave good eare.

'Such wolde I find,' quoth Lancelot,
   'For that cause came I hither';
'Thou seem'st,' quoth she, 'a knight full good,
   And I will bring thee thither.

'[In Mamecestre] a knight doth dwell,
   That now is of great fame;
Therefore tell me what knight thou art,
   And what may be thy name.'

'My name is Lancelot du Lake;'
   Quoth shee: 'It likes me than;
Here dwells a knight who never was
   Yet matcht with any man.

'Who has in prison threescore knights
    And four, that he did wound ;
Knights of King Arthur's court they be,
    And of his Table Round.'

She brought him to the [Irwell] side,
    And also to a tree,
Whereon a copper bason hung,
    And many shields to see.

He struck soe hard, the bason broke :
    Sir Tarquin soon he spyed ;
Who drove a horse before him fast,
    Whereon a knight lay tyed.

'Sir knight,' then said Sir Lancelot,
    'Bring me that horse-load hither,
And lay him down and let him reste,
    We'll try our force together :

'For, as I understand thou hast,
    Soe far as thou art able,
Done great despite and shame unto
    The knights of the Round Table.'

'If thou be of the Table Round ; '
    Quoth Tarquin speedily,
'Both thee and all thy fellowship
    I utterlye defye.'

'That's over much,' quoth Lancelot, tho'
    'Defend thee by and by : '—
They sett their speares unto their steedes,
    And eache att other flye.

They coucht their speares (their horses ran
    As though there had been thunder),
And strucke them each immidst their shields,
    Wherewith they broke insunder.

Their horses' backs brake under them,
    The knights were both astounde ;
To voyd their horses they made haste,
    And light upon the grounde.

They tooke then to their shields full fast,
   Their swords they drew out than ;
With mighty strokes most eagerlye,
   Each at the other ran.

They wounded were and bled full sore,
   They both for breath did stand ;
And leaning on their swords awhile,
   Quoth Tarquin : ' Hold thy hand ;

' And tell to me what I shall aske ; '
   ' Say on,' quoth Lancelot tho'.
' Thou art,' quoth Tarquin, ' the best knight
   That ever I did know.

' And like a knight that I did hate,
   Soe that thou be not hee,
I will deliver all the rest,
   And eke accord with thee.'

' That is well said,' quoth Lancelot ;
   But sith it must be soe,
What knight is that thou hatest thus ;
   I pray thee to me shew.'

' His name is Lancelot du Lake ;
   He slew my brother deere ;
Him I despise of all the rest,
   I would I had him here.'

' Thy wish thou hast, but yet unknowne,
   I am Lancelot du Lake,
Now knight of Arthur's Table Round ;
   King Haudes' son of Schuwake ;

' And I desire thee do thy worst ; '
   ' Ho ! Ho !' quoth Tarquin tho',
' One of us two shall end our lives,
   Before that we doe goe.

' If thou be Lancelot du Lake,
   Then welcome shalt thou bee ;
Wherfor see thou thyselfe defend,
   For now defye I thee.'

> They buckled then together soe,
> Like unto wilde boars rashing;
> And with their swords and shields they ran,
> At one another slashing.
>
> The ground besprinkled was with bloode;
> Tarquin he gan to yielde,
> For he gave back for wearinesse,
> And lowe did bear his shield.
>
> This soone Sir Lancelot espyde,
> He leapt upon him then,
> He pulled him downe upon his knee,
> And pushing off his helme;
>
> Forthwith he struck his neck in two,
> And when he had soe done;
> From prison three score knights and foure
> Delyvered everye one!"

THIS legend has been noticed by Hollingworth in his "Chronicles of Manchester," who, after quoting Chaucer respecting the state of the county when—

> "In al that lond dursten non Christen rout,
> Al Christen folk bin fled from the countrey;
> Through Paynims that conquered al about,
> The plagues of Northumbria by lond and see,"

gives in his own quaint manner the following particulars. "It is said that Sir Tarquine, a stoute enemie of King Arthur, kept this castle (of Manchester) and neere to the fooarde in Medlock, about Mab-house, hung a bason on a tree, on which bason whosoever did strike, Sir Tarquine, or some of his companye, would come and fighte with him; and that Sir Lancelot de Lake, a Knight of King Arthure's Round Table, did beate upon the bason—foughte with Tarquine—killed him—possessed himselfe of the Castle—and loosed the prisoners. Whosoever thinketh it worth his pains to reade more of it may reade the history of King Arthur. It is certain that about A.D.

520, there was such a Prince or King, and it is not incredible that hee or his Knightes might contend about this castle when he was in this countie ; and (as Minius sayeth) hee put the Saxons to flight in a memorable battle near Wigan, about twelve miles off."

Mr Roby, also, in the first series of his " Traditions," included a prose version of " Sir Tarquin," but this was suppressed in the later editions, and a short notice only was added to his tale of the " Goblin Builders." His first essay was evidently based upon the " Morte d'Arthur," and the extended metrical version of which he quotes the opening stanza.

> " Within this ancient British land,
> In Lancashire I understand,
> Near Manchester, there lived a knight of fame,
> Of a prodigious strength and might,
> Who vanquished many a worthy knight,
> A giant great—and Tarquin was his name."

INDEX.

ABBOT of Chester, 260
Accrington, notchel crying, 176
Ace of Spades, 4
Acorns, pelting with, 85
Acres Fair, 84
Adventures of a Skull, 67
Alfred, King, Legend respecting, 21
Amusements at Didsbury, 126
Ancient games, 132
Ancient houses, 120
Anderton's jewels, 145
Appeal of murder, 173
Apple catching for money, 162
Archery butts, 148
Ashton gyst-ale, 85
Ashton Manor, payment for, 3
Assheton's Journal, 94
Astbury Church, paintings at, 20

BACON, superstitions about, 124
Back-slamming, 175
Ballad quoted, 18
Bandy-ball, game of, 149
Barcroft of Barcroft, 4
Barley Brake, game of, 138, 141
Barton and Eccles, rhymes on, 89
Bear-baiting, 119
Beasts offered to the Devil, 124
Beheading a thief, 172
Benches in churches for women, 3
Bernshaw Tower, 5
Birds, superstitions respecting, 218
Biron, Lady, funeral of, 9
Blindman's buff, 141
Blackthorn, game of, 150
Boggart hole in Pendle Forest, 141

Book of Sports, 122
Bowt's bare, 202
Bradshaigh, Sir William, 45
Bradshaw chapel, skulls at, 60
Bradshaw, John, preaching, 109
Brank at Holme, lost, 167
Buck-thanging, punishment of, 175
Bull-baiting at Eccles, 127
Bull-baiting at Chatburn, 149
Burnley waits, 87
Burnley holidays, 161
Byrom, John, opposed to races, 154, 156

CASTLE Irwell, races at, 157
Cats, king of, 13
Cats, superstition respecting, 219
Chad's church, Rochdale, 52
Chapter of proverbs, 213
Chatburn, the tailor of, 15
Chests, carvings on, 65
Children put to death, 12
Children, superstitions respecting, 220
Christ's croft, 183
Christmas rhymes, 240
Christmas song, 88
Churches strewed with rushes, 109
Church feasts, 123
Churchyards, fairs held in, 125
Churning rhymes, 234
Chylde of Hale, dress of, legends, 31, 33
Cicely's hunting pranks, 253
Clayton hall, 8
Clegg Hall boggart, 11   [237
Clogs worn, clogs to clogs, 146,

Index.

Cockerham, the Devil at, 241
Cockfighting at Eccles, rules for, 128, 143
Coifi abandons paganism, 75
Courting on Fridays, 176
Courtship, superstitions respecting, 222
Cross and pile, game of, 139
Cuck stool at Liverpool, 167
Cucking stool at Ormskirk, 168
Cunliffes of Wyecoller, 79

DANISH sword dance, 153
Debtor relieved by a witch, 252
Decorations at rushbearings, 118
Demons, forms of, 77
Demon pigs, 7
Denton, derivation of, 28
Devil's bond, 6
Devil outwitted, 240
Devil's stride, 243
Derby, Earls of, crest, 22
Didsbury wakes, 125
Dilworth, written stone at, 13
Downham, King and Queen at, 88
Downes, Roger, superstitions respecting remains of, 66, 69
Dragon of Wantley, 265
Drawing dun out of mire, 140
Drowning female criminals, 172
Ducking pits at Burnley, 165
Dule upo' Dun, 15
Dun cow and old rib, 16
Drunk as blazes, 208

EAGLE Crag in Cliviger, 5
Eagle and child, legend of, 19, 259
Earl of Mexborough, cockfighter, 144
Eccles guising, 89
Eccles pageant, 92
Eccles tithes wagered on cocks, 145
Edward Longshanks "lifted," 143
Edwin of Northumbria, 75
Egerton lady and the skull, 70
Entwisel, Sir Bertine, ballad, 23

Eustace Dauntesey sells his soul, 42
Expenses of guising, 91

FAIR women of Lancashire, 206
Fairs at Manchester proclaimed, 84
Fairs, origin of, 125
Fairfax, General, 26
Farm house, description of, 17
Fighting "up and down," 145
Fish, superstitions respecting, 224
Fives, game of, 150
Fleetwood Habergham, ballad by, 30
Flodden Field, battle of, 35
Fox, Mr, and Earl of Derby, 51
Furness, rhymes and proverbs in, 202
Fylde, ducking stools in the, 170

GALLOWS at Manchester, 171
"Gaping Saturday," 161
Ghosts, vanishing of, 56
Goblin builders, 53
Godly lane, cross in, 7
Gorton, derivation of, 27
Great main of cocks, 144
Grinning through collars, 126
Grith, meaning of, 85

HABERGHAM Hall, 29
Habergham's, Mrs, lament, 31
Habergham, John, reckless life of, 30
Hair, superstitions respecting, 224
Hale, Chylde of, 31
Halper pots, 137
Hand-ball, game of, 149
Hanging ditch, origin of, 34
Hanging male criminals, 172
Harrop, Joseph, printer of race lists, 156
Heaving or "lifting," 142
Hector, speech of, 107
Helston, Mother, the witch, 6
Hidden treasure, 38
Higson, John, on plague stone, 54
Hoghton pageant in 1617, 93

Index.

Holt, Constance, saved from drowning, 62
Holy water, use of, 124
Hornby chapel, 34
Hot cockles, game of, 136
Hulme Hall, 37
Hunting at Extwistle, 147

IDIOT starved to death, 4
Ignanging and Ignagnus, 153
Ince Hall and the dead hand, 38
Inn, "Dule upo' Dun," 16
Inscription on written stone, 14
Inscription at Hornby church, 37

JEALOUS woman, revenge of, 175
Jem o' Bradeley, 212
Jeppe knave grave, 172

"KENT and keer," proverb, 193
Kersal Hall, traditions of, 41
Kersal moor, races at, 154
Kirkham, ducking stool at, 171
Knight murdered, 263

LADY in white, 22, 261
Lancashire v. Yorkshire, 144
Lancashire riddles, rhymes, 186, 188
Lancashire witches, revels of, 247, 257
Lancaster, mayor of, punished, 251
Lapland witches, account of, 258
Latham, Sir Thomas, 19
Latham and Knowsley, sayings, legend, 205, 259
Laws of Edward the Confessor, 133
Loggats, game of, 133
Lomax, James, otter hunter, 154
Lostock tower, description of, 44
Love's evil choice, 30
Lifting or heaving, 142
Liverpool fair, custom at, 95
Liverpool May-day customs, 96
Lucky bone, superstitions respecting, 236

MABEL Bradshaigh, penance of, 47
Mab's cross, 45

Manchester gallows and tumbrel, 171
Maid Marion, 108
Margery's pranks, 252
Marlock, meanings of, 86, 148
Marsh, George, footprint of, 77
Medicines, superstitions respecting, 225
Melletus on festivals, 124
Mellor Hall, 272
Men no seats in churches, 3
Milk or mickle stones, 54
Money, hidden, 55
Money, superstitions about, 227
Mischief night, 175
Miscellaneous superstitions, 217,
Moon superstitions, 238
Mortgage, the forfeited, 45
More of More Hall, 264
Morris dance, 137
Murder at Dilworth, 14
Murder, appeal of, 173

NICKER, derivation of, 29
Nine-holes, game of, 134
Norman punishment, 173
Notchel crying, 176
Nude men, races by, 159
Nuttall, William, ballad by, 11
Nuts, omens from, 222

OAT-CAKE lads, 239
Oat-cakes, presentation of, 127
Old Crambo, &c., 95
Omens or signs of death, 23
Omens from doves, specks, pippins, 228-230
O'Neal, rebellion of, 61
Origin of guilds, 97
Ormskirk, church bell at, 48
Osbaldeston Hall, legend of, 270
Oskatel, Sir, legend of, 20
Oswald's, St, Church, 61
Otter hunting, 154

PACE egg mummers, 101
Pack-sheeting, punishment of, 175
Pageants, maskings, &c., 81
Parker of Extwistle, hunting song, 147

2 M

282 *Index.*

Paulinus at Whalley, 74
Parker, Thomas Townley, cock-fighter, 144
Penance stool at Bispham, 170
Penance in Fylde, 174
Pendle hill rhymes, 186, 189
Personal appearance of Paulinus, 75
Peveril, Richard, his fate, 42
Pigs, demon, 8
Pilling Moss, eruption of, 243
Pillory at Manchester, 171
Pitching the bar, 133
Plague stone at Stretford, 53
Plott's, Dr, preference of brank, 167
Popular rhymes, 183
Preston guilds, merchant, 97
Preston festivities, 99
Prison bars, game of, 151
Proud Preston, 184
Proverbs, speeches upon, 97
Proverbs, 189, 201
Punching, meaning of, 146
Punishments, various, 165

QUOITS and bowls, 151

RACE course, the oldest, 155
Races, accidents at, 158
Rebellions, northern, 35
Rhodes of Rhodes defrauded, 50
Rhodes and Pilkington traditions, 49
Rib, old, and dun cow, 16
Ringing the pan, 176
Robin Hood, 108
Robbers robbed by a witch, 254
Rochdale proverb, 53
Rochdale rushbearing, 114, 119
Roger's transformation, 256
Rowland's rhymes for games, 132
Rooley moor, riddle, 159
Rushbearings, 109
Rushcarts, 110, 113, 115, 117

SADDLEWORTH rushcart, 111
Sale of a wife, 177
Sale, terms of, to the devil, 15
Samlesbury hall, its legend, 261

Samlesbury hall, views from, 261
Saxon cross at Burnley, 8
School holidays in 1790, 159
Scold's branks, 166, 167
Seathwaite, farms in, 204
Seise-noddy, game of, 136
Shoot-cock or shuttlecock, 140
Shovegroat, game of, 138
Signature by the dead hand, 39
Similes, sayings, &c., 190, 193
Skates, kind of, 151
Skittles, game of, 135
Slinging, methods of, 152
Southworth, Sir John, 262
Southworth, Dorothy's sad death, 263
Spectre horseman, huntsman, 79, 7
Spell and nur, game of, 149
Spell for witchcraft, 235
Sports at Southport, 161
Stang riding, 174
Stanley and the pig's ear, 260
Stanley, Sir Edward, 34
Stocks at Walton, Burnley, 166
Stool-ball, game of, 132
St George, speech of, 102
Sykes's wife, her appearance, 55

TAILOR killed by Downes, 66
Tarquin the giant, 54, 273
Ten-pins, game of, 134
Thick as Inkle weavers, 210
Tick-tack, game of, 135
Timberbottom, skulls at, 60
Timbered hall, description of, 65
Tip, game of, 150
Toothache charm, 226
Top and scouge, 140
Towneley, Lord William, 6
Towneley Hall, legend of, 57
Treacle dipping, 162
Trippet, game of, 152
Turton tower, wages when erected, 59
Tutelar gods, 93
Tyrone's bed, signature, 60, 63

UNSWORTH, Dragons of, 63
Unsworth, curious table at, 64

Index. 283

Unsworth's crest, 65

WAKES described by Drayton, 123
Wantley, Dragon of, 265
Wardley Hall skull, 65
Wardley Hall, owners, descrip- of, 70, 71
Warton rushbearing, 121
Weather rhymes, 188, 232
Weather wisdom, 231
Whalley crosses, rushbearings, 73, 121
Whitaker's opinion of Stanley, 36
White lady at Samlesbury, 264
Wife selling, 177

Wigan church, monuments in, 49, 72
Wigan nursery song, 182
Will o' the wisp superstition, 237
Wilson's proverb rhymes, 213
Winwick church and pig, rhyme, 76, 182
Wishes, tailor of Chatburn's 15
Witchcraft superstitions, 234
Witches' temptation, dance, feast, 248, 249, 255
Witches released from gaol, 257
Women's possessions, 121
Worsley giant, combats of, 78
Wyecoller Hall and spectre, 79

PRINTED BY BALLANTYNE AND COMPANY
EDINBURGH AND LONDON

Other Books Published By LLANERCH Include:

BOOKS BY W. G. COLLINGWOOD:

NORTHUMBRIAN CROSSES OF THE PRE-NORMAN AGE. Illus. ISBN 0 947992 35 9

THE LIFE AND DEATH OF CORMAC THE SKALD (KORMAC'S SAGA) translated from the Icelandic; illus. Facsimile. ISBN 0 947992 65 0

THORSTEIN OF THE MERE: A SAGA OF THE NORTHMEN IN LAKELAND. ISBN 0 947992 49 9

THE BONDWOMEN: A SAGA OF THE NORTHMEN IN LAKELAND. ISBN 0 947992 59 6

THE LIKENESS OF KING ELFWALD: A STUDY OF IONA & NORTHUMBRIA ISBN 0 947992 53 7

SCANDINAVIAN BRITAIN. Facsimile of 1908. ISBN 1 897853 21 1

DUTCH AGNES: A JOURNAL OF THE CURATE OF CONISTON 1616-1623. ISBN 1 897853 19 X

NORTHERN INTEREST/FOLKLORE

NORTHUMBRIA IN THE DAYS OF BEDE Peter Hunter Blair. A classic; a scholar's labour of love. First pb. reprint. ISBN 1 86143 012 4

NORTHANHYMBRE SAGA: A HISTORY OF THE ANGLO-SAXON KINGS OF NORTHUMBRIA. John Marsden. ISBN 1 897853 76 9

FÆREYINGA SAGA: THE TALE OF THROND OF GATE trans. F. York Powell. ISBN 1 897853 75 0

OLD SCOTTISH CUSTOMS. W.J. Guthrie. Fac. ISBN 1 897853 48 3

FRITHIOF'S SAGA trans. George Stephens. Fac. ISBN 1 897853 68 8

ICELANDIC LEGENDS trans Powell & Magnússon. ISBN 1897853 71 3

LAYS & LEGENDS OF THE ENGLISH LAKES. J. Pagen White. ISBN 1 897853 15 5

THE SAGA OF KING SVERRI OF NORWAY, trans. J. Sephton, Fac. ISBN 1 897853 49 1

COUNTY FOLKLORE: ORKNEY & SHETLAND. G.F.Black. Fac. of Folklore-Society edition. ISBN 1897853 53 X

LAKELAND & ICELAND: THE LANDNAMA BOOK OF ICELAND & A GLOSSARY OF WORDS IN THE DIALECT OF CUMBERLAND ETC. T. Ellwood. ISBN 1 897853 82 3

BANDAMANNA SAGA translated from the Icelandic by John Porter and illustrated by Andy Selwood. ISBN 1897853 13 0

NORTHUMBERLAND COUNTY FOLK-LORE, a reprint of the Folklore Society edn by M.C Balfour, 1904. ISBN 1897853 32 7

A HANDBOOK OF THE OLD NORTHERN RUNIC MONUMENTS OF SCANDINAVIA AND ENGLAND by George Stephens Small-paper reprint. ISBN 1 897853 02 5

For a complete list of c 200+ titles, please write to;

**LLANERCH PUBLISHERS
Felin Fach, Nr Lampeter,
Cardiganshire
SA48 8PJ**